ALSO BY BILL REYNOLDS

Born to Coach with Rick Pitino
Big Hoops

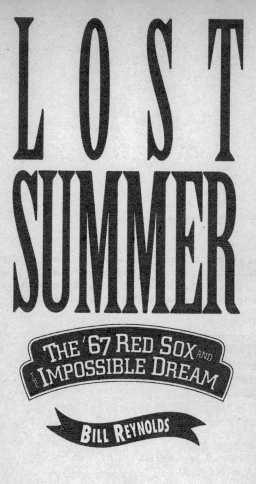

LOST SUMMER

THE '67 RED SOX AND THE IMPOSSIBLE DREAM

BILL REYNOLDS

WARNER BOOKS

A Time Warner Company

WARNER BOOKS EDITION

Book design: H. Roberts

Warner Books, Inc.
1271 Avenue of the Americas
New York, NY 10020

W A Time Warner Company

Printed in the United States of America

Originally published in hardcover by Warner Books.
First Printed in Paperback: May, 1993

10 9 8 7 6 5 4 3 2 1

ACKNOWLEDGMENTS

In trying to re-create the summer of 1967 I have relied primarily on newspaper articles from the time period, but have also benefited from several fine autobiographies, namely the two by Carl Yastrzemski; *Seeing It Through* by Tony Conigliaro; and *No More Mr. Nice Guy* by Dick Williams. In the beginning of the project I also discovered *The Impossible Dream Remembered*, Ken Coleman and Dan Valenti's fine day-by-day account of the season. They all offer excellent insight into the '67 season.

This book probably never would have happened without a phone call from David Vigliano in June of 1987. He became my agent then, and continues to this day, three books later. No one could ask for a better one.

Rick Horgan, a senior editor at Warner Books and a native New Englander to boot, believed in the project from the beginning and guided it at all the right times. No writer has the right to ask for more.

I also am fortunate to work for two great bosses at the *Providence Journal*, Dave Bloss and Art Martone, who've been supportive, and with colleagues who make the *Journal* sports department a wonderful place to work. Martone provided his vast knowledge of the Red Sox and their history. Bill Troberman always has gone out of his way to help me, and did it again this time. Linda Phelps loaned me her prized "Yaz" autobiography, Bob Leddy his '67 World Series program. Mary Jane Ryan of the Red Sox public relations staff helped with phone numbers. John Hanlon provided some past articles and a lot of background material on Carl Yastrzemski that was very helpful. Keith Rosenfeld, Tim Horgan, Dick O'Connell, and Don Fitzpatrick shared some memories. Wayne Worcester read much of the manuscript and gave me advice and encouragement when I needed both. Chris Zarcadoolas and Karen Anderson always believe, even in the bad times. They all have my enduring thanks.

And I would like to add a public thank you to the members of the '67 Red Sox who gave up their time to talk to me, especially Ken Harrelson, Dick Williams, Jim Lonborg, George Scott, and Rico Petrocelli.

PROLOGUE

I remember it as a cold, gray April afternoon.

I was sitting at my desk in a red-brick college dormitory in Providence, Rhode Island, doing homework, the radio tuned to the Red Sox against the Yankees, one of the first games of the season. It was 1967. I was a junior at Brown University. Pitching for the Yankees was the great Whitey Ford, now at the tail end of his career. Pitching for the Red Sox was some rookie left-hander named Billy Rohr. He was 21 years old, and it was his first major league start. I'd never heard of him.

Not surprising, really. I wasn't a fan anymore. Baseball was something that I'd come to associate with the past, just one of the things that had gotten stowed away in some childhood footlocker.

For the times they were changing. A high school friend had already been killed in Vietnam, his body sent home in a casket wrapped in the American flag. Every Wednesday at noon an assemblage of students and faculty held a peace vigil on the campus green. The war, and the specter of the draft, seemed inevitably to creep into our conversations at school. One of my roommates talked of maybe going to Canada to escape the draft. Another wanted to go to Vietnam to kill "gooks." I felt lost in the middle somewhere, unsure, beginning to be aware that life could be a lot more complicated than what they talked about in college classrooms. In a year I'd be out of school; there'd be no more student deferment. I looked at the future and saw no easy answers, looked at the world and saw everything more complicated than it was when my head had been full of adolescent dreams.

Baseball had been my first love, so every once in a while I'd listen to a game on the radio—the equivalent of taking a ride past an old girlfriend's house, a brief nostalgic visit to something that once had been important. One of the highlights of my childhood summers had been occasional trips to Fenway Park, the tiny oasis of green amid the urban bustle of Boston, a place that was a cathedral for generations of New England kids. My first memory of Fenway was from some lost year in the early '50s. It must have been one of Ted Williams' first games after he returned from the Korean War, because when he came to the plate, the big crowd around me standing and cheering lustily, my father said, "Remember this. This is a great moment." I must have been about seven or eight, certainly old enough to believe that one could yearn for nothing more noble than to play for the Red Sox and have people cheer as you came to the plate.

The next year there was a Little League outing, a two-hour bus trip complete with endless choruses of "100 bottles of beer on the wall," culminating in a dog day afternoon in the right-field grandstand cheering at anything that moved. After the game we hung around outside the players' gate, ready to kill for an autograph. Interspersed in there somewhere was an obsession with baseball cards, cardboard heroes lined up in the bookcase, childhood icons.

Throughout my adolescence there'd been annual pilgrimages to Fenway as the names changed from Jensen and Piersall to Runnels and Radatz. T. S. Eliot once wrote that we measure our lives in coffee spoons. But ole T.S. never could get around on the fastball. If you grew up in New England you measured your life in trips to Fenway Park. You got older; Fenway stayed the same, as timeless as sand castles at the beach. That had been back when I was still a fan, still glued to the daily box scores in the newspaper that served as links to the emerald green world of childhood.

By the time I was 19 there were other interests, seemingly more important things than a childhood game. Baseball was just something I used to love. My only real connection to it was a curious kinship I felt with Tony Conigliaro, one of the Red Sox's young stars, and that was by accident. I'd been in school at Worcester, Massachusetts, at the time and it wasn't a real good period for me. My longtime girlfriend was in the process of dumping me, and that realization had become an ache in my heart. I'd hitchhiked the 40 miles into Boston and was spending the afternoon sitting around a student apartment, drinking beer and feeling sorry for myself. On the radio was the ballgame. In his first at bat in Fenway Park Tony Conigliaro hit a home run. He too was 19.

I was suddenly struck by how different our lives were. Here we were the same age, yet *he* was hitting a home run in Fenway Park in his first at bat, and *I* was sitting in a seedy apartment just a few blocks away feeling sorry for myself. On that spring afternoon in 1964, in my particular view of the universe, Tony Conigliaro was everything I was not.

So all during college I checked the box scores to see how he was doing. In a sense he'd become a link to my youth. In some strange way his success became my success. Maybe it was because he was living out every New England kid's fantasy. Maybe it was something more elusive, undefinable, the little-understood reasons why we root for some athletes while others touch our hearts. But if he was doing well, then things seemed a little more right. As if in my mind our fates had become linked that day three years earlier when we'd both come to Boston on the same day, he to begin his major league career with the Red Sox, me to get dumped by a girl who had been the center of my little universe. No one ever said being a fan makes any sense.

Besides, rooting for the Red Sox was like rooting for my broken heart. If you'd grown up in New England in the '50s and '60s you never knew what a pennant race was. A pennant race was always something taking place in some other town, usually New York. Certainly not in Boston, where the Red Sox appeared to have failure and frustration all but seated on the bench with them.

But listening to that game on the radio seemed to resurrect all my old baseball memories, some lost childhood passion. In the beginning it had felt like just another early season game, nothing special, just another game in an endless string . . .

The Yankees are the most famous franchise in all of sports, but this is not a good Yankee team. The year before they'd finished last for the first time in 54 years, and for the first time in 13 years there's no talk of them fighting for the pennant. Roger Maris is gone to the St. Louis Cardinals. Bobby Richardson has retired. Mickey Mantle is aging and ailing, and there are rumors this might be his last season. Ford is near the end of his illustrious career. The great Elston Howard has become a part-time player. The Yankees seem a parody of themselves, as if the monuments of the great Yankee immortals that stare in from center field have turned their heads in shame.

There are only 14,000 people rattling around in huge Yankee Stadium. Two of them are Jackie Kennedy and her young son, John. It is three and a half years after President Kennedy was assassinated, a traumatic event that, in many ways, spawned much of the unrest currently sweeping the country. Jackie, though, is still the country's unofficial first lady. A month before, the *Saturday Evening Post* had done a cover story on her titled "The National Sport of Watching Jackie Kennedy." It called her a "public monument at 37," and detailed her life in New York down to such minutiae as where Caroline and "John John" go to elementary school and where Jackie's favorite Good Humor Man is located.

It's a year and a half before she will marry Aristotle Onassis, when her image will become infinitely more complicated, and she is called the most famous, best-dressed—and most admired—woman in the world.

Ken Coleman, whose voice, like Curt Gowdy's before him, has become synonymous with the Red Sox, is calling the game. As the innings go by, it's apparent this is not just another early-season game. Through five innings Rohr has not allowed a hit, a rare thing for any Red Sox pitcher these days, never mind a rookie making his first start in the major leagues. He'd appeared understandably nervous at the start, but has settled down and retired the first 10 batters he faced.

But the score is only 1–0, courtesy of a leadoff home run by Reggie Smith.

In the bottom of the sixth, with Rohr still breezing along, the Yankees' Bill Robinson rips a hard ground ball that comes off Rohr's shin. The ball ricochets toward third baseman Joe Foy, who throws Robinson out. Rohr limps around the mound, in obvious pain. Manager Dick Williams, also in his first year, and trainer Buddy LeRoux come out to see him. Williams is thinking of taking Rohr out. But Rohr walks around the mound for a while, testing his leg, and a few minutes later says he's okay.

There is some concern that Rohr is going to be affected by the bruise, and Williams tells catcher Russ Gibson, another rookie, to let him know immediately if he thinks Rohr has lost anything. He hasn't. In fact, Gibson thinks he's getting stronger. He gets through the seventh without giving up a hit, as the drama starts to build. Rohr's bid for a no-hitter has gotten serious. Rohr gets a cushion in the top of the eighth when Joe Foy hits a two-run homer to give the Sox a 3–0 lead. He gets through the bottom of the eighth. An early-season game in the cold of Yankee Stadium has become as good as baseball gets.

After the Red Sox go down in their half of the ninth inning all the people in the stadium stand and cheer as Rohr walks out to the mound, just three outs away from baseball fame. If ever there is someone who seems like an unlikely candidate for baseball immortality, it is Billy Rohr, this skinny stringbean of a left-hander. Even the fact he is on the Red Sox is unlikely.

He'd grown up in Southern California, began playing Little League when he was eight years old. He weighed only 145 pounds in high school, but he was 26-3 over his career, and when he graduated there were about a dozen major league clubs that had an interest. The Red Sox were not one of them. He eventually signed with the Pirates for a reported $25,000 bonus, and was sent to rookie ball in Kingsport, Pennsylvania, where the Pirates were trying to hide him and three other young players in hopes of ultimately leaving them off a list of protected players. They even played games in the mornings, never at night. Rohr knew something strange was going on, but wasn't sure what it was. The strategy failed. Mace Brown, a Red Sox scout, was tipped off, and the Red Sox drafted Rohr in the fall of '63. Just two years later, midway through the season, he was jumped to the Red Sox Triple A club in Toronto, bypassing Double A. It was a difficult adjustment, and the first thing he learned was that the better the league the less hitters chase bad pitches, an important lesson for any young pitcher. In 1966, still in Toronto, he pitched 10 complete games for Dick Williams and earned himself a spring training invitation.

But of course as I sit in my dorm room at Brown I know nothing of this. Nor do I know that last night Rohr had been so nervous he'd asked follow Red Sox pitcher Jim Lonborg to room with him, so that the two of them could go over the Yankee hitters, and that Lonborg will say later that Rohr had spent the night sleeping fitfully, tossing and turning. All I know is that he's three outs away from pitching a no-hitter in his first major league start, something no one in baseball history has ever done, and that I haven't been so absorbed in a baseball game in years.

Due to baseball etiquette, no one has mentioned the no-hitter to Rohr as he spent time in the dugout. No one has to. Coleman gets around it on the radio by saying there have been eight hits in the game and the Red Sox have all of them.

As the crowd stands and cheers Rohr's walk to the mound in the bottom of the ninth the young pitcher does not acknowledge the applause. He looks grim, determined. The suspense builds, the essence of baseball reduced to this one moment. This is baseball at its best, consequences riding on every pitch. He looks around at his teammates, and turns to pitch to Tom Tresh. The count runs to three and two.

"Billy Rohr on the threshold of fame, with a tremendous pitching performance today," Coleman says on the radio. "Rohr winds and here it is, a fly ball to deep left. Yastrzemski is going back . . . way back . . . way back."

Carl Yastrzemski, in his gray road uniform with "Boston" on the front in navy blue letters, and number eight on his back, starts running back as fast as he can. He can't see the ball, but instinctively knows where it figures to land. Behind him is the scoreboard. Behind it is the left-hand grandstand, with only a smattering of people sitting in it. On a dead run Yastrzemski dives, his body in full extension, left arm straining, his momentum carrying him away from home plate. He manages to catch the ball just before he hits the ground, landing on his left knee and doing a full somersault. His cap is off, lying near him on the grass. He quickly gets up, momentarily holding his glove with the ball safely tucked inside it over his head, as Coleman screams over the radio, "One of the greatest catches you'll ever see by Yastrzemski in left field. Everyone in Yankee Stadium is on their feet roaring as Yastrzemski went back and made a tremendous catch."

There is one out.

Yaz has done it, I think. He has saved it.

Joe Pepitone is the next batter. He hits a routine fly ball that Tony Conigliaro handles easily in right field.

Two outs.

One more, I tell myself. Just one more.

The batter is Elston Howard. Ironically, later in the season he will be with the Red Sox. But no one knows that on this afternoon. On this gray day he has become the one thing that stands between a rookie pitcher and a sliver of immortality. Before he steps into the batter's box Williams comes out to visit Rohr. The manager doesn't really have anything to say, just feels he should say something, anything, to calm his young pitcher. Howard digs in, a wide stance. He is a right-handed hitter and he rhythmically waves his bat toward Rohr. The count runs full. Billy Rohr is one strike away. Everyone in Yankee Stadium knows they are watching history. Sitting in a dorm room, rooting for the first time in years, I know I am listening to it. Can he really do it? Is it really possible? Gibson calls for a curveball.

"Russ Gibson gives the sign," Coleman says dramatically, the tension in his voice. "The left-hander delivers . . . a line drive into right field for a base hit. Tony Conigliaro takes it on the first hop. He had no chance."

Rohr's curveball has hung a fraction of a second too long, not breaking down and in to Howard as he'd envisioned it would. He looks over at Howard standing at first base and doesn't feel angry, just disappointed. He has come so close.

I turn the radio off, feeling somehow cheated, feeling that this is just one more example of an imperfect world.

When the game ends Rohr is greeted by several FBI agents. They tell him that Jackie Kennedy wants to come into the Red Sox clubhouse to meet him. He goes up the ramp toward the clubhouse and all he sees are reporters and TV lights. For a moment he wonders if he's about to be arrested or interviewed. Two days later he appears on the Ed Sullivan show, baseball's newest hero. The mayor of Boston sends him a telegram thanking him for giving all Red Sox fans everywhere an unforgettable day, and saying how he hopes Rohr's victory over the Yankees will be the first of hundreds of others in his career.

It isn't.

By the end of the year Rohr will be long gone from the Red Sox; the highlight of his career will be this afternoon in Yankee Stadium. But, in a sense, this early-season game, played before a sparse crowd in Yankee Stadium on this cold, raw April afternoon, comes to resemble that season that will forever be known as the "Impossible Dream," the season that becomes, as someone once put it, the time everyone forgot about the human race and worried about the pennant race: It is a complete surprise; it's an incredible, memorable performance by a player who isn't supposed to be able to deliver it; and, in the end, it just misses being perfect.

But I don't know that now.

Nobody does.

drugs in sports. The sports page doesn't look like a police
blotter. The problems of society rarely enter the locker
room, and if they do, we aren't told about them. There are
no astronomical salaries. The Red Sox's total payroll for the
season is roughly $800,000, not even a sixth of what a
superstar can make today in one year. Except for the few
superstars, playing major league baseball is not seen as a
way to get rich. Most players have second jobs in the
off-season, especially the players with families.

Nor is playing in the major leagues perceived as something that automatically will set up a player financially
for life, as it is today. Just the opposite. Rico Petrocelli,
the young, third-year shortstop, is afraid to buy a house,
for fear he will lose his job and be unable to make the
payments. Even Dick Williams, the new manager, is operat-
ing on a one-year contract. In a sense professional baseball
is more of a game than it will be years later, something one
does before going on to do something else. When a player's
contract is up he goes into the general manager's office and
essentially takes what is offered him. There are no agents.
There are few long-term contracts, thus the players are
under more pressure to produce. The owners run the game
and the players know it.

In many ways, baseball itself has been able to exist in its
own cocoon in this spring of 1967. There is only a fledgling
Players Association. There is no free agency, giving players
the right to make their own deals when their contracts
expire, thus giving them a certain freedom. In essence, the
players are bound to the team that owns them. The atmosphere is paternalistic, especially on a team like the Red
Sox, which is owned by Tom Yawkey, who's often accused
of running the club like some benevolent plantation. This is
the system the players have come of age in, and it's
accepted as if it came chiseled in stone. The players are still
products of the '50s. They have short hair. Many of them
are from small towns, haven't been to college, have married
young to their high school sweethearts.

If major league baseball appears little different from what
it had been a decade earlier, the rest of society is volatile.

alive with the sense of change. U.S. involvement in the war in Vietnam is in its sixth year, with more escalation, more casualties, more money spent; all without any end in sight. President Lyndon B. Johnson has recently committed an additional 50,000 combat troops to Vietnam, bringing the total number of American troops in Southeast Asia to 530,000. Casualties already have passed the 100,000 mark. Every day the nation's newspapers bring more reports from this far-off war, complete with once-strange names that are starting to be etched into the country's consciousness. Saigon. Da Nang. Quang Tri. Every night the fighting arrives in people's living rooms, complete in living color, an undecipherable war from some strange place that seems so different from all the other wars the country has fought.

Resistance is growing.

Throughout the spring there have been countless campus demonstrations. There have also been draft card burnings and protests against campus recruitment by the Dow Chemical Company, makers of napalm. Already, thousands of young men have been charged for refusing to enter the armed services, and the number of those who've fled to either Canada or Sweden is over 10,000. Senators William Fulbright of Arkansas and Mike Mansfield of Montana are starting to speak out against the war on the Senate floor. As is Robert Kennedy, now a senator from New York. In early April, speaking at Riverside Church in New York City, Martin Luther King calls for all blacks and "all white people of good will" to oppose the war by becoming conscientious objectors to military service. King goes on to say that blacks and poor people are bearing the brunt of the war, and this is a "reflection on the Negro's role in society."

At the same time Muhammad Ali, the former Cassius Clay, the heavyweight champ of the world, announces he's going to fight Floyd Patterson in late April, three days before he's scheduled to be inducted into the army. Ali has been at odds with the Selective Service, the euphemism for the country's draft board, for a while now, saying he opposes the war. Now he says he might give himself up for induction.

There is a new controversial play in New York. It's called *MacBird!*, and it's a vicious satire on Lyndon Johnson and American political life. It's a parody of Shakespeare's *Macbeth*, with Johnson plotting to assassinate John Kennedy. After saying he applauds irreverence in the theater, a drama critic writes, "This kind of irreverence we don't need." It is not a unique observation.

Then there is the music.

By 1967 it is clear rock music is having an increasing influence, not to mention significance, on the lives of young Americans, and, by extension, the larger society as well. The war. The civil rights movement. The free speech movement. The sexual revolution. All these seemingly disparate things are bound together by rock music, the music that has become an anthem for a generation coming of age. It's all the beginnings of a counterculture, one whose most obvious symbols will be long hair on young men, bell-bottom jeans, and the glorification of everything that shocks the main culture, especially marijuana and mind-altering drugs. It's the culture that first got spawned in rock music, and it's growing rapidly, setting off a generation gap that seems to be as awesome as the Continental Divide. In less than a year *Hair* will open on Broadway, billing itself as an "American tribal love-rock musical." It will celebrate long hair, opposition to the war, frontal nudity, draft card burning, and dropping out of society. It will become a symbol of this burgeoning counterculture, complete with its anthem that says this is the dawning of the Age of Aquarius, a new age "when peace shall guide the planets and love will steer the stars."

An article in *Fortune* magazine comments on how the business community is worried that a consumer revolution might be in the future, not because consumers won't be able to afford things, but because they won't want to. Timothy Leary, a former Harvard professor who's become the self-proclaimed high priest of LSD, predicts, "America will be an LSD country within 15 years." There are a reported

90,000 runaways in the United States, and the dropout rate at American universities is at an all-time high.

"Something's happening here," a rock group called Buffalo Springfield sings. "What it is ain't exactly clear."

Sports is one of the last arenas unaffected by all this change.

It still belongs to a simpler time, a time that will soon be gone forever. In a sense it's the last bastion of innocence. Everything else is touched by the war, and the reaction to it. Schools. Education. Politics. Families. The arts. Seemingly everything except sports, where the values have remained unchanged for decades, the assumptions unchallenged.

Shortly before the Red Sox leave Winter Haven, the small town in central Florida where they've held spring training for the second year, new manager Dick Williams will tell his team that they have to wear sports coats or suits on the road, no sweaters. He will tell them they can't wear dungarees, Levi's or chino pants on the road, and that he expects them not to "dress sloppy" when the club is at home either. "We'll leave the Bermuda shorts for the Beach Boys," he tells them.

No one objects.

The year before, the Red Sox had finished ninth, saved by the ignominy of last only by the inept New York Yankees. They finished 72-90, 26 games behind the Baltimore Orioles. It's not a new phenomenon. Under managers Billy Jurges, Mike "Pinky" Higgins, Johnny Pesky, and Billy Herman, the Red Sox had failed to finish higher than sixth in the last seven years. Now the Sox have been picked to finish near the bottom of the league once again. No one seems very surprised. The Red Sox have long been a team where futility and frustration have spots on the roster. The team hasn't won a World Series since 1918 and seems forever haunted by the sale of Babe Ruth to the Yankees, a deal made because Harry Frazee, the Broadway producer who owned the Sox at the time, needed money to support a sinking play. They'd won the American League pennant in 1946, but had lost the World Series when shortstop Pesky held the ball too long on a throw in from the outfield, a mental error that had allowed Enos Slaughter to score. Somehow it seemed symbolic. The Red Sox had acquired a reputation as a star-crossed franchise, one that forever seemed to have some dark cloud hanging over it. As if the trading of Ruth to the hated Yankees was the franchise's Original Sin, one they could never shake.

Two years later the Sox ended the season tied with the Cleveland Indians. A one-game playoff was held at Fenway Park. Red Sox manager Joe McCarthy opted to go with journeyman pitcher Denny Galehouse. He was routed. The Sox lost. The next year, in 1949, the Sox went into Yankee Stadium needing only one victory in their last two games to win the pennant over the hated Yankees. The Red Sox blew a 4–0 lead in the first game, then also lost the second.

The years after that had been bearable, if only for the presence of Ted Williams. He'd been the last player in the major leagues to hit .400, finishing the 1941 season at .406, an accomplishment that had become part of baseball history. He also seemed symbolic of the Red Sox. He was regarded as the best hitter in the game, yet was criticized for failing to hit in the clutch. He was such a great left-handed pull hitter that many teams invariably pulled the "Williams Shift" on him, sending all but two of the fielders to the right side of the diamond, thus opening up the left side of the field. Williams never budged. He continued to try to pull the ball, refusing to adjust. Early in his career he'd been nicknamed "the Kid," and it always seemed appropriate, even near the end of his career, as if he was frozen forever in perpetual adolescence, impetuous, independent, perhaps best exemplified by his refusal to wear a necktie. He was criticized for being selfish, for refusing to sacrifice himself for the good of the team. This too seemed symbolic of the Red Sox, suggesting that even the greatest of the Red Sox come with some tragic flaw, are victims of the franchise's Original Sin.

Williams' great career in Boston always was a bit tainted by his relationship with the Boston media. He derisively called the writers "the knights of the keyboards." They, in turn, largely considered him spoiled and arrogant, Yawkey's pet. Too often, Williams' relationship with the press became a sideshow that seemed to overshadow the team. He finally retired in 1960, hitting .316 at the age of 41. His last time at bat he homered, an event later turned into literature by John Updike in a magazine article called "Hub Fans Bid Kid Adieu." For years Williams had been occasion enough to come to Fenway. Even in the twilight of his career he was a drawing card, one of the only reasons to see the Red Sox.

But now the Splendid Splinter is gone, and the Sox have become a slow, one-dimensional team that never seems to have enough pitching. In theory, it's a team tailored for Fenway Park, the Red Sox's lyrical bandbox whose most distinguished feature is its left-field wall, a mere 315 feet from home plate, so close it always seems to be a siren song. The Red Sox are always looking for big, right-handed power hitters who can hit the wall. The result is they usually score a lot of runs. They also surrender a lot of runs. In the past 15 years they've been little more than an also-ran in an American League dominated by the Yankees. They finished 32 games out of first place in 1960, 33 back the following year. The next few years were not any better. The bright spots were few, centered around the arrival of young talent. In 1964 Tony Conigliaro hit 24 home runs as a rookie. The next year Carl Yastrzemski hit .312, and a young pitcher named Jim Lonborg won nine games.

Baseball has grown up with the country, a rural game that was born in the small towns of an earlier America. Not for nothing is it called the National Pastime. It is immortalized in literature, celebrated in song. There is not a school kid alive who hasn't heard of "Casey at the Bat," the famous poem written by Ernest Lawrence Thayer, who lived in Worcester, 40 miles from Boston.

Baseball is a part of the culture in ways that football and basketball aren't. Baseball is one of the few sports where the American ideal of the melting pot has been actualized. At least for white America. It's on the baseball diamond that the American Dream is visible to all, not just something discussed by learned men in the groves of academe. Baseball is the first sport to be broadcast on radio, the first sport on television. The premier sporting event in the country is the World Series. It's played in the afternoons, and has become such a national event that it's often broadcast into schools, part of the fabric of society.

The rising *new* game in the country, though, is professional football. Its popularity is growing significantly, spurred on by television and shrewd marketing. It is physical, violent, explosive. It seems more in tune with a changing America. By comparison, baseball seems dull, slow, rooted in some gone-forever time. Especially in Boston, where the Red Sox are boring, bad, and the victims of falling attendance.

The Red Sox's owner, Tom Yawkey, is a South Carolina plantation owner and gentleman farmer who has long been accused of running a baseball franchise disguised as a country club. His uncle, who adopted him when he was a baby, had owned the Detroit Tigers for three years in the early 1900s, and one of Yawkey's childhood memories was playing catch with Ty Cobb on his uncle's lawn. While a student at Yale, Yawkey was a second baseman. When he turned 30 he inherited a $500,000 trust fund. Later he inherited $4 million from his late mother's estate, and another $3 million from his foster father's estate. He also inherited the family lumber and metals business in Canada.

Yawkey bought the Red Sox in 1933 from Bob Quinn, who had no idea where he could get enough money to finance the season. The Red Sox had first come into existence in 1901, along with the American League, playing their games at a field on Huntington Avenue, not far from what eventually became Fenway Park. They had one of the game's first real stars, pitcher Cy Young, the man whose name eventually became synonymous with pitching excellence, the Cy Young Award going to the outstanding pitcher in each league. But by 1920 Ruth had been sold to the Yankees where he went on to become America's most famous athlete, and the most famous baseball player ever, not to mention the centerpiece of the great Yankee teams of the '20s and early '30s. All the while the Red Sox were languishing, never recovering from the selling of Ruth.

By the early '30s the team had hit rock bottom, having finished last for six straight years and nine years out of eleven. Attendance was poor. When Yawkey bought the team, interest in the Red Sox in Boston was below that of the Braves, who were in the National League and played at Braves Field, only a few miles away. Yawkey bought the club for about a million, vowed to spare no expense to make the team a winner. As proof of this, he promised to rebuild Fenway Park, which had undergone little change since it had opened in 1912. Between 1933 and World War II he spent millions of dollars in his attempt to win. He quickly transformed the team into a winner, but they never did win a pennant during that period, coming in second to the Yankees on four separate occasions.

When Yawkey first bought the team he loved to work out with the players, trading banter with such stars as Jimmie Foxx, Joe Cronin, and Lefty Grove. They were *his* stars, and he seemed to idolize them as much as the fans who flocked to his ballpark. He loved baseball in a way that few owners did, had a genuine passion for the game he'd played as a child. When the team was on the road and Fenway was empty, he would picnic with his wife on the grass. He had his own locker in the Red Sox clubhouse and liked to hit and take fly balls with his players, although the team members who joined him were called "ass kissers." But he was close to the age of his players, and often invited them to his South Carolina island to hunt with him in the winter. He paid them handsomely, never cut anyone's salary, and was known as the most benevolent owner in the game, to the point that the Red Sox were sometimes referred to as "Yawkey's Millionaires."

One of the knocks on the Red Sox organization was cronyism—Yawkey's habit of keeping people on the payroll who'd proven themselves incompetent. When the choice ultimately came down to hurting a friend or hurting the club, Yawkey reluctantly hurt the club, the one thing he loved the most. His first choice for general manager had been Eddie Collins, a once-great player whom Yawkey had idolized since childhood. The two had attended the same prep school in New York where, when Yawkey attended, the main prize had been the Edward T. Collins Medal for the best scholar-athlete. Yawkey had been runner-up. Collins had been a good general manager, organized, hiring people on merit. Within five years, the combination of Yawkey's money and Collins' baseball acumen had resurrected the team and made it a pennant contender. When in 1948 Collins was ailing and could no longer perform as the Sox's general manager, Yawkey selected his good friend Joe Cronin, his former All-Star and manager, as his replacement. Cronin hired his friends and stuck by them, the same way Yawkey stuck by him. The Red Sox had started the '50s as one of the best teams in baseball, only to get progressively worse as the decade played out, a victim of poor scouting and even poorer organization. By the time Cronin left in 1958 to become the president of the American League, the organization was in shambles. Two of his successors, Bucky Harris and Pinky Higgins, did little to change things, both being products of the same system. By 1965 the team had bottomed out. The manager then was Billy Herman, a friend of Higgins', who seemingly cared more about his golf game than developing his younger players.

As the years went by Yawkey became more removed from the players, working out instead with the batboys and grounds people. He was now older than the players and the age difference had changed his relationship with them. He still had a locker in the clubhouse, but fraternized less. A shy, reclusive man, Yawkey only felt comfortable around a handful of people, all the while doting on his stars, giving them his friendship while keeping a distance from the other players. This was one of the reasons the Red Sox were always criticized for being a selfish team, a team full of stars who all seemed to revolve in their own personal solar systems, a team stamped by little discipline and a preoccupation with personal statistics at the expense of team goals. One of Yawkey's pets had been Ted Williams, the only player who called him by his first name. So maybe it was only fitting that Carl Yastrzemski, Williams' heir, became another. In a sense they became the sons he never had.

Yaz had arrived in Boston in 1961, viewed as the next Red Sox superstar, the successor in left field to Ted Williams. As further example of his anointed status, the first time Williams saw him hit he supposedly said, "Don't ever let anyone change your swing." Coming from Williams, that was like a message from Mount Olympus.

The first year Yastrzemski went to spring training he was given a locker next to Williams, then in the last year of his career. Williams was forever talking to Yastrzemski about the intricacies of hitting, as if hitting a baseball was as complicated as nuclear fission. Yastrzemski didn't know what he was talking about. Williams talked about moving his hips and the science of hitting, and the young Yastrzemski had no idea what he meant. So he said nothing, nodding at the appropriate time. To him, hitting was instinctive, something he had done all his life, ever since being taught by his father as a young child. To Williams, it had become a science, something to be analyzed like some lab specimen.

Yastrzemski didn't like being billed as Williams' successor. He was too concerned with trying to make the club, with battling his own insecurities. The last thing he needed was to carry Williams' heavy baggage. He'd grown up, the son of a potato farmer, in Bridgehampton, New York, a tiny farming community at the end of Long Island, had learned the game by playing on a team coached by his father and made up of his uncles and cousins. His father once had his own major league dreams, ones that got sacrificed to the Depression. He worked long and hard, farming his 70-acre potato farm, and along the way transferred his dream to his son, setting out to give him the chance he never had.

Yastrzemski's boyhood was like being an apprentice in some baseball workshop. He practiced his swing in the garage. He did exercises to develop his wrists. He hit tennis balls thrown to him by his uncles. His entire childhood was devoted to one day being a major league baseball player, a blueprint orchestrated by his father, also named Carl. For 27 years the elder Yastrzemski spent two nights and one weekend afternoon throughout the summer playing semipro ball for teams with names like the Riverhead Falcons and the Bridgehampton White Eagles, and against such barnstorming players as Satchel Paige, Don Newcombe, and Roy Campanella. As young as six, Carl Jr. began tagging along after his father to baseball fields. Later, he and his father played in the same infield for a semipro team called Lake Ronkonkoma.

Yastrzemski grew up idolizing the Yankees, made pilgrimages in from Long Island to see them play, back when the big names had been first DiMaggio, then Mantle. The Yankees even worked out Carl Jr. in Yankee Stadium, offering $40,000 for him to sign. His father said no. His price for his son was $100,000, plus a college education—an almost unheard of sum in those days. Shortly afterward, Ray Garland, the Yankee scout who had first seen Yastrzemski play in leagues on Long Island, visited the house. He said the Yankees had authorized him to go as high as $45,000. Garland made some notations on a scratch pad, saying that since the Yankees were frequently in the World Series any player with them had the opportunity to make much more money. Yaz wanted to sign, wanted desperately to sign with the team of his boyhood. His father said no.

"What do you think?" Garland said to the elder Yastrzemski.

Yastrzemski's father took the scratch pad, wrote $100,000 in big letters across the top of it.

Garland reached across the table, took the scratch pad and the pencils and threw them up in the air. Yaz would later say he knew he'd never play for the Yankees the moment Garland heaved the pad into the air, that his father would interpret it as a sign of disrespect in his own house.

"The Yankees never offered that kind of money to anyone and they won't give it to your boy," Garland said.

"Then they'll never get him," said Carl Sr.

Yaz then spent a year at Notre Dame on a scholarship that was split between baseball and basketball. The following summer he came home to Long Island, played in local leagues, and once again the scouts were as much a part of his summer as mosquitoes and sunburn. At the end of the season, before he was scheduled to return to school, the Philadelphia Phillies offered him a package worth $102,000. But the elder Yastrzemski also wanted the Phillies to pay his son an additional $10,000 if Yaz dropped out of college. The Phillies balked, and Yaz went back for his sophomore year at Notre Dame. Shortly before Thanksgiving the Cincinnati Reds offered $125,000. His father asked for $150,000, and Yaz came to understand that his father, an uneducated potato farmer his entire life, was getting great delight in playing hardball with major league clubs.

During Thanksgiving vacation Yaz and his father visited Boston for the first time. By this time the elder Yastrzemski had decided the Red Sox were the right team for his son. Not only did he like the idea of his son playing in Fenway Park—known in baseball circles as a hitter's park—he also liked Bots Nekola, the Red Sox scout who had been pursuing Yaz long and hard. Yaz signed that weekend for $108,000, a two-year Triple A contract at $5,000 a year, plus the rest of his college tuition.

While Yaz and his father were signing the contract, Joe Cronin wanted to have a look at the new Red Sox phenom. Cronin was the Sox general manager at the time, a once-great player who had come of age at a time when unproven kids weren't offered big money before they ever put on a big league uniform.

"He doesn't look very big," Cronin said.

"He hits big," said Johnny Murphy, the Sox's farm director.

Cronin grunted.

By the end of 1966 Yastrzemski had played six seasons in Boston, and though he hadn't accomplished the sort of heroics that would make anyone forget Williams, he'd hit over .300 twice, winning the batting crown in 1963. He'd also been moody, even petulant at times, with a reputation for not running out routine outs and playing only as hard as he had to. One reason for this was that he'd joined the team when it had been mediocre for years, and morale was poor. By his second year, in 1962, he knew there was a certain antagonism toward him, that there were many players who resented the size of his signing bonus and the attention he was receiving. It got so bad that he realized there were some of his teammates who actually were rooting against him, hoping he would fail.

By the end of the year the team was mired in the second division, and many of the players had completely lost interest. Don Fitzpatrick, the Red Sox's clubhouse boy, kept telling Yastrzemski to forget the others and just play for himself; that if he listened to most of his teammates he would end up just like them, losers. Throughout the '66 season there had been rumors he might be traded. His relationship with manager Billy Herman had deteriorated, and it was no secret Herman would have loved to be rid of him. Yastrzemski had the ceremonial title of captain, a role he neither wanted nor was particularly suited for. Not only was he moody, he was a loner. He also wasn't close to any of his teammates. That dated back to spring training in 1960 in Scottsdale, Arizona. It was Yastrzemski's first spring training with the Red Sox, a year before he would stick with the Red Sox. He was newly married. It was when he first felt resentment from many of the older players because of his large signing bonus. His wife, Carol, away from home for the first time, was lonely and couldn't make any friends. Nor could Yaz. His only true friend the year before in the minors had been Chuck Schilling, whom he'd played against as a kid on Long Island. But Schilling was at the Sox's Triple A camp. The Yastrzemskis stayed in the same apartment complex as the other players and their wives, but they were never included in any social activities. With the exception of Frank Malzone, the veteran third baseman, and his wife, no one else went out of their way to make either Yaz or Carol feel a part of the team. It was a slight he hadn't gotten over yet.

"Because of that dreadful spring I never found it easy to fraternize with teammates," he wrote in his autobiography, published in 1968. "Although I got along all right with everybody, the only true close friend I had on the Red Sox was Schilling. Except for him, I was always a bit of a loner, which is not my nature at all. I would have been more gregarious, friendlier, and much happier if it hadn't been for the deep freeze Carol and I lived in during those first weeks of our marriage.''

For a while during the '66 season he'd tried to function as a go-between between Herman and the rest of the players, but as the season progressed he stopped doing it. Soon after, Yastrzemski started hearing rumors Herman was trying to get rid of him. Eventually, Herman told Yaz he wasn't hustling. Yastrzemski objected. Herman countered by saying that one of them wouldn't be there the following year. But even when Herman got fired, Yastrzemski worried about his future in Boston. It was all over the papers that he was being shopped around, and now here was a new manager, a symbol of a new era. Yaz had just bought a new house in Lynnfield, a suburb north of Boston, and had come to like the city. He was comfortable with the Red Sox and had no desire to uproot his family and go somewhere else.

Shortly after the '66 season Yastrzemski went to the Colonial Inn in Lynnfield, partly to take his mind off the trade rumors and his uncertain future. There he met Gene Berde, who'd once coached the Hungarian boxing team. He was a little gnome of a man who ran the health club at the Colonial.

"So you're the great baseball star Carl Yastrzemski," Berde said. He reached out and touched Yastrzemski's stomach. "You think you're in shape?"

"Well," said Yastrzemski. "I'm not in bad shape."

"Huh," said Berde. "You the big baseball player. You the big champion. You the best player. You can't even run a hundred yards. You no athlete. In my country you are nothing, because in this kind of shape you are only a third-class athlete. All right. You do what I say. I put you in shape."

He put Yastrzemski through a series of exercises and Yaz was winded.

"You're soft," Berde told him. "You have a good body, but you're flabby. You have no resistance. You are not an athlete in my country in this shape. I am surprised in United

States you are one of the biggest athletes, your picture in the paper every day almost.''

So began an almost daily six-week conditioning program.

"He put me on a schedule of ninety minutes a day, six days a week,'' Yastrzemski said in his autobiography. "I was skipping rope for 10 minutes straight, and then I was sprinting until I thought my lungs would burst. He gave me every exercise, except lifting weights, that anybody ever heard of. And he made me do them. Soon I was feeling better than I ever had in my life.''

This is before the time when professional athletes were careful to work out in the off-season. Most of them worked, either in some business they hoped to one day get involved in after their playing days were over, or for a second income. There were no Nautilus machines. Weights were thought to make ballplayers muscle-bound and blocky. No one talked about nutrition, aerobics, stretching. The prevailing thinking was that spring training was plenty of time to get in shape for the season.

Yastrzemski arrives at Winter Haven in the best condition of his life, and immediately starts showing more power.

The other star is Tony Conigliaro, who is in the middle of some sandlot fantasy. He is young, Hollywood handsome, with a talent as deep as the hole in right-center in Fenway. He also is a right-handed pull hitter and hits the long ball, born to hit in Fenway Park. Though Yaz has always seemed uncomfortable with his star label, Tony C. seems destined for it—a homegrown hero direct from Central Casting. He was born in Revere, little more than a long fly ball from Fenway Park, and grew up first in East Boston, then in suburban Swampscott. He also might just be the most popular Red Sox player since Harry Agganis in the early '50s. Agganis was from nearby Lynn, had been a great high school athlete, and an All-American quarterback at Boston University. He was called "the Golden Greek.'' In his first season with the Red Sox in '54 he hit 11 home runs. The following June he was hospitalized with a fever and chest pains, and died soon after. He was 25.

Conigliaro had gone to high school in Lynn, at a parochial school called St. Mary's. When he graduated in the spring of 1962 he was signed by scout Milt Bolling, a former Red Sox infielder, for $20,000. He bought a Corvette, the ultimate teenage status symbol. He was sent to the Instructional League, where he hit .220. The next winter was spent swinging a weighted bat in the basement of his parents' home in Swampscott. He also worked as an extra in the movie *The Cardinal*. The following year in Class A in the New York–Penn League, he was the league MVP.

That earned him a trip to spring training with the Sox in March of 1964 in Scottsdale, Arizona, even though no one thought he was ready. But he homered in one of the first intrasquad games, and immediately became one of the big stories in spring training. He was local. He was cocky. By the end of spring training he was being called the best young Red Sox power hitter since Ted Williams a quarter of a century earlier. He also had star quality. Throughout that spring training Conigliaro, Petrocelli, and some of the younger players often spent their nights at a local nightspot called J. D.'s. Downstairs was rock 'n' roll. Upstairs was country and western. Sometimes Conigliaro would sing, a harbinger of things to come.

In his third time at bat, in fabled Yankee Stadium, he complained to the umpire behind the plate that veteran Yankee great Whitey Ford was throwing a spitter, unheard of for a rookie in his first major league game. In his first time at bat in Fenway Park he hit a home run. On his ceremonial home run trot, near second base, he smiled and shook his head, as if at the wonder of it all. He went on to hit 24 home runs that year, more than any other teenager in major league history. By June he was getting 200 fan letters a week, mostly from teenage girls who thought he was as cute as a rock star. In the *Boston Globe,* his rookie year was being compared to Williams' first season. That July there was a feature story headlined, "Will Conig Follow Ruth, Speaker, to the Hall of Fame?" He was 19 years old.

During the off-season he cut a record. On one side was "Playing the Field," a song that seemed aptly suited to Conigliaro's life-style. Tony C. was young, handsome, single, famous, and never saw a lady he didn't like. The other was a ballad called "Why Can't They Understand?" Within a month it was number 14 in Boston. The next year he led the American League in homers, the youngest ever to do so.

In 1967 Conigliaro is well on his way to becoming one of baseball's biggest names. He also is visible in the singles bars in Kenmore Square, where he lives in a 10th-floor penthouse apartment with Tony Athanas, whose family owns Anthony's Pier Four, one of the city's most popular restaurants. He continues to be one of the best power hitters in the league. He also has another record out, "Little Red Scooter" and "I Can't Get Over You."

There is no obvious friction between Yastrzemski and Conigliaro, yet there is an underlying tension, two large egos that have yet to feel comfortable with each other. Some of it is life-style—Yastrzemski the homebody, Conigliaro the swinging young single. Some of it is personality—Yastrzemski the loner, moody, as if always at war with private demons. Conigliaro, brash, cocky, the star in his own movie. Some of it is territorial—Yastrzemski the symbolic leader of the Red Sox and Conigliaro the emerging young star. Yet Conigliaro has never been able to understand how Yaz can seem so outwardly blasé about the Red Sox's failures, how he sometimes seems to only go through the motions.

Conigliaro also doesn't like Dick Williams. This is the result of an incident that goes back to Conigliaro's first spring training in Scottsdale when Williams had been a veteran. Rookies were to be seen and not heard then, their presence rarely acknowledged by the older, established players. One of the first days, Conigliaro was coming out of the dugout when he suddenly saw a ball coming for his head. He dove to the ground, only to hear Williams say, "Watch where you're going, bush." The next day Conigliaro was playing catch with the veteran Dick Stuart when he saw Williams coming out of the dugout, oblivious. He rifled a ball at him, and down Williams went, sprawled in the dirt. "Watch where you're going, bush," Conigliaro said. Williams jumped to his feet and came charging, only to be intercepted by Stuart. It was the first friendly thing a veteran had done for Conigliaro, and he began a friendship with Stuart because of it. Not with Williams, though. As fate would have it, their relationship worsened shortly afterward when, for a short while, the two were assigned to be roommates in spring training, part of the Red Sox policy at the time of pairing a rookie with a veteran. Williams was regarded as a good company man at the time, a veteran player who might be a positive influence on an impulsive rookie. Every night he stayed in his room and talked to his wife on the phone while Tony C. and the younger players went to J.D.'s. Williams said that when he went to bed at night Conigliaro wasn't there. When he woke up in the morning Conigliaro wasn't there. "It was like rooming with a suitcase." Talk about the odd couple. Early into the season Williams went to manager Johnny Pesky and said that his rooming with Conigliaro had become a joke. Shortly after the two separated, the Red Sox caught Conigliaro missing curfew and fined him $1,000. Conigliaro always thought Williams had set him up.

If the Red Sox of 1967 promise to be better, it's because the seeds were sown in 1965. Dick O'Connell, who'd been the organization's business manager and all-around troubleshooter, became the general manager. He replaced Pinky Higgins, a former manager whose primary credential for the job of general manager seemed to be he was one of the few people Yawkey felt comfortable around.

There always seemed to be a card game in the clubhouse, and not too many players spent a lot of time working on their imperfections. The tradition was passed on to the younger players like some fraternity handshake, presided over by managers who either didn't have the ability or inclination to deal with the situation, and by an eccentric owner who didn't show up in Boston until June and seemed to grow more aloof, more eccentric, as he got older.

O'Connell set out to completely overhaul the team.

He'd grown up in suburban Winthrop, had gone to Boston College, class of '37. He'd been an air force pilot in World

War II in the Pacific, and when the war ended he'd walked into the Red Sox offices at Fenway, ostensibly to deliver a message to Joe Cronin from a mutual friend. One thing led to another, and he was offered a job running a Sox farm team in Lynn. He gradually worked his way into the front office, and in an organization full of Cronin's buddies, immediately distinguished himself as competent and effective. For a while he was listed as business manager. What he really did was all the things that no one else did in an organization where the owner essentially hid from people. It was O'Connell who dealt with City Hall. It was O'Connell who dealt with the parking problems around Fenway Park. It was O'Connell who was the man who said either yes or no, the one who came, almost by default, to make the decisions.

When he became the general manager in 1965 his game plan was to unload players he considered past their prime. Pitcher Bill Monbouquette went, though he had won 20 games two years before, and had grown up in suburban Boston. He was traded to Detroit after the '65 season, after winning only 10 games. Traded too was Dick Radatz. Only a couple of years before he'd been the most dominant relief pitcher in the game, a large, hulking man who threw smoke and was nicknamed "the Monster." For a while in the early '60s he was one of the few reasons to watch the Red Sox. But he tried to come up with a breaking pitch and hurt his arm. O'Connell traded him to Cleveland in early 1966. The Sox got pitchers Lee Stange and Don McMahon in return.

And for the first time in years the Red Sox farm system was sending some young, quality players to the big leagues, the legacy of Neil Mahoney, who'd become the farm director in 1960. The seeds were there for a new era.

Enter Dick Williams.

He'd been managing the Red Sox's Triple A farm team in Toronto for two years, leading them to the International League pennant in 1966. Before that, he'd spent 13 years in the major leagues, mostly as a reserve. He'd joined the Red Sox in 1962, coming over from Baltimore via Houston for reserve outfielder Carroll Hardy, whose only claim to fame was that he was the only man ever to pinch-hit for Ted

Williams. After the '64 season Dick Williams was offered a minor league managing job at half his major league salary.

By the '66 season there were rumors manager Billy Herman was in trouble. Gary Waslewski, who was playing for Williams in Toronto, remembers one night early in the year in some hotel bar when Williams told a group of players that next year Herman would be out, and whoever played well for Williams was going with him to the big show. One time in the middle of the season O'Connell flew to Columbus, Ohio, where Williams and his Toronto team were playing. After the game, the two went out to dinner at the local air force base, where O'Connell had privileges due to his air force status. Williams knew why O'Connell was there, but the job of being the next Red Sox manager was never discussed. Williams and O'Connell had always gotten along back when Williams had been a Red Sox player and O'Connell had been the business manager.

That September Herman was indeed fired, replaced by veteran Pete Runnels, who managed the remainder of the season. At the end of the year Williams drove to Boston with Mike Andrews, who had been his second baseman at Toronto and already had been told he was being called up to Boston. Williams checked into the Howard Johnson's hotel in Kenmore Square, little more than a fly ball from Fenway Park. Also there was Eddie Popowski. He had already been told he would be a coach in Boston the following season. Two days went by, as the Red Sox held their minor league meetings. Williams continued to wait. He was sure he was there to be named the next manager, but no one had told him anything yet. He kept asking Popowski if he knew anything. Popowski kept telling him not to worry. He kept worrying.

On the third day most everyone in the Red Sox organization went to lunch at Jimmy's Harborside, a popular seafood restaurant on Boston's waterfront, across the city from Fenway Park. Afterward, O'Connell told Williams and Popowski he would give them a ride back to their hotel. He left the restaurant parking lot, drove around the corner. Then he stopped the car.

"I want to shake hands with the next manager of the Red Sox," he said to Williams.

They went back to O'Connell's house to talk about specifics. O'Connell offered him a one-year contract at $25,000. Williams was elated. He'd never made that much money in his life. His tops as a player had been $18,500 his last year with the Red Sox. His first year managing in Toronto he'd made $10,000, receiving a $2,000 raise the following year. He and his wife, Norma, had always been poor. Now they were dirt poor. They'd had their third child shortly before the '65 season, and he hadn't been able to be present at the birth because he was in spring training and Norma was in California. By his second year in Toronto he was so strapped financially his family didn't come with him to Toronto for the summer because they couldn't afford it, and if he hadn't gotten the Red Sox job he would have given serious thought to getting out of baseball. Now he was the manager of the Red Sox, and was perceptive enough to realize O'Connell had pushed for him, perceptive enough to know he was the first Red Sox manager in years who was not a drinking buddy of Yawkey's. It was a realization that later would haunt him, this feeling that Yawkey never had wanted him. In truth, he didn't particularly like Yawkey. To the people who worked at Fenway Park, and to several of the players who'd come of age in the organization, Yawkey was almost sainted. Williams didn't see it that way. To him, it was more personal. His suspicions about Yawkey had been formed in the two years he'd played with the Red Sox, a veteran has-been at the end of his career. Yawkey never introduced himself, never paid any attention to him. He would see Yawkey in the clubhouse and it was like he didn't exist, just one of the faceless marginal players Yawkey seemed to have no time for.

By the time he left O'Connell's house his salary had jumped to $35,000. He was 37, the youngest manager in the American League.

As spring training opens Williams knows all too well the club's country club image. In his two-year stint as a Red Sox player Williams had distinguished himself as bright, tough, a needler, and someone who lived and breathed baseball. Last winter, at his home in Arcadia, California, near the Santa Anita racetrack, he knew that would be his first priority. Throughout the off-season, while he waited to go to Winter Haven, he spent his time fiddling with lineup cards and talking to O'Connell, all the while knowing that without a significant change in attitude all the new lineups in the world wouldn't change anything.

One of the first things he does upon arriving in Winter Haven is call a team meeting.

"Look," he says, "I was here when this was a country club. I've been here and I've been a lot of other places. I'm not going to tell you that I'm the greatest. But I've been everywhere and I've done everything. And the buck stops right here with me. If you don't want to be proud, then I can't put pride in you. I'll get rid of you. This is a one-year deal with me. I can put you up in the first division. I can make you proud to be a baseball player. And I can get rid of you and I can embarrass you. You pick. From this moment on, the fine for missing curfew is $500 and there isn't any way to get upstairs to Mr. Yawkey. It stops right here with me. The fine is $500 and it sticks and it comes out of your paychecks and that means every two weeks, and if your paycheck is $500 short, then you don't have to account to me. You can account to your wife—and you just try explaining that to your wife. Because I don't want to hear about it. I saw guys lose every bit of pride they had, playing for this team. I got one year—and I'm going to give you the chance to be proud."

He adds one more thing.

"There won't be any team meetings without coaches and the manager. And there won't be any team captain this year. I don't need a team captain. I don't need a spy and I don't need anyone crying cop. I run this team. I'm the boss. You live with me, you play for me, and if you screw up on me, then there's one solution—as long as I'm here you're gone."

During spring training Williams stresses fundamentals. Hitting the cutoff man. Bunting. Baserunning. Backing up the bases on a ball hit to the outfield. All the boring things most major-leaguers think is beneath them. One of the things he does is take the entire club around the field, stopping at each position where he explains, often up to as long as an hour and half, the responsibilities and demands of each position. It takes him three days to do it. Most of all, he vows to bring some discipline to a team that never has had any. From the beginning he says he has no interest in keeping his players happy, a goal of past Red Sox managers. He says he doesn't care if he antagonizes the veterans, several of whom are former teammates. He doesn't care how the players perceive him.

It's a lesson he learned in his two-year stint at Toronto. One time infielder Joe Foy made a mental error in the field, and as he came into the dugout at the end of the inning, Williams started harping on him. Foy started walking away. Williams told him, in no uncertain terms, that if he didn't want to listen he could keep on walking right into the clubhouse and out of his life forever. Foy stayed. He went on to be the International League player of the year.

"I thought, if that's what it takes, fine," Williams would later recall.

He has come to believe that players will never give 100 percent because they want something, but only because they hate something. And if they hate him, so be it.

"I hated losing," he'd say later. "Some guys hate failure. For the ones who treated winning and losing lightly, I figured I'd give them something to hate. Me. I tried to make some players win just to show me up."

He insists the players be on time. If they're not playing in a game, they are expected to either run or play volleyball out near the left-field foul line. He believes playing volleyball is a good way to get in shape, certainly better than sitting around doing nothing. Workouts are timed, organized.

The very first day camp had officially opened veteran pitchers Dennis Bennett and Bob Sadowski arrived 25 minutes late, saying the motel switchboard had failed to wake them on time. Williams called the motel and barked that all players were to be wakened at 7 A.M. sharp. Then he told the two veterans, in a voice that could be heard throughout the locker room, that their tardiness was not to happen again.

The Red Sox long had been used to an easy spring training, a leisurely chance to stretch out the kinks of the long winter, sit in the sun, and gradually get into shape, the type of spring training that dominated baseball. Instead, they get a baseball boot camp, with Dick Williams as drill sergeant. He is brash, caustic, authoritarian, manipulative. He wears his hair in a crew cut, marine style, looks like he just stepped off a recruiting poster. Sometimes he umpires intrasquad games because he feels it gives him a better look at his pitchers. He proclaims that winning is the only thing he's interested in, and he isn't real concerned what it takes to reach that end. He also gets into a minor tiff with Ted Williams, who always comes to spring training as a sort of unofficial hitting instructor. Ted Williams traditionally spends a lot of time kibitzing with the players, a custom that bothers Dick Williams and creates some tension between him and Ted. Sensing this, Ted eventually leaves spring training.

"The players probably thought I was crazy," Dick Williams would say later, "but, hell, I had a one-year contract, so if I was crazy I was going to be crazy all year and give it the best I had. I didn't make too many friends among the players, but I don't care if they like me or not. I am concerned, though, about them respecting my knowledge of the game. If they do, though, they'll play for me, and they'll play at the top of their ability."

Throughout spring training he constantly criticizes first baseman George Scott for his tendency to gain weight. Scott doesn't like the criticism, but he also puts it in a certain perspective. He sees Williams yell at everyone else. He sees Williams pushing every player to be better. Anyway, Scott had grown up in the Deep South, where the Man is always in charge, one way or the other.

Scott had arrived in Boston the year before, complete with a home run swing and a gold tooth in the front of his mouth. He was from Greenville, Mississippi, talked big, and was a dose of culture shock to the staid Red Sox. He was black on a team that had been the last to integrate in the major leagues. That had happened in 1959, only a few years before, when the Sox roster included Elijah "Pumpsie" Green, a reserve infielder whose most famous moment occurred in 1962 when he and pitcher Gene Conley jumped off a team bus in New York, supposedly to go to Tel Aviv, Israel.

Now there are five blacks, Scott, Joe Foy, pitcher John Wyatt, infielder George Smith, and rookie Reggie Smith. Scott is flashy. He wears a necklace that he says is strung with second basemen's teeth. He refers to home runs as "taters." In short, he is the antithesis of the typical Red Sox player. He'd only hit .245 as a rookie and had struck out 152 times. But he knocked in 90 runs and connected for 27 taters.

Scott quickly learns that Williams is the chief, and everyone else is an Indian. One day Williams tries Scott out as an outfielder, much to the first baseman's dismay. One apparent reason is that Williams would like to get Tony Horton's bat in the lineup. Horton had played two years for Williams in Toronto, and Williams likes him. He is a big right-handed hitter with power, the type of young player the Sox always seemed to covet. But he can play only first, while Scott is more versatile. Scott doesn't want to hear any of this, however. When he sees his name penciled in for right field, he shakes his head, and begins mumbling to himself.

"This is going to ruin my hitting," he says to Eddie Popowski, the third base coach. No matter that Popowski fails to see how playing right field is going to affect Scott's hitting. Scott is convinced Williams is playing with his head.

Told of Scott's reaction, Williams says, "I hear Scott doesn't like right field. Well, if he doesn't want to play, that's all right with me."

"I'm not a right fielder," Scott tells Williams.

"You are today," counters Williams.

The experiment ends three days later when Scott runs into the right-field wall in Winter Haven and knocks himself out.

"I want George's bat in the lineup, but I don't want him running into fences," Williams says.

So much for Scott's career as an outfielder.

It's also part of Williams's overall game plan that all spring training games are treated like the real thing. He is concerned about instilling a winning attitude, and treats even minor indiscretions as if they had just cost his team some mythical pennant. About a week before the season starts, pitcher Dennis Bennett fails to back up third base. Williams shouts some angry words from the dugout. Bennett glares at him. Williams sprints to the mound, loudly reminds Bennett he will not tolerate griping from his players.

Near the end of spring training, a sportswriter approaches Williams at Chain o' Lakes Park, home base for the Red Sox in Winter Haven. On the field in front of them the team is working out. The sun is beating down like an accuser. Still, it's obvious everyone is working hard, going all out.

"They obviously like school," the sportswriter says.

"They do," replies Williams. "They see what the fundamentals can do for them. They're not going to beat themselves by making mistakes. Let the other team make mistakes."

Williams is then asked if he thought the club already had achieved a certain unity, one of Williams' main goals throughout spring training.

"Definitely," he says. "We've done that. We're running a tight camp and the players like that, because now they think they're playing for a cause."

Williams goes on to say he's pleased with the ways the players are responding, and that he thinks the team will not only "win more than we lose," but that already they're better than five clubs in the league. "I told them that nobody would have any trouble with me as long as he gave 100 percent at all times."

Williams is smart.

He quickly establishes a good rapport with Yastrzemski, the symbolic leader of the team. When Williams said he didn't think the Red Sox needed a captain it was interpreted as a symbolic swipe at Yastrzemski, a way of telling his star that the manager was the boss and Yaz should expect no special treatment. But since Yastrzemski never wanted to be the captain in the first place he was glad to be rid of the role. He felt trapped in the middle, caught on one side by complaining players; on the other by management who expected him to be a clubhouse leader. Neither role suited his personality. He is too self-absorbed, too focused, too concentrated on his own performance. He is not a backslapper by nature. He'd become the captain almost by default, a symbol of some supposed new era. Now he doesn't have to be saddled with that baggage. All he has to do is perform.

Yastrzemski's arrival in Winter Haven was full of speculation. Would he and Williams clash? If they did, who would win the power struggle? Right away Yastrzemski told Williams he wanted to win, and he would do whatever it took to win. If Williams wanted him to bunt, he would bunt. If he wanted him to hit-and-run, he would hit-and-run. If he wanted him to steal, he would steal. He told Williams that if Williams gave the orders he would obey them. He wanted Williams to know that just because he had played on losing teams he hadn't gotten used to losing. And he also told Williams that he'd begun his career in Boston, and if it was up to him he would finish his career in Boston.

"I know you," Williams told him, "and you know me. You give me your best and we'll get along fine."

Williams had known his way of managing was not only going to come as a shock to many of the players, it was going to be grating on their psyches. So he added Popowski as his third base coach, proclaimed him the second-in-command. Popowski had either coached or managed in the Sox farm system for decades, had become a bit of father-confessor to some of the younger players, especially Scott and shortstop Rico Petrocelli. A small gnome of a man, Popowski had broken into baseball playing for the House of David, the bearded barnstorming team that used to tour the country in the '30s playing local teams. Their trademark, of course, was their beards, and their clowning. A favorite trick was for the first baseman to hide the ball in his beard, then tag out the local hero as he went to take a lead off first. The House of David also used to play against many of the old Negro League teams, so Popowski was well acquainted with such Negro League greats as Satchel Paige and Josh Gibson. After a minor league career as a Sox infielder, Popowski had gotten into managing, working his way through the organization: Alpine, Texas; Roanoke, Virginia; Lynn, Massachusetts; Reading, Pennsylvania; Pittsfield, Massachusetts; the Red Sox instructional camp in Florida. Odds were that any player who came through the organization had run into Popowski somewhere along the way. Everyone liked Eddie Popowski.

In 1967 Williams and Popowski become the Sox version of "good cop, bad cop." But from the time the Sox leave Winter Haven and begin working their way north there is no denying that, for better or worse, this is Dick Williams' team.

But even with all the changes during spring training, no one expects anything serious from this year's edition of the Red Sox. The defending American League champions are the Baltimore Orioles, who last year won the pennant in a breeze and then swept the Los Angeles Dodgers in four games to win the World Series. They appear to be loaded again, and there is even talk of the Orioles dominating the American League for years to come, like the old Yankees did, winning 29 pennants in 46 years. Lee McPhail, who was one of the architects of building the Orioles' organization and is now the Yankees' general manager, thinks the Orioles can emulate the Yankees' dominance if their young pitchers develop. Certainly, the other pieces are there. Frank Robinson is the most feared hitter in the league, last year's Triple Crown winner. Boog Powell and Curt Blefary provide additional power. Brooks Robinson, no relation to Frank, is the best third baseman in baseball. Veteran Luis Aparacio is at shortstop, though figures to be pushed by rookie Mark Belanger, who arrives in Baltimore with the reputation of having a great glove. Catching is in the capable hands of Andy Etchebarren, last year's hot rookie. There is also another touted rookie, left-handed slugger Mike Epstein. The pitching staff includes Jim Palmer, Wally Bunker, Dave McNally, and Moe Drabowsky. All had exceptional seasons last year, and the O's are also high on Tom Phoebus, who joined the team too late to be eligible for the World Series, but still won two big games for them in September. The bullpen was the best in the league last year.

The Minnesota Twins appear to be the main contenders, primarily because of trades that brought them right-hander Dean Chance, a former Cy Young winner, and quality reliever Ron Kline. They join a pitching staff that already includes Jim Kaat, Jim "Mudcat" Grant, Dave Boswell, Jim Merritt, and Jim Perry. The new Tigers' manager, Mayo Smith, puts it this way: "The Twins have pitching they've never had before."

There's no doubt they have the hitting. Harmon Killebrew, the big, balding strongboy with the arms of a blacksmith, is one of the most productive longball sluggers in the game. Bob Allison gives them additional power. Left-handed Tony Oliva has only been in the major leagues three full years and already has won two batting crowns. Zoilo Versalles is a mainstay at short, Cesar Tovar and Ted Uhlaender are two good young players. A rookie slap hitter named Rod Carew is supposed to be another.

In recent years the Detroit Tigers have been contenders, but not winners. They have one of the league's superstars in Al Kaline, who hit .288 with 29 homers last year, and good power with Norm Cash, Jim Northrup, Gates Brown, Mickey Stanley, and Willie Horton, no relation to the Sox's Tony Horton. The good-hitting Dick McAuliffe has been inconsistent at shortstop and there's talk of switching him to second. The Tigers also are expecting catcher Bill Freehan, who slumped at the plate last year, to rebound. It's a good, solid lineup. Then there's the pitching staff.

The Tigers were third last year, primarily because their pitching staff betrayed them. But this year they have Mayo Smith, who is known as being able to communicate with his players, an art that seemed in short supply in seasons past, and a new pitching coach in Johnny Sain, someone much celebrated for his ability to resurrect slumping pitchers. His two greatest reclamation projects appear to be Mickey Lolich, whose ERA ballooned to nearly five runs a game last year, and Bill Monbouquette, the former Red Sox right-hander, who was a major disappointment. He is being sent to the bullpen while the Tigers try and regroup with Lolich, Denny McLain, Earl Wilson, and Dave Wickersham.

The Chicago White Sox have great pitching, and a team that seems to mirror the intensity and smarts of manager Eddie Stanky, described in Street & Smith's *Baseball Yearbook* as "the resident genius in the White Sox dugout." Once again, the White Sox will bleed for runs, will try to get enough production out of the speedy Tommie Agee, last year's Rookie of the Year, Walt Williams, Ken Berry, and third baseman Don Buford. If Stanky gets any offense at all, the White Sox figure to make a splash, for the pitching staff, anchored by Joel Horlen, Gary Peters, and Tommy John, with Hoyt Wilhelm in the bullpen, is as deep and good as anyone's in the league.

Cleveland has a new manager in Joe Adcock, and questions. The biggest concerns flame-throwing left-hander Sam McDowell, often called the American League's answer to Sandy Koufax. McDowell had arm trouble last year, but if he returns to his '65 form when he led the league in earned run average, the combination of Sonny Siebert, Steve Hargan, Luis Tiant, Gary Bell, and McDowell gives the Indians a formidable staff. Rocky Colavito and Leon "Daddy Wags" Wagner supply the power. But the Indians have defensive woes, especially in the infield. They have been fifth the last two years in a row, and appear to be looking at a similar finish.

The young Kansas City Athletics have new white shoes, the brainstorm of their owner Charlie Finley, and hopes of reaching the first division. For years the Athletics have been the doormat of the American League, a team that seemed to need a periscope to even be able to see the first division. That is starting to change. Last year they finished seventh, spurred on by a new attitude and manager Alvin Dark, who seems to be the perfect manager for this young club. The A's are committed to a youth movement, and they have several young players, including shortstop Bert "Campy" Campaneris and outfielder Rick Monday, who have "can't-miss'' stamped all over them. The other young A's player who is said to have great potential is outfielder Reggie Jackson from Arizona State, the A's first draft choice.

The California Angels are another team also headed in the right direction, finishing sixth last year. Their theme for the season is ''a major leaguer at every position,'' and though they gave up Dean Chance to the Twins they have obtained Don Mincher and Jimmie Hall, two much-needed hitters, to give Rick Reichardt, one of the league's young stars, some help in the lineup.

Age and the ongoing rush of time have finally caught up with the Yankees, and the talk now is of rebuilding and playing for the future. The Yankees' front office is very high on Bill Robinson, the young outfielder who was obtained from the Atlanta Braves for Clete Boyer. They have young proven players in Joe Pepitone and pitcher Mel Stottlemyre, who won 20 games in '65 but was 12-20 last year.

For years the old joke has been ''Washington, first in war, first in peace, and last in the American League.'' They haven't finished in the first division in 20 years, and this year figures to make it 21. They have a right-handed slugger in Frank Howard, and not a whole lot else. Gil Hodges, the old Brooklyn Dodger, is the manager and he's trying to shake things up. He traded for pitcher Camilo Pascual, once one of the top pitchers in the league before arm trouble two years ago complicated his future.

The Red Sox?

Oddsmakers in Vegas have the Red Sox as a ''100-to-one'' shot to win the American League pennant.

Opening Day at Fenway Park is scheduled for Tuesday, April 11.

The park, built in 1912 between Lansdowne and Jersey streets, was called Fenway because it was in the "Fens," a residential area of the city dominated by a large park that had been designed by noted architect Frederick Law Olmsted. Major John "Honey Fitz" Fitzgerald, the grandfather of John F. Kennedy, threw out the first ball. It had been laid out to conform to the narrow streets surrounding Kenmore Square. The result is an idiosyncratic ballyard full of odd angles and grandstands that hug the field, allowing the fans sitting alongside both the left- and right-field foul lines to almost reach out and touch the players.

In the 1934 season Yawkey replaced the wooden grandstands with steel and concrete ones. He also did away with a 10-foot incline in left field that was known as "Duffy's Cliff," so named for Sox left fielder Duffy Lewis. Yawkey had wanted to enlarge the left-field bleachers, to the point that he discussed with Boston city officials the possibility of acquiring some of Lansdowne Street, which paralleled the left-field bleachers. The city said no; thus was born the famous left-field wall, known to baseball fans everywhere as "the Green Monster." It is Fenway Park's most distinctive feature. It is only 315 feet away from home plate down the foul line, 37 feet high. On top is a large screen designed to prevent balls from ending up on Lansdowne Street. Its completion removed nearly 7,000 seats, reducing the park's capacity to about 34,000.

The other distinctive feature is a triangle in right-center field, 420 feet away from home plate. In 1940, Sox management added bullpens in right field. They shortened the area in right field and for a while other people around the American League referred to it as "Williamsburg," the feeling being that Red Sox management had shortened the dimensions for Ted Williams, the young Sox left-handed slugger. Still, the bullpens are 380 feet away, before curving in dramatically near the right-field foul pole at 302 feet. With few exceptions, Fenway is still the same park it was then.

It's the city of Boston that's different.

It is, of course, a city rich in history. The Boston Tea Party. The Old North Church. Paul Revere's ride. Tourists can walk the Freedom Trail and get a sense of Boston and neighboring New England as the "cradle of liberty." Across the Charles River in nearby Cambridge are the ivy-covered buildings of Harvard, the oldest college in the country, and the austere, geometrical buildings of the Massachusetts Institute of Technology. The city has long been called "the Hub," a local reference for hub of the universe.

By the mid '60s Boston is, for all practical purposes, as segregated as any city in the country; a city of strong ethnic neighborhoods where the values are all about turf and family, places where the Old World looms heavy. The Italians are in East Boston, the North End. The Irish are in South Boston and Dorchester, a legacy of the 1840s when the potato famine in Ireland sent scores of immigrants to America, to Boston. The different ethnic groups are almost separate duchies, insular, parochial, complete with their own rules and customs. To the point that when Ray Flynn who later became the mayor of Boston, was a basketball player at Providence College in the early '60s, he asked the team's broadcaster to announce that he was not from Boston; he was from *South Boston*.

The blacks are in Roxbury, removed from downtown geographically as well as spiritually, tucked away in the city's west side, out of sight and usually out of mind. They never go to Fenway Park, one of the unfortunate legacies of the Red Sox being the last team in the major leagues to integrate. Blacks comprise roughly 10 percent of the city's population of 697,000, and none of its power structure. Ironically, the early blacks had gotten along well with the Brahmins, Boston's ruling class. Slavery had been ruled unconstitutional in Massachusetts as far back as 1783. By the middle of the nineteenth century, blacks in Boston had achieved a degree of freedom unprecedented in the United States. Schools had been desegregated in 1855. Boston had been the center of the abolition movement, founded at the African Meeting House, the city's first black church. The movement's two main goals had been the eradication of slavery in the South and the end of Northern discrimination. Many blacks were educated, cultured, closely aligned with whites. That had begun to change as the city's ethnic makeup changed. More blacks, uneducated, unskilled, arrived from the South, establishing distinct divisions in the black community. The poorer blacks competed for marginal jobs with the Irish, increasing tensions that would last for generations. From 1940 to 1960 the black population in Boston tripled, as the influx of more uneducated Southern blacks flooded the city and settled into ghettos.

Though at one time the Boston public school system was arguably the best in the country, by the early '60s it was entrenched in de facto segregation. In 1963, thirteen of the city's schools were 90 percent black, 11 of these were at least 50 years old, and the amount of money allocated for black students was appreciably less than that allocated to predominantly white schools. The NAACP has called for an end to these conditions. Yet it only seems to make the Boston School Committee more rooted to the concept of neighborhood schools, a euphemism for the status quo. Its leader is Louise Day Hicks, one of the most popular, if notorious, politicians in the city. She is a South Boston housewife, the daughter of a popular South Boston judge, and has become the foremost symbol of white opposition to the busing of students to achieve racial balance in the Boston public schools. Raised "lace-curtain Irish," her campaign slogan is "You know where she stands."

The day before the opener Fenway had been too wet for practice, so the team used the batting cage at Harvard. Spring in New England usually arrives late, and even then in dribs and drabs, complete with afternoon winds that seem to bring March back for a rerun. It's the kind of weather that conjures up Mark Twain's famous line about New England weather: *If you don't like it, wait a minute*. The forecast is for cool temperatures, but sunny. It's wrong. The next day is in the upper 30s, complete with a 40-mile-an-hour wind. The field is called unplayable and, for the first time in 14 years, the home opener is called off.

It is a young team, with a sprinkling of veterans.

At first base is Scott, in his second year. He is 23. Rico Petrocelli, in his third full year, is the shortstop. He is 24. Joe Foy, in his second year, is at third. He's also 24, grew up in the Bronx where he was a three-sport star at Evander Childs High School. He originally had been signed by the Twins, who tried to convert him to either a catcher or a first baseman, and had been acquired by the Red Sox following his first minor league season. Two years ago he had been the minor league player of the year in Toronto. Last year he had come on strong the second half of the season, hitting nearly .300 after July 4.

Rookie Mike Andrews, who played for Williams the year before at Sox's Triple A club in Toronto, is penciled in at second, but he is out with a back injury and will be replaced in the opening day lineup by rookie Reggie Smith, although Williams envisions Smith as his center fielder. Andrews, a former All-American end at El Camino Junior College in California, had started in Toronto as a shortstop. He had been signed by scout Joe Stephenson, whose son Jerry is pitching for Toronto.

Smith is raw, but extremely talented. Early in spring training Dom DiMaggio, former Sox outfielder and brother of Joe DiMaggio, the Yankee great, had visited Winter Haven and worked with Smith. He taught him how to field ground balls in front of him, not to the side. He taught him to run fast to a ball, then wait for it, instead of gliding over and catching it on the run. He also predicted that within five years Smith would be a great player.

He is only 22, and he came to the Red Sox almost by accident. He grew up in Compton, on the outskirts of East Los Angeles, the second youngest of eight children. He was a three-sport star at Centennial High School, considered a great athlete, six foot, wiry-strong, a good enough acrobat to be able to do flips. There seemed to be nothing in sports he couldn't do. It was there in high school he became a switch-hitter.

"I started out hitting right-handed until my junior year in high school," he says. "Then one day my coach suggested I try left-handed. I used to fool around with it. When I first got to the minors the good right-handed pitchers threw the ball right by me when I was hitting lefty."

He was signed by the Twins in June of '63, shortly after his high school graduation. They first projected him as a shortstop, but failed to protect him after his first season in the minors and he was selected by the Red Sox for $8,000.

"The Twins gave up on me because I made a lot of errors and Zoilo Versalles, who had a wonderful year for them at shortstop, was only 22. The Red Sox drafted me as a third baseman. Then I played second for a while at Waterloo before they moved me to center field. The decision was made by Matt Sczesny, the Waterloo manager, and Neil Mahoney, the scouting director. The next year at Pittsfield I started at second base."

Throughout his year at Pittsfield in Double A in the summer of '65 he commuted every day from New York City, over two hours away, where his wife, Ernestine, lived. They had met in high school. The next year he was in Toronto playing for Dick Williams. That September he was called up to the Red Sox. One of the first people who befriended him was Yastrzemski.

"Yaz helped a lot of black players, including Joe Foy and myself, at a time when the Red Sox were being criticized for not signing too many blacks. Yaz always has been very open-minded."

Conigliaro, now in his fourth season, is in right field. He is 22. The old man is Yastrzemski in left, and he is only 27. The catchers are two local Massachusetts products, Mike Ryan of Haverhill and Russ Gibson of Fall River. Ryan is considered excellent defensively, but weak at the plate. Gibson had performed well for Williams last year in Toronto, his 10th season in the minor leagues. He is about to be 26.

The pitching staff is as thin as a New York model. Lonborg is being counted on to be the ace, but he is 19-27 in his two major league seasons. Behind him are José Santiago, Dennis Bennett, Darrell Brandon, and Hank Fischer. Santiago, 26, went 12-13 for the Sox last year, after they bought his contract from a Kansas City farm club after the '65 season. Bennett is 29, broke into the majors six years ago with the Phillies. He had some arm trouble last year, but is considered a smart pitcher, a left-hander who changes speeds and knows how to pitch. Brandon was originally signed by the Pirates as an outfielder, and came over to the Sox in September of '65 in the trade that sent Jack Lamabe to the Houston Astros. Fischer joined the Red Sox last season after he was released by the Cincinnati Reds. It's not exactly a group to send fear into the hearts of the American League hitters.

Also in the mix are Lee Stange, considered a gutsy competitor, who was voted last year's "Unsung Hero" by the Boston baseball writers after pitching eight complete games near the end of the year, and Billy Rohr, whose fine work in spring training moved him into the rotation.

In the bullpen are Don McMahon, Galen Cisco, Dan Osinski, and Bill Landis. Osinski is 34, came over to the Red Sox last year from the Milwaukee Braves. Cisco, a former Ohio State football star, is 30. None have distinguished themselves, although McMahon has knocked around the major leagues for years, and the rookie Landis looked good in spring training. The top man is John Wyatt, a veteran who has bounced around and is reputed to load up the ball with Vaseline. Later in the season the Yankees' Joe Pepitone will say Wyatt has so much Vaseline on him that if he slid into second base he would keep right on going until he hit the outfield fence.

Eventually, the age of specialization will come to baseball, with one of the main differences being the increased use of relief pitchers and the realization that the bullpen is equally as important as the starting rotation. But not in this summer. Now, with few exceptions, relief pitchers are the flotsam and jetsam of the staff, usually either failed starters, or veterans near the end of their careers. There is still the macho belief that the great pitchers work the entire ball game, that the complete game is a mark of excellence.

The year before, the Sox staff had been the worst in the league, with an ERA of 3.92. Dick Williams notwithstanding, no one expects it to be any better this year.

There is little depth, with the exception of good-hitting Tony Horton, whom Williams would love to find a spot in the lineup for. Second baseman George Smith hurt his knee during spring training; he's not ready to play. The best reserve infielder is Dalton Jones. He is only 23, from Baton Rouge, with the reputation of swinging a good bat. But already he's become a victim of being a left-handed hitter with minimum power in Fenway Park. He'd come to Boston four years before when the prevailing strategy was to play for the big inning, and the lineup was geared to right-handed hitters who might be able to jerk one into the screen. There is still a certain prejudice against left-handed hitters in Fenway, especially ones with little power. He'd also struggled in the field in his first season, when he'd been only 19 and nervous, and had gotten the rap that he was a defensive liability. He feels it's unfair, an example that in baseball young players can get labels on them that are tough to shake.

The outfield has José Tartabull, now in his sixth year in the major leagues. He had come over to the Sox last year in the multiple trade that also brought Wyatt over from the Athletics. He has speed, and is a contact hitter, though considered shaky as a fielder with a weak arm. He is also known as a good person in the clubhouse, always happy and upbeat, the ideal personality for a reserve player. He loves to sing, sometimes accompanying himself on bongo drums. Another great person in the clubhouse is reserve outfielder George Thomas, who'd come to the Sox in the '65 trade that sent pitcher Bill Monbouquette to the Tigers.

Thomas is the team's court jester, quick with a quip. He sees his role as keeping his teammates loose, at times being the buffer between them and Williams' sarcasm. One day, later in the season, he will tie a piece of string to a June bug and walk him near the dugout as if he were a house pet. Anything to keep his teammates loose. He likes to banter with Williams, has quickly come to know that Williams also enjoys the verbal jousting—as long as he has the last word. Thomas accepts this. He is 29, can play both the outfield and the infield. Sometimes he throws batting practice, and sometimes he catches in the bullpen. During games he often charts pitches, is always involved in the game, thinking about it. It's a trait Williams likes, for he knows that despite Thomas' irreverent attitude, he's into the game, a team player in the best sense of the word.

The players' respective attitudes are not to be underestimated. Even the best of teams are a fragile assemblage of different personalities and egos. What they don't need are reserve players who are unhappy with their status, so both Tartabull and Thomas are perfect role players. They realize they're not going to break into an outfield of Yastrzemski, Smith, and Conigliaro, and so they're not going to grouse about it.

Also on hand is veteran Don Demeter, who first got to the majors in '56 and came over to the Sox from the Tigers last season. He is seen as insurance in the outfield, and a right-handed pinch hitter.

Wednesday, April 12. It is still uncommonly cold, even for a Boston spring, temperature in the 40s. Massachusetts governor John Volpe throws out the first ball, and Johnny Mathis sings the National Anthem. There are 8,324 fans rattling around in Fenway.

The Red Sox beat the Chicago White Sox, 5–4. The star

is Petrocelli, who hits a three-run homer into the screen in left in the third, and also knocks in another run. In a sense this is symbolic, for perhaps no Red Sox player had suffered more under manager Billy Herman than Petrocelli, the young shortstop.

Petrocelli is extremely sensitive, needing constant reassurance. He often doubts his ability, and bad days can get him into a personal funk that can last a week. Herman rarely gave him the reassurance he was searching for, often ignoring him. Petrocelli had also been bothered by a succession of nagging injuries the year before, injuries that Herman looked at with scorn. Herman was forever telling sportswriters Petrocelli was loafing, that he had a shortstop who didn't want to play, and that if he ever got fired it would be Petrocelli's fault. One day Petrocelli told Yastrzemski, who had an adjoining locker, that he was going to quit. Yastrzemski talked him out of it, but Petrocelli still spent most of his time worried Herman didn't like him. Early last season, concerned about his wife, who was home sick, Petrocelli had actually walked out of the locker room in the middle of a game and gone home. Club officials were shocked. A player leaving in the middle of a game was unheard of. No matter that Petrocelli had gone home to find his wife writhing in pain on the kitchen floor. Herman demanded he be either traded or released. Yastrzemski lobbied to Yawkey on Petrocelli's behalf, and Herman ended up fining Petrocelli $1,000, one-ninth of Petrocelli's salary.

The winning pitcher in this season opener is Lonborg. He goes six and a third innings. The year before he'd been 10-10, but had been groomed throughout spring training to be the Red Sox starter on opening day. Lonborg is an anomaly among baseball players. He's put in three years at Stanford, one of the most prestigious colleges in the country. He's tall, blond, handsome. He's also a classic power pitcher, considered to have great potential.

Over the years there have been a lot of Red Sox pitchers with great potential. Usually, it never got actualized. The closeness of the Wall has always had a psychological effect on pitchers. Many young pitchers never adjust, and end up changing the style that got them to the majors in the first place. Today, Lonborg pitches well in the cold. Between innings he keeps his arm warm with a heating pad. He also gets rubdowns from trainer Buddy LeRoux. He is replaced in the seventh by Wyatt before McMahon closes out the game in the ninth. Throughout the spring Williams had promised a new look. On this first day it is here, a fact duly noted in the Boston newspapers the next morning. But the next day the Sox lose 8–5 to the White Sox, committing five errors and giving up five unearned runs in the ninth, so the opening day victory is quickly put in perspective.

It's the same old Sox, right?

The Red Sox leave after the game by bus for New York and the first road trip of the season. Rohr wins the first game in his quest for immortality, but then Stottlemyre throttles the Red Sox on four hits the next afternoon. Not that that's the big news in New York City on Saturday, April 15. Over a quarter of a million people meet in Central Park and march to the United Nations to protest the war. It is 10 times the number of people who had gathered just a year ago for a similar demonstration, and one of the highlights is when 75 young men burn their draft cards.

It also doesn't take long for Williams to begin venting his frustrations over losses, something that is rare in baseball. Since there are so many games, the prevailing wisdom is that the season is too long to get too emotional over a particular game. The rhythm of the game negates that. A major league season is geared to the long haul, the even emotional keel, the feeling that there's always tomorrow, always another game, another chance. Williams doesn't manage that way. Each game is an island in itself, life and death. He doesn't have the emotional temperament to be able to put losses into some perspective. Losing tears at him, resurrects old hurts, the emotional pain of growing up with a martinet of a father, the memory of a St. Louis childhood where the only thing that mattered was winning, the winning that gave him respect, identity, the winning that defined life. To Dick Williams, it isn't that winning makes him feel complete, satisfied. It is that winning is not losing, and he isn't emotionally capable of dealing with losing.

He'd grown up in his maternal grandfather's house in Depression St. Louis, a few blocks from Sportsman's Park, since his father, who alternated between being out of work and doing menial jobs he thought were beneath him, was often unable to support the family. His father had been a frustrated man, a blunt man, but in his house he was king. Williams' father taught him and his older brother how to swim by taking them to a river in southern Missouri and throwing them in against a raging current and telling them to swim against it, even while the current kept pushing them backward. If the two sons disobeyed they were taken into the basement, tied to a pole, and whipped. His mother would stand there watching and crying. Williams learned early that for there to be order there had to be one authority figure. It's a lesson he's never forgotten, this simplistic view of the world, and he's always wanted to be the one in authority. There is no gray in Dick Williams' world. Nothing infuriates him more than players who don't play all out, who don't care as much as he does, hurt as much as he hurts. If he thinks someone doesn't care as much as he does, he will damn near kill him. Later, he would wonder if the reason he managed so hard was that everything else in his life was so bad.

When he was in junior high school the family moved from St. Louis to California, to northeast Los Angeles. The Depression was over. California had become the new promised land, complete with the promise of steady work for Williams' father. Shortly afterward his father got sick. When Williams was 16 he was injured in a high school football game. His father, recovering from gall bladder surgery, had a heart attack while running out onto the field to see how his son was. He died at 47. Dick Williams was 16.

Less than 24 hours after his high school graduation in 1947 he packed all his belongings and got on a Greyhound bus bound for Santa Barbara, where the Dodgers' Class C team played. He lived in the clubhouse, sleeping on a cot in the shower area, then slipping out in the morning before the manager arrived at the ballpark. The next spring he went to Dodgertown in Vero Beach, Florida, the first year it opened. Dodgertown was the culmination of Branch Rickey's vision, the first state-of-the-art spring training site. There were so many players they wore different-colored shirts. They were divided into smaller groups and they spent the day rotating around six different fields, each one emphasizing a different skill such as bunting or sliding. This went on for six weeks, an obsession with fundamentals.

But in the spring of '52, Williams' fifth year in pro ball, finally getting a chance to start for the Dodgers in left field, the culmination of every adolescent dream he ever had, he hurt his shoulder diving for a fly ball. He was helped off the field by Eddie Stanky. The injury changed Williams' life. He went from someone who'd always gotten by as a player on his ability to someone who now had to try to get by with his head. He began studying opposing pitchers. He studied strategy. And he studied human nature. He became a journeyman player, bouncing from team to team, six in 13 years. As he spent many long hours on the bench he managed games in his head, learning what to do from some of the men he played for, learning what not to do from the others. He knew that when his career ended he wanted to be a manager. And through it all, through this time that ultimately served as his apprenticeship on how to manage a baseball team, Williams carried his Dodgertown experience with him, his own little moveable feast. Bunt. Hit the cutoff man. Take the extra base. Fundamental baseball. The kind of baseball he learned at Dodgertown when he was just beginning in baseball, his career all ahead of him. The kind of baseball he's trying to instill in his Red Sox.

Williams knows that in the grand design of things he's probably slated to be little more than an interim manager. That he only has a one-year contract is his first clue. Sam Mele, a former Red Sox player who'd grown up in the Boston area, is rumored to be on the outs with the Minnesota Twins, and there already is speculation he could become the new Red Sox manager. In this scenario Williams is to be little more than a symbolic break with the good-old-boy network of the past, a transitional figure linking the Sox's past with the Sox's future.

On Sunday, still against the Yankees at the Stadium, the Sox strand 20 runners in an 18-inning one-run loss, a game played in the biting spring cold. The Sox have 13 opportunities to knock in the winning run from scoring position, but fail each time. Scott, in particular, strikes out three times in extra innings with the winning run in scoring position. This is coupled with the failure of relief pitcher Bill Landis to throw strikes. Few things infuriate Williams more than pitchers who give up a lot of bases on balls. Williams considers throwing strikes the first step in learning how to play winning baseball, and pitchers who don't soon feel Williams' wrath. After Landis walks three batters Williams comes to the mound, tells him that if he doesn't start throwing strikes he soon will be pitching from the back of his doghouse. It isn't an empty threat. After Landis walks another, it will be 28 days before he pitches again. Williams' doghouse is real, and he likes everyone to be aware of it. Not pitching Landis for almost a month isn't merely to punish Landis, but to let everyone else know the same fate could happen to them if they fall out of favor with the new manager.

Afterward, Williams is in a foul and nasty mood. The next day he orders 17 players to have an early-morning workout in Comiskey Park in Chicago, though it's an off-day and the club had just played a five-hour game the day before. He also decides to bench Scott for one game against the White Sox in favor of Tony Horton. At the beginning of spring training Williams had said Scott and Horton would contend for the first base job. It was Williams' way of lighting a fire under Scott, keeping him on edge. He believed that when Scott felt secure he lost some of his drive, let himself get heavy. He also felt Scott's lack of self-discipline carried over to his habits at the plate, fueling his propensity to chase bad pitches. When a sportswriter commented that Scott didn't appear to be fishing for as many low pitches as he had in the past, Williams snapped,

"No. He lets them come up to his shins now." Throughout the spring Williams made no secret how difficult he thought it was to get through to Scott. There was even a strong rumor at one point that Scott was going to be traded. Now he says, "Scott has been awful hitting and his fielding hasn't been so fabulous that Horton will hurt us out there. The last three times he struck out with men on base. Trying to talk to him is like talking to cement."

It's a cruel statement, one that will haunt Scott throughout his career. An example of Williams at his worst.

Williams isn't through.

The Red Sox lose to the White Sox, a game marked by sloppy play, a succession of errors and missed cutoff men. After an error by Foy in the sixth, Williams benches him in favor of Dalton Jones, and proclaims afterward that both Scott and Foy will be fined heavily if they don't start losing weight. He says Foy has gained 10 pounds since the end of spring training, and Scott now weighs 220, compared to the 198 he weighed two years ago when he had his great year at Pittsfield. He also says Foy and Scott will continue to stay on the bench.

Four days later Williams is thrown out of a game after heckling plate umpire Red Flaherty on a ball-strike call. Not that Williams was necessarily upset at the call. Part of his strategy is to periodically argue with umpires. He feels it not only shows his players he's battling for them, it also serves notice to the umpires that the Red Sox care, are involved in the game, that an umpire just can't go through the motions. It's Williams' first ejection as a big league manager. It's also the first time in three years a Red Sox manager has been thrown out of a game. It won't be the last.

It's late April and already certain things have become apparent. First, this *is* Dick Williams' team. Both Foy and Scott have been sent the message that they better stay in shape, or else. During spring training Williams had been unhappy that Foy had been six pounds over his allotted weight of 205, though he still was lighter than he often had been the previous season. Last year he'd gotten off to a very slow start, his average mired in the low .220's, until going on a tear the latter part of the year, which saw him finish with a .262 average and 15 home runs. Williams thought Foy, like Scott, played better the lighter he was. Now Williams thinks nothing of changing the lineup. Mental errors will not be tolerated.

The second thing that's become apparent is Lonborg's dominance as a pitcher. On April 28 he throws a six-hit shutout against Kansas City, striking out 13, handcuffing the Athletics in the cold at Fenway before 9,000. The year before he had a good fastball and a mediocre breaking ball. He'd worked on the breaking ball playing in the winter in Venezuela. He also is pitching inside, not afraid to throw the brushback pitch. The American League is regarded as more polite than the National League, the pitchers less likely to brush back hitters. Lonborg has become different. He is throwing inside and that has changed everything. That and a better breaking ball has made him a dominant pitcher, the stopper around which to anchor the pitching staff.

The third revelation is that the Sox have a different attitude than in years past, perhaps best symbolized by a game the following day. The Sox and the Athletics are tied 9–9 in the 15th inning when the A's celebrated bonus baby, rookie Rick Monday, hits his first big league home run, against Don McMahon. Conigliaro opens up the bottom of the 15th with a single off the A's excellent reliever, Jack Aker, and Petrocelli sacrifices him to second. Scott singles, leaving Conigliaro at third. Catcher Russ Gibson is scheduled to hit, but Williams sends up the left-handed hitting Dalton Jones instead. He walks, loading the bases. Williams plays the percentages, sending left-handed José Tartabull to hit for Mike Andrews.

With one out, and Tartabull possessing good speed, the Athletics have their infield in, trying to prevent the tying run from crossing the plate. At the plate, Tartabull is guessing. A notorious high-ball hitter, he suspects Aker is going to try to keep the ball low. So he looks for a low pitch, gets it, and singles through the drawn-in infield, scoring both Conigliaro and Scott. The Sox have won their most dramatic game of the young season. As Scott crosses home plate for the winning run, the entire dugout empties onto the field in celebration. The Red Sox are in a first-place tie, the first time they've been at the top at this point in a season in four years.

The clubhouse is ecstatic, so different from what it was the year before. Unlike many of the past Red Sox teams, which were older, more jaded, full of veterans who long ago had come to view a game as just another day at the office, this is a young team. Baseball is still fun, the season is still young. In the bad times a clubhouse is full of cliques, pockets of people who seem to huddle in corners and whisper about others, the bad feeling as prevalent as the discarded tape that lies on the floor. Everyone in baseball knows that it doesn't take too many clubhouse lawyers, too many people always griping and second-guessing, to poison a clubhouse. In the good times it's a baseball version of a fraternity, full of sophomoric humor, a place that belongs to the players and the players alone. The sportswriters can come in after games to get their quotes, grist for the mill, but they don't belong. Nor do the fans. The clubhouse is the players' sanctuary, and now it's a happy one. That in itself is a small sign that things are changing.

APRIL STATS

BATTING	AB	R	H	HR	RBI	AVG.
Dan Osinski	2		1			.500
Don Demeter	2		1			.500
Dalton Jones	21	6	8	1	2	.381
Tony Conigliaro	48	6	16	1	7	.333
Rico Petrocelli	54	8	18	2	10	.333
Hank Fischer	6		2		1	.333
Darrell Brandon	6		2			.333
Mike Andrews	28	6	9	1	6	.321
Russ Gibson	40	3	12		6	.300

BATTING	AB	R	H	HR	RBI	AVG.
Carl Yastrzemski	61	6	18	2	9	.295
George Scott	40	7	10		3	.250
Reggie Smith	59	10	13	2	6	.220
José Tartabull	24	4	5		2	.208
Mike Ryan	10		2		1	.200
George Thomas	16	3	3		2	.187
Tony Horton	22	2	4		3	.182
Jim Lonborg	8		1			.125
Joe Foy	40	4	4	1	2	.100
Billy Rohr	6					.000
Bob Tillman	5					.000
Dennis Bennett	3					.000
John Wyatt	3					.000
Don McMahon	2					.000
Lee Stange	1					.000

PITCHING	IP	H	BB	SO	W	L	ERA
Wyatt	12⅔	6	6	12	2	0	.000
Osinski	7	4	2	2	0	0	.000
Galen Cisco	3	3	2	1	0	0	.000
McMahon	8⅔	6	4	3	1	0	1.00
Fischer	15	14	4	9	1	1	1.80
Rohr	21	14	8	10	2	0	2.57
Bennett	14	9	6	6	0	1	3.21
Lonborg	25⅔	23	9	26	2	0	3.46
Brandon	24⅔	23	13	11	0	2	4.32
Jose Santiago	2	3	1	2	1	1	4.50
Stange	4	7	2	2	0	1	18.00
Bill Landis	⅓	1	3	1	0	0	54.00

Though the next day they lose a 1–0 game on a Danny Cater homer into the screen, they end the first month of the season 8-6, one game out of first place, behind Detroit. Conigliaro and Petrocelli are among the top 10 in batting average, both at .333, while Detroit's Al Kaline is first at .383. Lonborg and Rohr are both 2-0, both of Rohr's wins coming against the Yankees. Yaz is at .295, with a team-leading nine RBI's and two homers, same as Petrocelli and Reggie Smith.

May begins with General William Westmoreland asking President Johnson to increase the number of American soldiers in Southeast Asia to 600,000, a 160,000 addition. The original plans had called for a slow troop buildup, but increased Communist pressure in northern South Vietnam and a disappointing operation in the Mekong Delta, south of Saigon, have combined to make Westmoreland seek more troops. A couple of days later three U.S. pilots, shot down over North Vietnam, are put on display in Hanoi. The day before, members of the House Armed Services Committee decided that the Justice Department must disregard the First Amendment protecting free speech and prosecute those who urge young men to defy the law.

There is the expected backlash. The Senate Republican policy committee questions whether Republicans should continue to support an "open-ended unilateral commitment to an Asian land war." In Stockholm, a "War Crimes" trial conducted by Bertrand Russell finds the United States guilty of aggression in Vietnam and war crimes against the civilian population.

On the political front, former Alabama governor George Wallace, who has become the leading symbol of the Old South and first achieved national notoriety when he stood on the steps of the University of Alabama to prevent the school from being integrated, visits New Hampshire, trying to decide whether he will enter the fall presidential primary. The highlight of the trip comes when Wallace visits Dartmouth College. Hundreds of students protest his appearance and rock his car; Wallace is visibly shaken. George Romney, another presidential hopeful, is in Atlanta endorsing "Negro Civil Rights" and calling Wallace's proposed third party a move to legalize racism. A few days later Muhammad Ali pleads not guilty to a federal grand jury charge of refusing to be drafted into the armed forces. The action comes 10 days after Ali refused to take the traditional step forward at a Houston induction center, symbolic of joining the armed forces.

The Red Sox seem to mirror the turbulent times.

They begin a nosedive that begins to look like déjà vu, at one point losing nine of 11. Back in Boston the news is met with little surprise, a chance for the skeptics to say that though this is supposed to be the start of a new era, it appears to be the same old song, another season when the pennant race will be taking place in some other city.

The big news back home is a mini-riot in downtown Boston. It has nothing to do with the war, or racial tensions, or any of the other issues that so dominate the news, however. It is about the Boston opening of the new James Bond spoof *Casino Royale,* with Ursula Andress, who shortly will be named the worst actress of the year by the *Harvard Lampoon.* The Savoy Theater, in a special promotion, advertises it will let anyone in free for a 4 A.M. showing of the film, providing they are wearing a "super-sleuth trenchcoat." Fifteen thousand kids show up, end up battling with police. Eventually, 30 people are injured and 15 arrested. It's big news at the time, but a month later it will seem like some tame prelim to more serious trouble.

The principal reason for the Red Sox's slide is a road trip that goes from southern California, to Minneapolis, to Kansas City. The dreams of many a Red Sox season lie buried in these places, faraway ballparks where the Sox's lack of speed, lack of pitching, and their one-dimensional wait-for-the-big-inning baseball make them especially vulnerable. Even in the bad years, the Red Sox are difficult to beat in Fenway Park, where their right-handed power always is a factor. It's on the road where all their warts show. In Minneapolis, for example, they are 3-27 over the past three years.

Lonborg loses a game in Anaheim 2-1 in the ninth inning when he throws a pitch that bounces in the dirt in front of the catcher, and it rolls back to him. He grabs it, all set to try to throw out the Angel runner coming in from third. But he drops the ball, the runner scores, the Angels win. Lonborg leaves the ball on the grass and walks to the dugout. It's his first defeat of the year. Williams attributes it to Lonborg trying to pitch too carefully in the ninth after he'd blown the ball by the Angels for eight innings.

"He was too cute, he was trying to finesse them," Williams says in the dugout.

In Williams' view of the world being too cute is another sin. He likes pitchers who challenge hitters, pitchers who throw strikes, not pitchers who are always trying to nibble at the corners, finessing hitters. He also believes that for a pitcher to be effective he has to pitch inside, not to hit batters, but to set up his other pitches. It's probably the only thing he and pitching coach Sal Maglie agree on. Nicknamed "the Barber" for his habit of brushing back hitters he thought were digging in on him, Maglie pitched 10 years in the major leagues, playing for five teams and appearing in the World Series with both the Giants and the Dodgers. Williams had inherited him from Billy Herman's staff, primarily because the Red Sox were not willing to unload Maglie's $20,000-a-year contract, and their relationship was doomed from the start. Williams and Maglie once had been teammates on the Dodgers, but since Williams hadn't wanted him, he rarely relies on Maglie's judgment, and Maglie will spend much of the year feeling left out, unwanted. At the end of the year Williams will cut him loose, hiring Darrell Johnson, an old teammate from his Baltimore Oriole days and a onetime rival International League manager.

Maglie will retaliate, telling a Boston sportswriter at the

end of the year, "I got a lousy deal from Williams. The guy never listened to me and only gave me sarcastic answers. It got so frustrating during the season that I just shut up. But then I thought again. I knew I was being paid to speak up and I did. That's what I get paid for. But it didn't do any good. All I ever got was sarcasm or a deaf ear. Williams may be the toast of the town now, but I've seen people hit the popularity skids before and I'll see it happen fast again."

After his heartbreaking loss, Lonborg goes into the dugout and sits down, staring out at the field. Most of the players already are gone. The crowd is filing out of Anaheim Stadium. Lonborg continues to sit there, staring straight ahead, looking out on the field where the ball continues to lie there on the grass.

"Great game, Lonnie," says Petrocelli, trying to comfort him.

"Great game, hell," retorts Williams.

After that, Lonborg decides not to be cute, not to think, decides to just throw the ball. Williams will say, "It was worth it. It cost the game, but it taught him a lesson. He's the best pitcher in baseball."

That night Williams imposes a curfew, even though the team has a day off the next day before they move on to Minnesota. This is the baseball equivalent of the father taking the car keys away, especially in southern California where visiting teams are infamous for chasing the local nightlife, and the prevailing motto is "Anaheim, lose a game, win a dame."

Shortly after the curfew, Williams and two of his assistant coaches, Doerr and Al Lakeman, are cruising the hotel corridors knocking on doors when they bump into George Thomas, on his way to Dennis Bennett's room for an afterhours card game.

"You're a little late, George," Williams says.

"Which way are you guys going?" Thomas asks, thinking he'll call ahead to alert the guys playing cards.

No such luck.

Williams eventually catches several players not in their rooms. In the morning he tells them it's a freebie, but the "next time it's $500 and you can explain that to your wife."

Though the trip is a losing one, there are a few interesting highlights that give glimpses that things are different, regardless of the swoon. The curfew when there was no game the next day certainly was one. Before a game in California against the Angels, Popowski was hitting ground balls to some of the Red Sox reserve infielders when he became disgusted with the poor play. To the amazement of the players, he walked off the field and told Williams it was obvious the players weren't overly interested in infield practice. Williams, of course, was furious, and let the players know it as only he could.

The other is that Yaz was benched in Minnesota for lack of hitting. Not only is this something that never would have happened under either Billy Herman or Johnny Pesky, it's also the first time since he publicly stripped Yastrzemski of his captaincy that Williams has publicly treated Yastrzemski as if he's no different than anyone else.

"I don't care how much they're making," Williams says afterward. "I'm trying to win ball games." The next day he goes a step further. "I don't care what a man's name is or if he's a rookie or a star. If he isn't hitting he isn't playing."

There is some speculation Yaz will react negatively, thus beginning the start of a power struggle between the star and the new manager.

He doesn't.

The Sox return home on Thursday, May 11, to prepare for a weekend series against the Tigers. Once again, they do little to convince anyone that this isn't just the same old story. They lose the first game, allowing the Tigers to score three runs without a hit, and the Tigers add a fourth when catcher Bob Tillman, attempting to throw out Al Kaline, hits pitcher John Wyatt in the head. Kaline went to third on the play, then scored on a sacrifice fly. The next day the picture of Wyatt lying on the ground is in all the papers, the kind of bizarre play that once had seemed to characterize the Red Sox, a play out of some bad Little League game.

The Sox drop the second game when the Tigers score si. runs in the ninth. All the runs are charged to Wyatt, whom Williams left in, though the crowd got on Williams for leaving him in when it was obvious it wasn't his day. In the clubhouse afterward some pitchers feel that Williams, disgusted with Wyatt's performance in the ninth, left him in to humiliate him. Wyatt, though, is not about to be baited into that trap. He'd broken in with Kansas City in 1961, coming over to the Red Sox last year, and has come to know that one of the things that keeps a black player in the big leagues is not being in the center of too many controversies.

"I'm a pro, and I got to eat," he says, "so I don't say nothing. That's all, man."

After the game, Yaz, who's been struggling at the plate, asks coach Bobby Doerr if he will come out early the next morning to throw him some batting practice. Doerr had been one of the all-time great Red Sox players, the second baseman from 1938 until 1951. He was considered the best fielding second baseman of his era, and is one of the few in baseball history to hit over 200 home runs. He had been a special scout for the Red Sox for a decade, thus is familiar with the Red Sox players who've come up through the organization. He also is respected, the respect he gets for having been a great player.

The next day, a Sunday, Doerr and Yastrzemski get to Fenway at nine in the morning. It has been a wet spring but the day is mostly sunny, temperature about 60. The park is quiet. The batting cage is already set up for the afternoon's game. Doerr suggests Yaz hold his hands higher, about the level of his left ear. Doerr thinks Yaz's lower hands are making him uppercut more, thus hitting the ball with more topspin and causing a lot of well-hit balls to sink in the outfield. Yaz makes the adjustment and immediately begins hitting Doerr's practice pitches with more power, spraying the ball all over the empty park. The sound of the ball ricochets through the stillness of the morning. That afternoon, in a doubleheader, Yastrzemski homers in his first at bat, then hits another in the second game. The Sox win both games, breaking out of their slump.

Afterward, Williams barricades himself in his office. He refuses to talk to reporters. He knows that talking to reporters is part of his job, and he usually likes it. His experience in the Dodger organization, where there always were reporters around, has trained him well. He is neither intimidated by them, nor threatened. He feels he gets along with most of them, although he and Larry Claflin of the *Record-American* had gotten off to a bad start in spring training when, at a reception during one of the first nights, Williams argued with Claflin and threatened to end it with his fists. But he is still upset at the criticism in the papers for leaving Wyatt in the day before. This is his way of getting even. Popowski talks to the press instead, once again playing his appointed role of Williams' alter ego.

By the middle of the month the Sox have slipped to 13-14, six games behind the White Sox, and five behind Detroit. They also face the prospect of losing Conigliaro, who must go away for two weeks to Camp Drum, New York, with the Army Reserves. Demeter is slated to replace Conigliaro in right field.

The placement of major leaguers in the Army Reserves and the National Guard is a common practice. With high monthly draft calls needed to supply the troops, the Reserves and National Guard have become popular alternatives, to the point that their rosters are full, with long waiting lists. Baseball teams are often able to circumvent this, using their influence and the player's celebrity to secure coveted spots. Besides Conigliaro, such players as Lonborg, Petrocelli, Rohr, Bill Landis, and backup catcher Mike Ryan are all in the Army Reserves—virtually all of the single guys, since married men are exempt.

Conigliaro had joined the Reserves in the summer of 1965, his second season. After the season he went away for six months of active duty at Fort Dix, New Jersey, standard practice for Reservists and National Guardsmen. Afterward, he was placed in an "inactive control group" in St. Louis, which meant he did not have to attend any meetings, or go off to summer camp for two weeks, no doubt because he was a major league ballplayer. But the Defense Department recently decreed that all Reservists be in an active unit or risk being drafted into the army. Conigliaro had been given to May 11 to comply. At the last minute, after the company commander had threatened not to let him join unless he showed up by the appointed date, he joined the 412th Engineer Company based in nearby Lynn.

Several days before, Ken Holtzman, a young pitcher for the Chicago Cubs in his second season, was called for six months' active duty in the National Guard. He's become the season's most visible reminder of the war, a war that seems to drag on with no end in sight. Symbolic of that, the Senate votes to keep the draft for four more years. U Thant, the United Nations' secretary-general, says he feels the Vietnam War is heading the world toward World War III.

The national media have discovered hippies and start quickly turning them into the All-American freak show. The *Village Voice* does a story called "Freaking Out in Mid-America," an account of the Southwest's first "love-in" where 500 people danced and rolled around in the mud in Tulsa, a city that just three years before had given Barry Goldwater a 30,000 vote plurality. The *New York Times*, the old gray lady herself, publishes an article linking LSD use with cell damage, and the *Times* Sunday magazine starts doing articles on dropout culture, everything from Hell's Angels to a young freelance writer named Hunter Thompson doing a story about the deterioration of Haight-Ashbury, the section of San Francisco near Golden Gate Park that's becoming the focal point for this strange new counterculture.

A couple of years earlier the neighborhood had been inundated with an influx of young white kids who wore bright, psychedelic clothing, or any kind of clothing that came from a different era. Victorian dresses. Old military uniforms. Flowing robes. Bell-bottom pants. LSD, or acid, was often given out free on the streets. San Francisco always had been known as a tolerant, liberal city. In the late '50s it had been the spiritual center of the Beat movement, cultural outcasts who had rebelled against the mind-numbing conformity of American life. It had been across the bay in

Berkeley, at the University of California, where the free speech movement had started in 1964, widely perceived as one of the beginnings of the counterculture. In the summer of 1967 Haight-Ashbury becomes a symbol of this new culture, and it comes complete with its own musical sound, the San Francisco sound. The Jefferson Airplane. The Grateful Dead. Country Joe and the Fish. They are three area bands all getting big airplay, and a promoter named Bill Graham has given them a local showcase. It's called the Fillmore Ballroom, an old warehouse in downtown San Francisco, and it represents this new scene with strobe lights, liquid light, Day-Glo paint, black light, films and slides, all designed to re-create the psychedelic experience, the effect of taking mind-expanding drugs. It's become the forerunner for a new kind of rock club, and soon starts to be replicated in other large cities around the country.

In January an event happened in Golden Gate Park that seemed symbolic of this new era. It was called a "Human Be-In," and it was billed as "A Gathering of the Tribes," a meeting of the acid-heads of Haight-Ashbury and the old Berkeley radicals. Some of the organizers were former Beat poets Allen Ginsburg and Gary Snyder, Timothy Leary, the avatar of LSD, and several of the San Francisco bands, including the Dead, the Airplane, and Big Brother and the Holding Company. Between 10,000 and 20,000 people showed up. It was free, there were only two policemen, and afterward the hippies cleaned the park of all debris. The *San Francisco Oracle,* one of the city's main underground newspapers, had heralded the event, saying, "A new concept of human relations being developed within the youthful underground must emerge, become conscious and be shared so that a revolution of form can be filled with a Renaissance of compassion, awareness and love in the Revelation of the unity of all Mankind."

Or something like that.

Basically, this growing counterculture is a reaction against the middle-class, work-hard-and-save-for-a-rainy-day values the young have grown up with. Its members are against materialism and competition and virtually all of the values that define society. They believe drugs are the pathways to a higher consciousness, mind expanders. They believe in love, spirituality, free sex, sharing, poverty, political anarchy, long hair as a symbol of freedom, and living communally. They are against money, consumerism, bank accounts, cleanliness, structured education, hate, living for the future, and the conveyer belt of American life. They are also against the business suit, which they perceive to be the ultimate symbol of the structured, uptight, repressed American male.

Not all kids are part of this, of course. Most are not. The boys have short hair, still look like products from the '50s. They still believe in the same things their parents believe in, traditional values. Work hard, get a good job, make money, and the future will take care of itself. The girls, with their styled hair and pleated skirts, believe they will grow up and get married and live in the suburbs and have 3.2 kids and drive station wagons and live like their mothers do. It is, at least on the surface, very traditional, particularly in the South and Midwest.

But even among the so-called straight kids there is a strong undercurrent that the world is changing. The main clue is the music, the one thing that sets them apart from their parents, even if on the surface they seem to believe in the same things. Rock 'n' roll, which always had glorified youth culture, is all-pervasive, constantly sending out messages about the new counterculture. There are an estimated 1,000 psychedelic bands in the San Francisco area alone, and more and more of the music being played on the radio is psychedelic rock. Feedback. Loud amplification.

Marijuana is as much a part of the scene as long hair and flowing robes. It's thought to not only get you high, but also change your consciousness. There is a certain innocence to drugs. They are not supposed to lead to harder drugs like heroin, or push anyone into a cycle of drug dependency. Instead, they are viewed as training wheels on the ride to a richer, fuller, more spiritual life. Taking LSD is thought to be one of the ways to understand the universe. Drugs ''blow your mind,'' the saying goes—the implication being that the contemporary American mind, full of closed doors, merely needs a key. Drugs are the key, and many rock 'n' roll songs seem to be sending out subliminal drug messages. Among the hit songs whose titles supposedly contain drug references are "Along Comes Mary" by the Association, "Eight Miles High" by the Byrds, and "Mellow Yellow" by Donovan. These are not underground songs, played on obscure radio stations. They are played constantly on AM radio, songs of a new generation, for a new generation. Drug slang already has become part of the language. Bummer. Bad trip. Blow your mind. Spaced out. Strung out.

The hippies are also soul mates of the movement, or new left, a loose, often unstructured collection of radicals, revolutionaries, and civil rights workers whose goal is nothing less than the complete transformation of American society. The movement identifies with leftist youth movements all over the world that are struggling to overthrow oppression. Although its members are virtually all white, they identify with the American Indian, the third world, and people of color, and their heroes are Che Guevara, Fidel Castro, Ho Chi Minh, and other revolutionary leaders. They also support rising black leaders like Eldridge Cleaver, Stokely Carmichael, and H. Rap Brown.

But the movement is not structured, and that is much of its appeal. Its parameters are wide enough to encompass rock musicians, folk singers such as Bob Dylan and Joan Baez, activists, long hairs, idealists, disaffected college kids who feel anonymous in the American university system, dreamers, pot heads, leftist professors, underground filmmakers, high school kids who sit at home listening to rock 'n' roll and don't want to grow up to be like their parents, virtually anyone who is counter to the grain of American society. The movement's enduring myth is that it's the beginning of a new culture that one day will make America just and kind and truly democratic.

The times they are changing.

Over in Fenway, on May 17, the Sox are being shelled by Baltimore. They give up seven home runs, four in the seventh inning alone. The day before they'd given up eight runs in another loss. In the past six games the pitching staff has given up 56 runs, very much resembling last year's staff, which had been the worst in the league. The only consolation is that in this game against Baltimore the Sox get three home runs of their own—two by Yaz. He now has five in four days, the best streak of his career. Galen Cisco gives up five runs in the seventh, but when Williams comes out to replace him Williams is booed. Williams replaces Cisco with Bill Landis, who quickly gives up two more homers.

"Were you glad to see the Orioles leave town?" Williams is asked afterward.

"It's not so much them leaving town," he responds. "I think some of our pitchers will have to leave town."

In the six-game home stand, four of which were lost by the Sox, Red Sox pitchers had surrendered 18 home runs, and were tattooed all over Fenway. Two days later Lonborg puts a stop to the ignominious streak, with a four-hit, 12-strikeout performance. Even with that, the Sox trailed 2–1 going into the ninth, thwarted by the Indians' Gary Bell. But Tartabull, pinch-hitting, singled to begin the bottom of the ninth. Reggie Smith tripled in Tartabull with the tying run, then scored on Tony Horton's pinch-hit single.

"After I hit the ball into right field I almost forgot to run," Tartabull said after the game. "That's how excited I was."

Two days later, on May 21, the Sox come back to sweep the Cleveland Indians on a Sunday afternoon in Fenway. It is a sunny spring day in Boston, temperature in the 60s. The Sox come from behind in the first game, the third time they've come from behind in late innings to either tie or win. At the end of the day the Sox clubhouse is a happy place. Darrell Brandon has won his first game in five decisions. George Scott is hitting, and when he is hitting he is happy and outgoing, making everyone around him laugh. The team is back to within one game of .500. Williams is particularly pleased with Scott, who's raised his average to .298. Williams knows he needs Scott's bat in the lineup, that outside of Yastrzemski and Conigliaro there is little power.

"He's found himself," Williams says the following day. "Scotty's just trying to hit the ball up the middle, not aiming for the left-field fence. He doesn't have to pull the ball. He has proven he's so strong he can hit it out in any direction, in any ballpark."

Williams believes Scott has become a victim of the Wall. He is not the first. Red Sox history is full of right-handed hitters who couldn't get the Green Monster out of their sights. Dick Gernert. Norm Zauchin. Dick Stuart. They all were classic right-handed pull hitters, supposedly made to order for Fenway Park. Invariably, they tried to pull everything, and invariably pitches on the outside part of the plate became ground balls to shortstop. Or else they lunged at everything, changing their swings, so desperate to pull everything. Scott seems caught in the same trap, unwilling to use all the field, trying to pull every pitch. Williams is forever on Scott for this, just one of many Scott idiosyncrasies that irritate Williams. He offers Scott a deal. For every base hit that Scott gets to the right of the shortstop Williams will give him $20. The flip side is that for every hit Scott gets down the left-field line he must pay $5 to Williams.

The Sox go to Detroit, to Tiger Stadium, the old ballyard on Michigan Avenue, where they climb back to .500. But the game isn't without a small confrontation between Williams and pitcher Dennis Bennett. In the fifth inning, the bases loaded, Kaline up, Williams went out to the mound to visit Bennett.

"He told me if I didn't get Kaline out he was coming after me," Bennett said later.

It's not the first time Williams has come out to the mound for a confrontation with Bennett. He had done it near the end of spring training, after Bennett had failed to back up third base. Bennett is one of the great all-time Red Sox characters, one of the last links to the days when the franchise was known as a country club. He'd joined the team in 1965, having been traded for the irrepressible Dick Stuart, the big first baseman who seemed to symbolize the

Red Sox in the early '60s, all right-handed power, and so deficient in the field that he was called "Dr. Strangeglove." Stuart once hit 66 homers in the minor leagues, and cared about little else other than home runs and his personal statistics.

Bennett is in the same mold, someone who rarely lets baseball get in the way of a good time. Once, during spring training in Arizona, he positioned himself at the door of his hotel room and fired shots from two pistols. Asked why, he said, "I had these two pistols and it was Arizona, so why not?" It was inevitable that he and Williams would clash. Bennett has been around too long, has seen too much to embrace Williams' gung-ho view of the world, an approach infinitely more suited to younger players who still can be molded, still are hungry. By the end of June the Red Sox will sell him to the New York Mets for cash and a minor league outfielder.

The Sox continue on their roller coaster.

They move into sole possession of third place when Lonborg strikes out 11 in a 1–0 win. But three days later they get shelled 10–0 at Memorial Stadium in Baltimore when Frank Robinson hits his 11th and 12th home runs of the year, tops in the American League. The day before Scott had struck out four times, has now struck out eight times in his last 15 at bats, prompting Williams to announce that Scott is going back to the bench and Tony Horton will replace him at first base. It's a classic example of how hitting a baseball is often a mysterious thing that seems to take on a life of its own, riding along on streaks and slumps, events that can change in a couple of days. Just six days before Scott had been hot, Williams happily proclaiming that the Boomer had found himself, was no longer trying to pull everything. Now Scott is back in the middle of a terrible slump. He seems so pathetic at the plate, overswinging, trying to pull everything, that even Popowski, Scott's mentor, says despairingly, "He chirped for 15 miles on the bus from the airport last night telling everybody how far he was going to hit the ball. Did you see any balls go over the fence? Neither did I. Jerking his head and trying to kill everything. If he thinks about getting 35 home runs, he'll hit two.''

Yet there is the feeling that this season is different, this team is different. Already they seem to hustle more, have a better attitude. Williams has said all along this team will win more than it loses, and if that's the case maybe a first-division finish is really possible. After years of failure that would be wonderful, a sign that this is a club finally moving in the right direction.

The Sox return home on Memorial Day, May 30, and things have changed. The crowd is the most obvious example. It's the largest in five years, 32,012. They see the Sox sweep a doubleheader from the California Angels, the third time already the Sox have swept a doubleheader at Fenway. The next day Yaz hits two more homers, his ninth and 10th of the season, as the Sox win another to push their record to 22-20, only four and a half games behind the Tigers. For the second straight game the Sox have squeezed in a runner from third base, the kind of baseball rarely associated with this team, adding credence to the growing theory that this is an unusual Red Sox team, so different from the others that have preceded it for nearly two decades.

"I said it before the season, this team will win more games than it loses, and I still believe that," Williams reaffirms publicly.

This has not been the biggest story in baseball over this Memorial Day, however. Whitey Ford, who has won more games than any other pitcher in Yankee history, has announced his retirement. He is 38. It's one more visible symbol that a great era in Yankee history is over. But, once again, world headlines are pushing baseball into the background. Tensions in the Middle East are like kindling just waiting for a match. Egypt's Gamal Abdel Nasser has said his forces are ready for war against Israel, and the United States has countered by warning Egypt that it views any blockade of the Gulf of Aqaba as "aggression." Arab leaders in the UN Security Council raise the ante by threatening "all-out war" if Israel challenges Egypt's control of the gulf. Moshe Dayan, the hero of Israel's 1956 Sinai campaign against Egypt, is named Israel's defense minister. Within a week war breaks out. Israeli planes will push deep into Egypt's Gaza Strip and Sinai Peninsula, downing 374 Arab warplanes in the first two days. The war only lasts six days.

But as this Memorial Day weekend comes to a close, so does the second month of the season. It has been the coldest May in half a century in New England, an average of 52 degrees. It also has been the second wettest in 99 years, with twice as many bad days than an average May.

Only the baseball is better. The Red Sox are 22-20 and in third place. Chicago is a half game out of first. Cleveland is a half game behind the Red Sox, then come Baltimore, Minnesota, Washington, New York, Kansas City, and California.

The Sox also have three batters in the league's top ten. Petrocelli, off to the best start of his young career, is fourth at .325, Conigliaro seventh at .304, and Yastrzemski eighth at .299. Kaline continues to lead the league at .347, followed by Don Mincher of the Angels, and Frank Robinson. Rod Carew, a rookie with the Minnesota Twins, is fifth. Yaz also is fourth in home runs, behind Robinson, Mantle, and Frank Howard of the Senators, and is fourth in RBI's, trailing league-leader Robinson by six.

Already, Yaz has been reborn. For the first time in his career the Sox are in a pennant race on Memorial Day, and he realizes the difference, how each game means something, each at bat. It's so different from his other years where after the first few weeks it was all too apparent that the only realistic goals worth pursuing were individual ones, the season already beginning to stretch out like a forced march across a desert, the clubhouse lifeless, the excitement somewhere else.

It's also apparent no one is going to run away and hide in the American League. Baltimore, which most experts had thought would have command of the pennant race by now, is wallowing. So is Minnesota, the other team everyone fears. Already, it seems to be a race that has made the preseason form charts obsolete, though there is still strong sentiment that the Red Sox are not for real, that once the summer comes they'll start to sink, just like always. In the Red Sox front office Dick O'Connell knows the Sox need more pitching help if they are going to be able to stay in the race. McMahon has walked seven men in two relief appearances. Williams has lost confidence in Rohr, believes that though he has the talent to win in the major league, he lacks the required toughness. Santiago has arm trouble. After Lonborg, the starting pitching is very suspect. In other years O'Connell might have let the lack of pitching slide, viewing it as something to try to solve in the off-season. Not this year. O'Connell looks around the league and thinks the Red Sox can be in the race until the end. That, in itself, means this is a different year.

MAY STATS

BATTING	AB	R	H	HR	RBI	AVG.
Santiago	7	1	3	1	3	.429
Petrocelli	154	23	50	6	24	.325
Horton	37	2	12		9	.324
Conigliaro	92	13	38	2	15	.304
Yastrzemski	154	30	46	10	31	.299
Ryan	64	10	19	1	8	.297
Andrews	124	16	36	2	11	.290
Demeter	42	7	12	1	4	.286
Jones	60	10	17	2	7	.283
Scott	144	18	39	3	19	.271
Fischer	8		2			.250
Osinski	4		1			.250
Gibson	56	4	14		6	.250
Tartabull	97	14	24		3	.247
Brandon	18	1	4			.222
Smith	146	22	31	2	13	.212
Thomas	20	3	4		3	.200

BATTING	AB	R	H	HR	RBI	AVG.
Foy	120	17	23	4	9	.192
Tillman	26	2	5		2	.192
Bennett	19	1	2	1	3	.105
Lonborg	25		2			.060
Rohr	10					.000
Wyatt	5					.000
Cisco	3					.000
Stange	2					.000
McMahon	2					.000

PITCHING	IP	H	BB	SO	W	L	ERA
Osinski	21	16	5	14	2	0	1.29
Fischer	23⅔	22	8	16	1	2	2.62
Cisco	16	11	5	5	0	1	2.81
Lonborg	70	57	22	71	6	1	3.09
Bennett	51⅔	45	16	18	3	1	3.12
Wyatt	27⅔	15	14	21	3	2	3.21
McMahon	16⅓	15	13	3	1	2	3.37
Brandon	65	55	28	42	2	5	4.03
Rohr	36⅓	35	17	13	2	2	4.25
Stange	17⅓	21	5	22	1	2	4.76
Santiago	30⅓	37	11	26	2	2	6.30
Landis	5	6	6	6	0	0	10.80

June arrives with the announcement that last week was the bloodiest yet for American forces in Vietnam, with 313 killed and 2,616 wounded. The television nightly news continues to bring the war into the nation's living rooms, the agony and sorrow, the pictures of the wounded, the firecracker sound of gunfire, the anguished looks on the faces of the Vietnamese peasants, the chaos, the endless talk of body counts, the sound bites of American military spokesmen saying they are starting to see the light at the end of the tunnel, the lasting images of American soldiers coming home in body bags.

The signs of change are everywhere in Boston, the new colliding with the old, two cultures in collision. Television has yet to grasp this, so that on a Thursday evening in this June of '67 one can watch *Batman*, *F Troop*, *Bewitched*, and *That Girl*.

But *MacBird!* opens in Boston, and Kevin Kelly of the *Boston Globe* calls it a "scathing and relentless indictment of the current political establishment." There is a coming-out party for 260 debutantes in downtown Boston, while

Timothy Leary appears outside of Hartford, Connecticut, a white flower tucked behind his left ear, and tells a crowd of 600 about the virtues of "flower power."

Lady Bird Johnson, here to inaugurate her New England tour for her "Beautify America" program, is met by throngs of schoolchildren in nearby Quincy who have been let out early to see the First Lady. Out in the western part of the state, at Amherst College, one-third of the graduating class signs a petition calling on her husband to provide alternative service for draft age men, and over 100 faculty at nearby Smith sign antiwar statements and protest the campus visit of one of her husband's cabinet members, Undersecretary of State Nicholas Katzenbach.

Lonborg runs his record to 7-1, beating the Indians 2-1 at Fenway on June 2. Lonborg had a no-hitter for seven and a third innings before catcher Duke Sims doubled to right. Afterward, he is down about losing the no-hitter because he knows that getting it would have put him in the national spotlight. It's one more indication that underneath the blond good looks and the placid exterior lurks a burning desire to succeed. Yastrzemski's two-run homer in the sixth is the game-winner. It's his 11th of the year, placing him four behind Frank Robinson's 15. Yaz is fourth in the league in RBI's with 33, 10 behind Robinson.

"This is a fine ballclub and a fellow who deserves some of the credit is Dick O'Connell for putting it together," Yastrzemski says. "He has done a good job of molding it. There's a new life on the ballclub under Dick Williams, and then there's O'Connell. I know in my case I was always reading stories about trading Yastrzemski. That's a very upsetting influence on a player. Dick O'Connell assured me the club wasn't planning to trade me and he talked to me in a way that gave me a lift. Just today I had a chat with Mr. O'Connell and he said, 'Best of luck, get a couple of hits.' We haven't had that around here. I'm not the only one who feels this way either. On the bench too there's a new enthusiasm. You should hear the noise and encouragement in the dugout. Everybody is pulling for each other. And we're winning. It used to be we'd be 10 or 12 games behind the other clubs. Nothing is more discouraging.''

Yastrzemski jokes that his young son, Mike, is starting to take an interest in baseball, that he now saves soda caps that have pictures of players on them, is starting to watch games on television, so ''I've got to play good ball.'' But he's also getting praise from two of the Red Sox coaches, two men who've seen him in previous years and see the difference this year. Maglie says Yaz has matured, that he goes about the game with more discipline and a better attitude. ''He always was a good hitter,'' says Maglie. ''But now he's a terrific all-around player.'' Popowski takes it a step further. ''Yaz is a great player on this club,'' he says. ''He talks hitting with the younger players and they listen. You don't find the stars of the game giving equal time to the younger guys who are coming along. That's the thing I like about Yaz. He's great for that.''

It's the first tangible example that Yastrzemski is finally beginning to emerge as the leader of this team, the role that had been cast on him the year before when he'd been both unwilling and unable to do it. Now it's evolving naturally, largely the result of so many younger players on the club. The younger players not only respect his ability, they also respect his experience. No longer is he the young kid, complete with the near-impossible baggage of being the next Ted Williams. He's become one of the role models, almost a veteran. He likes to talk baseball, likes it when the younger players ask him questions. He's befriended Foy and Reggie Smith. He watches Foy struggle at the plate and tells him he should hold his hands up higher. Foy immediately starts to hit better. Foy likes to joke that the reason he stays close to Yastrzemski is that Yaz always carries an attaché case around with him that has all the checks in it. Regardless, Yastrzemski has become a real leader, not some cheerleader.

Yastrzemski has sensed the players are relying on him and that's changed his approach. He's also found that many of the players want his advice. That too is different from past years when, as the captain in name only, he felt that his teammates weren't particularly interested in being led.

Not that Dick Williams seems too enthused when several writers point out Yaz's emerging status as a team leader. Like a terrier patrolling his turf, he snorts, "He may be an inspiration to the other players, but there's only one leader on this team."

Williams doesn't have to say who he thinks it is.

But the big news occurs the next day when the Sox trade reliever Don McMahon and a minor league pitcher to the White Sox for veteran infielder Jerry Adair. Adair is light-hitting, his average at .204, but can play second, short, and third. He also knows Williams, the two of them having been teammates for a while in Baltimore. Williams considers him the ultimate professional.

Then the next day, June 4, shortly before a game in Cleveland, the Sox announce another trade. This time it's Tony Horton and reserve outfielder Don Demeter for pitcher Gary Bell. Bell is 30, originally from San Antonio, Texas, where he grew up with White Sox pitcher Joel Horlen, playing on the same high school team.

"I was a pitcher and outfielder and Joel played shortstop and also pitched," he says. "We were both quarterbacks in football and the coach switched me to fullback and we both played in the same backfield. The Red Sox talked to me about signing but I picked Cleveland. I thought I'd have a better chance with them. Their pitching was getting older."

He is a 10-year veteran, a good-looking, dark-haired man nicknamed "Ding Dong" primarily because of his flaky, outgoing manner and a personality that sometimes gives off the impression he doesn't take baseball seriously enough. He only has won one of six decisions this year, but had 194 strikeouts last year. He has not gotten along very well with new Indian manager Joe Adcock, who replaced Birdie Tebbetts, and the Red Sox are hoping a change of scenery will do him good. Bell agrees. His best year was eight years ago when he was 16-11, but he comes to the Red Sox with the imprimatur of Frank Lane, the old trader himself, now with Baltimore, who believes Bell still has a good rising fastball and that the Sox have made themselves a great trade. Bell doesn't know any of the Red Sox, but has been rooming on the Indians with Radatz, the former Sox reliever, and thus is more aware of the Red Sox and their players than he would be otherwise.

Both Horton and Demeter have been in Williams' doghouse. Horton is only 22, but has been unable to break into the starting lineup due to defensive deficiencies and the presence of Scott. He is hitting .308, but half of his hits have come as a pinch hitter. Demeter is an eleven-year veteran, now going to his fifth team. It also was a symbolic move, one that says the front office believes in the team, is willing to do what it has to do to make it better. Williams is overjoyed.

"I think this gives us a shot at the pennant," he says, although no one takes him very seriously.

The next day Williams says he plans to start Adair at third in place of Joe Foy, who is hitting .204.

"Maybe this will light a fire under Foy," Williams says, which is another way of saying that Foy is back in Williams' doghouse.

For the first time this season the Red Sox appear on the front page of the *Boston Globe,* yet another indication that the Sox are starting to make New England take notice. The story is about Williams, and is headlined, "Can He Keep the Sox Going?" The gist of it is that Williams is not afraid to bench his regulars, not afraid to defy the Sox's tradition. What it doesn't say is that this strategy also can make a team jittery, players afraid to make mistakes and playing with one eye on the bench. So far it doesn't seem to have happened. Or if it has, Williams is oblivious.

The Sox are in Cleveland, at Municipal Stadium, the big, cavernous ballpark on Lake Erie, but all the excitement is back in Boston where the city is undergoing its third straight night of racial violence. It had begun on Friday night, June 2, when a group of Roxbury mothers demanded to see the city's welfare director. They complained of long waits to see social workers, and of being insulted and harassed when they finally did see them. The mothers locked themselves in the office on Grove Street in a sit-in and prevented welfare workers from leaving. Police charged through the windows, attempting to force out the demonstrators.

This started a riot that lasted 11 hours in the streets of Roxbury and the South End, a four-square-mile area that contains roughly 65,000 blacks and Puerto Ricans, about 10 percent of the city's total population. The police fired shots into the air. The next night a police officer was wounded by a sniper in another night of rioting and looting. It is the worst riot in the city's history, and Mayor John F. Collins calls it "the worst manifestation of disrespect for the rights of others that this city has ever seen." Several of the welfare mothers charge that the police beat and kicked them; several black leaders blame the police for the escalation of violence.

The rioting continues for another night. It coincides with the first hot weather of the year, the beginning of summer. Blue Hill Avenue, a main thoroughfare, is closed to traffic. The police, outfitted in full riot gear, patrol Roxbury and parts of the South End. By the second night there are 1,900 police, and even as the rioting ends—with 65 arrested and 75 injured—150 police are still stationed in the area, with another 500 on alert nearby.

Boston has become, for all practical purposes, a segregated city, a city where whites and blacks live in worlds that rarely intersect. Even in sports. For the past decade the Celtics have been the best basketball team in the world, one of the most successful in sports history. They have banners that hang from the Boston Garden rafters to prove it, symbols of world titles in 1957, and from 1959 through 1966. Yet the Celtics rarely sell out the Boston Garden, while the Boston Bruins, a perennial NHL doormat, always sell out the same building. Since the arrival of Bill Russell in the late '50s, the first great black athlete in Boston, the Celtics have become increasingly a black team, so that now many of their key players are black, Russell, Sam Jones, K. C. Jones, Tom Sanders. They also have become the first NBA team to have five blacks on the floor at the same time, a practice considered taboo in a league that still supposedly has an unofficial quota system regulating the number of blacks on each team.

Boston is not a particularly good place to be if you're a black athlete. Russell has gone on record calling Boston a racist city, saying he and his family had trouble buying a house in Reading, a Boston suburb, and have been the target of discrimination. Russell has the clout to be able to say these things and get away with it. Other black athletes don't.

The city takes its sports cue from the Red Sox. As far as the black community is concerned the Red Sox might as well be playing on the far side of the moon. In turn, the Red Sox do virtually no public relations in the inner city.

It's never been determined just why the Red Sox were the last team in baseball to integrate. The most common theory is that because Yawkey is a South Carolina plantation owner, the club's failure to sign young black players is attributable to him. Yawkey always denies this, saying he would have loved to have signed a good black player earlier but his scouts never found him any.

Ironically, the Red Sox are rumored to have given Jackie Robinson and two other blacks, Sam Jethroe and Emory Wright, both of whom had played in the Negro Leagues, a brief tryout in Fenway Park as early as 1945. As the story goes, the tryout was little more than a cursory look, conducted by a scout who had little influence and no power to sign anyone. Another oft-told story is that the Red Sox had the chance to sign a young black player in Birmingham, Alabama, named Willie Mays, having sent a scout to see him play. But the game got rained out, and rather than stay around and wait for another game, the scout essentially filed a report saying Mays couldn't cut it. Interestingly, Al Hirshberg, a Boston writer, once wrote that in the late '50s Pinky Higgins told him, "They'll be no niggers on this team as long as I have anything to say about it."

Back in 1957 Joe Cronin had said in an interview that the Red Sox would have "a couple of them" in a year or two, but it wasn't until 1959 that Elijah "Pumpsie" Green was brought to spring training in Scottsdale, the first black player. Not that he was allowed to stay in the hotels the Red Sox used, having to stay instead in Phoenix 17 miles away, at the same hotel several of the New York Giants stayed in, including Willie Mays, Willie McCovey, and Orlando Cepeda. Green was soon sent down to Minneapolis, even though he'd hit well in spring training, and his demotion caused the Boston chapter of the NAACP to pressure the Red Sox front office. Red Sox management tried to counter the attack in a prepared statement saying they had five black players in the organization.

It's now a decade later, and though Higgins' statement seems the product of some antediluvian time, many of the black players realize that they are little more than hired hands, glorified "field niggers" with little margin for error. They're also aware that they live in two different worlds. Consider Scott, for example. He socializes in Roxbury. But he knows that Roxbury and Fenway Park have little in common.

Scott grew up in Greenville, Mississippi, a Delta town on the Mississippi River. It was the segregated South, the Faulkner South, where blacks stayed to themselves, the air thick with humidity. Mississippi was the heart of darkness then, the most backward state in the country, and the Delta had a reputation as the poorest, most repressive area of the country. The median income of blacks was below $2,000, a third of what it was for whites. Only 5 percent were registered to vote, and many lived in shacks with no running water. Scott's family was typical. His father had died when he was an infant, his mother worked a succession of menial jobs trying to keep food on the table for Scott, his brother, and sister. The family lived in a tar paper shack. Scott went to Coleman High School, the black school, even though the white school was only a few blocks from his house and Coleman was three miles away. It was the early '60s, still a couple of years before civil rights workers would come to Mississippi and begin the process that would change the South forever, but to Scott it was just the way things were. He didn't grow up rebelling against the existing social order. He didn't grow up militant. He just wanted to play ball. His mother, Magnolia, always taught him to work hard, be respectful of people, and good things would happen. She was a Jehovah's Witness and young George grew up in the church. School, church, sports, working part-time—these were the cornerstones of Scott's life.

By the time he reached high school he was a great athlete, excelling also in football and basketball, and he began to think baseball could be a ticket out of a sleepy Delta town. He heard about a local kid named Tommie Agee getting signed out of Grambling, a black college in Louisiana, and figured that if he followed his mother's advice the same thing might one day happen to him. When he was a senior there were scouts looking at him, and signing with a major league team had become a reality. The night he graduated from high school, still in his graduation robes, he went into the principal's office. There were seven scouts there. They made their pitch. Scott listened to all of them and signed with the Red Sox for $10,000, more money than he knew existed in the world. The scout who signed him was Ed Scott, a black who was no relation, and who years later would sign Dennis "Oil Can" Boyd from the same area. George Scott knew nothing about the Red Sox, or their racial history. He had no idea where Boston was, or anything about it. He bought some land for his mother and a used black-and-yellow GTO for himself, and a few years later was in Olean, New York, in the New York–Penn League, out of Mississippi for the first time in his life. It was the summer of 1962.

"I went to play ball," he would say later. "I didn't know anything else."

The only other black on the team was a kid named Homer Green from Pittsburgh. Scott quickly realized that "none of them white boys was going to talk to me," so he put it out of his mind. He was there to play baseball, not worry about racial prejudice. He had grown up with prejudice and discrimination, it had been as much a part of his life as baseball, so why should it come as any surprise now? He spent his time off-field with Green, tried to forget about being homesick, about being so far from anything that seemed familiar. It worked on the field, but it took him two years before he got over being homesick.

The next summer he went to Winston-Salem, North Carolina, still the Jim Crow South. It was the summer of '64, civil rights workers had arrived, tension was everywhere. Scott was the only black on the team. Sometimes people brought black cats to the games.

"This is your sister," they would yell at Scott, holding up the cat. "This is your mother."

Scott vowed to block it all out, to just try to concentrate on playing ball. On the field, within the white lines, the world made sense. Outside the white lines nothing made sense. He'd grown up with segregation, yet everything had been structured, orderly. Now everything seemed in flux, changing. He worried about his mother and sister back home in Mississippi where it had become "Freedom Summer," and the violence and hate was on the nightly news. Three civil rights workers were found murdered that summer, their bodies discovered in shallow graves in woods near Philadelphia, Mississippi. Scott kept persevering, a long way from home.

By the next year, when he went to Pittsfield, Massachusetts, to Double A, where Popowski was the coach, he knew the worst was over. He was no longer homesick. He knew he was going to eventually get to the major leagues. He won the league's Triple Crown that year, was named MVP, and the next year came to Boston. He played third base in the home opener in 1966 and was so scared his knees shook. After a few games he was moved to first, and right away he became one of the flashiest first basemen in the game, showing a combination of slick fielding and style that had been forged in the Mississippi sandlots of his youth.

It is summer, and with the advent of summer come racial outbreaks in Cincinnati, Tampa, Dayton, and Lansing, Michigan. Already, the images have become a part of the times, angry black youths throwing rocks and bottles, police in riot gear, buildings in flames, the rhetoric of hate. The outbreaks all begin as random incidents, just like Boston. In Cleveland,

Muhammad Ali reaffirms his stand against the draft at the "Negro Industrial and Economic Union," headed by football great Jim Brown. Ali refuses to enter the service on the grounds he is a Muslim minister. He is scheduled to go on trial later in the month in Houston.

It is a simpler world for Carl Yastrzemski, who keeps on rolling along, beginning to emerge as the leader he never had been before.

White Sox manager Eddie Stanky, nicknamed "the Brat," tries to rattle him, calling him "an All-Star from the neck down" in the newspaper. But on June 8, in Comiskey Park, Yastrzemski makes three great catches, gets four hits, including his 12th homer, and tips his cap to Stanky as he rounds third base after the home run.

It's not the first time, of course, that Stanky has been in the middle of a controversy. His epitaph as a player was that no one ever got further on less ability, and he'd been known as one of the meanest, scrappiest, toughest players in the game, in addition to being one of the game's most acerbic bench jockeys. In fact, it was Stanky who prompted Leo Durocher to make his famous "nice guys finish last" remark. Stanky was with the Dodgers at the time and Durocher told a group of sportswriters to look at Mel Ott of the Giants, who "is a nice guy and he finishes second. Now look at the Brat. He can't hit, can't run, can't field. He's no nice guy, but all that little SOB can do is win." Stanky only hit .268 as a player, but had played in three World Series. In the mid '50s he'd become player-manager of the Cardinals, then manager. Now 51, he's in his second year as the White Sox manager, and his team has come to reflect his personality. The White Sox have no offense, no power, a team batting average that hovers at around .230. It's said that watching the White Sox is like watching paint dry. What they do have is quality pitching centered around Joel Horlen and Gary Peters, and an aggressive approach to how the game should be played. They are called the "Go Go White Sox," which comes as no surprise to anyone who remembered Stanky as a player. Not that Stanky takes any credit for this.

"My job is to entertain the gentlemen of the press, radio, and TV, make up the lineup, then fall asleep," he says.

So much for the mystique of managing.

Ironically, it was Stanky who had helped Dick Williams off the field when he hurt his shoulder diving for a routine foul ball in May of 1952.

On June 10 the Twins fire manager Sam Mele. He is 45, had managed the Twins for six years, winning the pennant two years ago. Not that it comes as a great surprise to Mele. Before the season he had said he knew he was in trouble, that if the Twins didn't get off to a quick start he didn't think owner Calvin Griffith would keep him around. The Twins hadn't. They had played stupid baseball, missing cutoff men, making mental mistakes, all the signs of a team that's lost its focus. Tony Oliva has not hit. Left-hander Jim Kaat, a 25-game winner last year, is struggling. Kaat supposedly is still upset at the Twins for letting pitching coach Johnny Sain get away to the Tigers at the end of the last season. He even wrote a public letter to Twins fans saying if he were a club owner he would hire Sain as a pitching coach, then get a manager who could take advantage of him. It was a slap at Mele, one more nail in the coffin.

The Twins are in sixth place, 25-25. Former Yankee infielder Billy Martin, already known as feisty and combative, had been rumored to be Mele's successor, but Griffith chooses Calvin Coolidge Ermer, the manager of the Twins' Triple A franchise in Denver instead.

Since Mele comes from nearby Quincy, he's long been considered an ideal candidate to be a Red Sox manager. Supposedly this was the main reason Williams was only offered a one-year contract, the Red Sox front office unwilling to commit themselves to an unproven manager if a proven winner like Mele became available. The one-year contract also was a not-so-subtle message to Williams. Although he later said it had no effect on the way he managed, his contract status also told him he had to make the team better right away, for he wasn't going to get too many second chances.

* * *

June also means the arrival of Tom Yawkey.

Every summer he comes to Boston, to his suite in the Ritz-Carlton Hotel, one of Boston's swankiest, an elegant establishment overlooking Boston Common. He arrives almost surreptitiously at Fenway Park, going to his private box where he sits by himself and watches his team.

He is rarely seen by the public. After the 1949 season, which supposedly broke his heart, he became more and more of a recluse. For years the only picture of him in the newspapers showed a man in middle age, looking fairly robust. But the Yawkey of 1967 is frail, old, emaciated, so anonymous that he could walk through Fenway Park in the middle of a Sunday afternoon doubleheader and go unnoticed. He has diabetes and there are rumors he is dying of cancer.

The batboys and clubhouse attendants certainly are around Yawkey more than the players are. The ritual is always the same. They go out on the field in the afternoon of night games and work out. It begins with Yawkey hitting. Then everyone else hits, usually six or seven guys. Then Yawkey hits again. It is a time when Yawkey is completely relaxed, at peace in the personal kingdom he's created. He is comfortable with this small group of employees. They, in turn, revere him, view him as the benevolent owner, the old uncle who always gives you money for candy and never judges you. On many afternoons, when the Red Sox are out of town, Yawkey comes down to the clubhouse to sit around with the guys and listen to the game on the radio, just sitting around and talking baseball. This is the side of Yawkey the public never sees.

One of the guys is clubhouse boy Don Fitzpatrick, who first started working for the Red Sox in 1944. He is from neighboring Brookline, virtually grew up in the center-field bleachers. He had been there in '46 when the Red Sox clinched the pennant in Cleveland on Ted Williams' inside-the-park home run. He was working as the Indians' batboy in the 1948 playoff game to determine the American League pennant, in the dugout with Lou Boudreau and Ken Keltner, all the while rooting for the Red Sox with all his heart, crushed when the Indians won. Fitzpatrick thinks the world of Yawkey, considers him a marvelous man, someone who's always loyal to the little people who work for him.

Yawkey is happier this summer. The team is in the pennant race. Attendance is the best it's been in years. Fenway Park is alive again, full of spirit and passion, so unlike other years when by this time in the season Fenway would seem too full of the echoes of yesterday's cheers. He takes great delight in this team, as if they have become some consolation for all the summers spent sitting by himself in his private box watching a team that was out of the pennant race by Memorial Day, sitting there by himself, thinking who knows what.

But though he's happy with his team for the first time in years, he throws a bombshell at New England. There are rumors that the financial people who govern Yawkey's estate are putting pressure on him to sell the team. In a story in the *Boston Globe* he says if the city does not build a new stadium within five years he will take the Red Sox out of Boston.

"I'm losing money with the Red Sox and no one—unless he's a damn fool—likes to lose money," Yawkey says. "I cannot continue indefinitely under present circumstances. This is not a threat. It's a statement of fact."

He is rumored to have lost $3 million in five years, a conservative estimate.

"There have been at least a dozen new stadiums constructed in the past five years," he continues. "St. Louis, Oakland, Atlanta, New York, and Los Angeles come to mind. In Boston we have done nothing. The situation hasn't changed one bit, and you can only live with a bad situation for so long. I've come to that realization. We need a new stadium for the Red Sox and for pro football and the Boston Patriots."

He not only hates the parking situation around Fenway Park; he is irked as well by rumors that the Kansas City Athletics are about to move to Oakland and a new stadium where the Oakland Raiders play. Previously, it had been thought that only Billy Sullivan, the owner of the fledgling football Patriots, wanted a new stadium in Boston. Yawkey punctures that myth.

Despite the fact that Yawkey is starting for the first time to play hardball with the city of Boston, he likes his new team, and his new manager.

"I knew about 10 days after I got here that I wanted Dick back with us," Yawkey says. "It wasn't any one particular thing, but it was the way he was running the whole show. He was doing an outstanding job of being the manager, but he also was running things well. What was more important, he was running things off the field. He was handling the men well. He had control. Nowadays, I think handling the players is the biggest part of the job."

Williams, though, never feels secure around Yawkey. After games Williams often goes upstairs to Yawkey's lounge, where the club officials have an informal gathering. But Williams doesn't feel a part of it. The Red Sox family has always been insular, like some special club with its own secret initiation rites, its own codes. For years it's included Yawkey and a handful of the few people he feels comfortable with. Williams has never belonged, never has been Red Sox family, even though he spent a few years with the team as a player. He always feels like an employee, an outsider. Within the organization he feels comfortable around O'Connell because he knows O'Connell wants him, fought to get him hired. He doesn't trust Yawkey. He also doesn't like Yawkey's starting to spend more time in the clubhouse now that the club is winning. Williams sees this as phony, for he knows Yawkey was rarely around in the years he himself had been a player in Boston. So he goes upstairs to the lounge after the games, always feeling like the guest at the party who knows he better not use the wrong fork or he'll never be invited back.

The trade for Gary Bell is already paying dividends. On June 12 the Sox beat the Yankees in Fenway as Bell wins his second game for the Red Sox. Besides Bell, the hero is catcher Russ Gibson, who hits his first major league home run. He is from Fall River, Massachusetts, a tired textile city about an hour south of Boston, the city immortalized in

American folklore for Lizzie Borden. He is a 28-year-old rookie, having spent 10 years in the minor leagues. His father Jim is in a Fall River hospital, listening to the game on the radio.

"First homer," says a New York writer, approaching Gibson afterward in the Red Sox clubhouse. "What took you so long?"

"Pitching," Gibson deadpans.

Gibson is not the only new hero for the Red Sox.

Another is pitcher Gary Waslewski, called up from Toronto to replace Billy Rohr when he went away for two weeks' active duty with the Reserves. Waslewski, a Connecticut native who'd been the property of the Pittsburgh Pirates until the Sox had signed him in 1964, had played last year for Williams in Toronto and had found him to be different from his previous managers. Unlike the others, who still clung to the notion that a starting pitcher should pitch complete games, Williams' philosophy was "Give me six or seven good innings and we'll get someone else to finish it for you." Waslewski also quickly became aware of Williams' obsession with fundamentals. "We practiced fielding bunts until we couldn't walk," he says. "He used to love to stand there with a fungo bat and hit rockets off your kneecaps."

The next night begins with the promise of being memorable. It is Thursday, the 15th of June.

Before the game Stanky announces to the press how he's instructed his wife to sue for $300,000 if anything happens to him, because of what he calls the "inadequate police protection at Fenway Park." He then ups the ante, saying he will sue Yawkey and Players Association rep Marvin Miller $1 million each "if I am killed or maimed."

"I might have been killed or maimed because of the inadequate protection here," Stanky says. "Mr. Yawkey thinks more of the deer and pheasants on his farm in South Carolina than he does of human flesh on his ballfield."

It's a reference to the night before when fans sitting near the visitors' dugout along the third base line had showered him with debris as his White Sox had lost the second game of the twi-night doubleheader. Stanky had been ejected in that game by umpire Jerry Neudecker. He'd been reacting to a call earlier in the game by umpire Larry Napp, who'd ruled that a J. C. Martin line drive that went into the seats along the right-field line had been foul. Stanky had run out on the field to argue with Napp, but hadn't been ejected. But later, as the umpires crossed the field, he again had words with both Napp and Neudecker and Neudecker ran him off.

Afterward, the writers had found Stanky reclining on a table in the trainer's room in the visitors' clubhouse in back of the third base dugout, though the trainer's room was usually off-limits to the press.

"You saw it," barked Stanky, referring to Napp's call. "Write your own story. Of course it was a foul ball. I don't have to have people tell me what I saw. It was a home run, but you'll write what you want anyway."

Stanky knew that American League president Joe Cronin, the former Red Sox general manager, had been at the game.

"I just hope Mr. Cronin—and I said *Mr.* Cronin, get that—saw that play," he continued, getting angrier. "They ought to chew somebody out in the American League office after a play like that."

Somebody asked him if it had been a judgment call.

"Judgment?" he said. "I've been bucking judgment all my life. That's all I get. What about justice? The whole world is based on judgment. Does that make the Communists right because they don't like our president? I know what I saw and a lot of you guys don't have the guts to write it. You are all negative. That's what's hurting the game. It's the number one game, but it won't stay number one the way you guys are writing it."

Now, on this June 15 night, the Red Sox are positioned only four games back of the White Sox.

The game is scoreless, one of those games where every movement, every act, seems to take on added significance. This is a game right out of a Stanky playbook, one dominated by pitching and defense. The two pitchers are Bruce Howard for the White Sox, and Waslewski, two little-known names in this baseball summer. But through 10 innings neither team has any runs. Waslewski leaves the game, complete with a well-deserved standing ovation. He is replaced by Wyatt. The suspense builds.

Then, in the top of the 11th, the White Sox score, and when both Yastrzemski and Scott go down easily in the bottom half of the inning, it appears the Red Sox are going to lose and the 16,000 or so fans in Fenway are going to go home unhappy. But Joe Foy singles to left, bringing up Conigliaro.

He has been struggling at the plate ever since he returned from his two weeks of summer camp at Camp Drum. He'd even been dropped from fourth to sixth in the order.

"The army was tougher than I thought it would be," he says. "The first week we lived in a tent and I was on bivouac. When you got back at night it was dark and you were tired out. It was all-army. You got up at 5 A.M. and you were completely played out, and no playing around either."

Now he's in a slump, one that has played with his head. Slumps are especially hard for Conigliaro to deal with, primarily because he's so cocky, so outwardly confident. It's part of his persona, this confidence, and a slump upsets the natural order of things, allows for small doubts to sneak into his life.

"When things are going bad everybody becomes an expert," he'd said a few days earlier, the incredulity in his voice. "When I was driving over here earlier the attendant on the Mystic River Bridge recognized me and started telling me what I was doing wrong. He said I was snapping my head or something. I suppose now that I got a hit he'll take the credit. But I was starting to lose my confidence. You can't help feeling down when you're in a slump. Everyone is telling you what to do except your grandmother."

Now he's at the plate with two out and Foy on base in the bottom of the 11th, the game tied. He is crowding the plate, as usual, being aggressive, which is his trademark. He is a firm believer that home plate is his territory, and that the more he can control it the more effective he will be. He is what is known in the game as a tough out, someone who's always going to battle the pitcher, crowd the plate, be aggressive, take his cuts. Veteran reliever Johnny Buzhardt, whose been pitching in the big leagues for 10 seasons now, is on the mound and the count is three and two. Conigliaro had swung and missed at two Buzhardt curveballs, looking overmatched, but then Buzhardt had missed with three pitches, adding to the suspense. Over and over, almost like a mantra, Conigliaro tells himself to be ready, to be quick with the bat. Sitting in the dugout minutes earlier he'd felt that if Foy had gotten on he was going to hit a home run, one of those rare, fleeting moments when you convince yourself that the improbable is possible. But now that he's at the plate, with the count full, it's much more compli-cated. He figures Buzhardt will throw another curve, be-cause not only has he gotten him on two already, the book on Conigliaro is he's a fastball hitter. Buzhardt throws again, another curve, Conigliaro swings, and the ball seems to leap from his bat in a high parabola, the white ball streaming across the darkened night sky. The crowd seems to come out of their seats collectively in a massive roar, as the ball keeps going and going until it lands in the screen above the Green Monster in left, a classic Tony C. home run. The Red Sox win, 2–1.

The Red Sox bench runs out on the field surrounding home plate, waiting for Conigliaro to finish his home run trot, his most dramatic since his home run in his first time at bat in Fenway four years earlier. The first player to greet him is Yastrzemski. This is important for a couple of reasons. First, it is out of character. Second, Conigliaro never could figure out how Yaz could play on such a lousy team and seem so blasé about it. So Yastrzemski greeting him at the plate is a symbolic moment. Never again will Conigliaro think Yaz doesn't care. The rest of the players, seeing Yastrzemski reacting that way after a game-winning hit, makes them question their own reactions.

This is one of the games that will stand out, as if outlined in neon. On one hand, it reinforces the notion that this season will be more successful than previous ones. On the other, it's an indication that pettiness and selfishness are a thing of the past. This had been the main theme in Williams' first address to the team back in Winter Haven, the belief that if they played hard and played with pride good things could happen. From the first day of spring training everything had been geared to strip away at the age-old attitude of selfishness that pressed down on the Red Sox like some sedimented rock.

But words only have so much effect. So not only has this been a dramatic victory, it has been an important one.

"It reminded me of the Polo Grounds and Bobby Thomson's home run in '51," says Dick Williams, a reference to the home run that won the pennant for the New York Giants over the Brooklyn Dodgers, one of the most dramatic moments in baseball history. "But, hey, this was better. I'm a winner this time."

Three days later this young Red Sox team receives another lesson in how ephemeral baseball success can be, losing three out of four to the lowly Senators in Washington, once again back on baseball's roller coaster. They also learn that baseball is a marathon, not a sprint. They are back to .500 again, six and a half games behind the White Sox, and scheduled to go to New York for a short midweek series with the Yankees. First, though, they have to suffer through a bad airline flight from Washington to New York, the worst one of announcer Ken Coleman's long career.

Coleman is the main Red Sox broadcaster on a radio and television network that stretches throughout New England. The Red Sox on the radio have long been a New England tradition and it's virtually impossible to go anywhere in the region without hearing a Sox broadcast, the soundtrack to a New England summer. Coleman, who grew up in Quincy, had broadcast the Cleveland Indians for years when in 1965 Curt Gowdy, the longtime voice of the Red Sox, left to go to NBC. For Coleman, who'd gotten his start in small radio stations throughout New England, the offer to come to Boston was a dream come true. One of his partners is Ned Martin, who'd been broadcasting minor league games in

Charleston, West Virginia, before hooking up with the Sox in 1961. The other is former Sox pitcher Mel Parnell, who along with Babe Ruth is considered the top left-handed pitcher in Red Sox history.

No one likes the airplane flight to New York, least of all Yastrzemski. Years before, he'd developed a fear of flying, partly the legacy of Jackie Jensen, the former California football star who had been the right fielder when Yastrzemski was breaking in with the Red Sox, a player whose fear of flying eventually led to the premature end of his career. Every time Yaz gets on an airplane he either plays cards fervently, or engages other people in conversation, anything to distract himself. Other players are more fatalistic.

"I don't care if this thing goes down," quips Gary Bell. "I'm only three and six."

Over the weekend U.S. planes carried out the heaviest raids of the year on North Vietnam, and simultaneous with the Sox's arrival in New York Soviet premier Aleksei Kosygin pays a visit to the United Nations and prepares for a summit meeting with President Johnson. In sports, the headlines belong to 27-year-old Jack Nicklaus, who wins the U.S. Open at the Baltusrol Golf Club in New Jersey. A few days earlier Arnold Palmer, who is 37 and the most popular golfer in the world, had predicted he himself would win. In Times Square, along the Great White Way, the marquees advertise *The Sand Pebbles* with Steve McQueen and *I, a Woman*.

The next day, as Williams prepares for the series with the Yankees, he shuffles the batting order again. Andrews, who'd been second and is hitting .261, moves up to first. The year before he'd led off for Williams in Toronto. He is from Los Angeles, was signed by Red Sox scout Joe Stephenson in 1962 while he was going to a junior college preparing to go to UCLA to play football. He already had been offered a scholarship, but had failed to take a second year of a foreign language in high school, thus had to go to junior college to get academically ready. But when Stephenson offered him the opportunity to sign he did.

He was a shortstop until his second year at Toronto where

he was switched to second, primarily because Petrocelli already was the shortstop in Boston. He and Reggie Smith joined the Red Sox last September and couldn't believe the attitude of some of the players, how some of them were just playing out the string, waiting for the season to end. Already he knows Williams has made a difference, totally revamped the attitude. Not that Andrews needs any refresher on how demanding Williams is. He likes Williams off the field, but knows firsthand how caustic and driven he is on it.

Smith, who is struggling with a .187 average, moves down to eighth. There was some speculation that Tartabull, who's hitting .250, might be moved into the lineup for Smith, but Tartabull has defensive liabilities and Williams wants Smith's speed in center field. Foy, who is swinging the bat better after being benched earlier, moves into the second slot in the order.

"We have to get more people on for Yaz," says Williams.

The new order now reads, Andrews, Foy, Yastrzemski, Conigliaro, Petrocelli, Scott, Tillman, and Smith. Tillman hasn't played since May 12 when he inadvertently hit pitcher John Wyatt in the head while attempting to throw out a stealing Detroit base runner. In retrospect, it was one of the funnier scenes of the Red Sox season, a little déjà vu of the way things used to be. Not that Tillman thought it was funny. "The play was very serious for me," he says defensively, "I don't see why people think it was funny."

Tillman and Williams once had been roommates on the Red Sox.

"Is it just a coincidence that Tillman hasn't played since he hit Wyatt in the head?" Williams is asked.

"Oh yes," he says.

What he doesn't have to say is that Russ Gibson and Mike Ryan, the two other catchers, are hitting .232 and .247 respectively.

It is not a good Yankee team. The Yankees dominated baseball for an entire generation, towering over the rest of the sport, the premier attraction in the American League. But in 1964 the Yankees were sold to CBS, their demise also correlating with the fall of attendance in the American League. Their fall also highlighted the problems in the American League. For years the National League has been more balanced, stronger from top to bottom. Six different teams have won the National League pennant in the past eight years. The NL has won five out of the past eight World Series, and dominated the last dozen All-Star games. This obvious superiority of the National League was not so apparent as long as the Yankees dominated the American league. But the Yankees fell into the second division two years ago, their long era over. Ford is gone. The great Mickey Mantle is near the end of his career, hobbled by bad knees. So is Elston Howard. Now the names are Horace Clarke, Ruben Amaro, Mike Hegan, Joe Pepitone, Jake Gibbs, Tom Tresh. Names that are mortal, that don't come wrapped in legend. Now the Yankees are lodged deep in the second division, another season going nowhere. One bright spot of news is that they've just signed the number one pick in the free agent draft for $75,000, 18-year-old Ron Blomberg from Druid Hills High School in Atlanta.

But there is still something special about a Red Sox–Yankees series, regardless of the records, or how their seasons are going. Some of it is history. Some of it is that the two franchises were forever linked back in 1920 when the Red Sox sold Ruth to the Yankees, the event that led to the Yankees becoming the greatest dynasty in sports, and the Red Sox becoming a team of frustration. Throughout the '40s and '50s the Red Sox and Yankees had, in Ted Williams and Joe DiMaggio, two of the greatest names in baseball history. The Yankees always have been the Red Sox's alter ego, what the Red Sox would have been if Yawkey's vision had been fulfilled. They have even infiltrated New England, their fans everywhere, the legacy of years of success, and the fact that DiMaggio became the hero of everyone with an Italian-American surname.

Part of it is Yankee Stadium itself, the "House That Ruth Built." Forced to leave the Polo Grounds in 1920, Yankee owner Jacob Ruppert set out to build the most famous stadium in baseball, complete with triple decks. He chose an old lumber yard in the Bronx near the Harlem River as his site, across the river from the Polo Grounds. It opened in 1923, and ironically the Yankees beat the Red Sox in the first game, a Ruth home run the difference. The Stadium became the perfect showcase for the great Yankee teams of Ruth and Gehrig, making everything seem larger than life, as indeed the Yankees were then. It was the site for Ruth's 60th home run in 1927, and Roger Maris' 61st in 1961. It was the place where Don Larsen pitched his perfect World Series game in 1956. Now, the Stadium has remained virtually unchanged. The left- and right-field corners are close to home plate, only 301 and 296 feet away, but center field is an incredible 463 feet away, and the power alleys in both left and right long ago became known as "Death Valley," places that long drives go to die. Stone monuments honoring Ruth, Gehrig, and old-time Yankee manager Miller Huggins are deep in left-center, and are part of the field of play.

So maybe it's only fitting that in this trip into New York this young, still unproven Red Sox team takes another symbolic step on the road to establishing their own identity. It happens on Wednesday, June 21, a cool night, temperature in the 60s.

The Sox are leading 4–0 in the second inning when Foy, who'd hit a grand slam the day before, comes to the plate. Yankee pitcher Thad Tillotson throws a ball that bounces off Foy's helmet. As Foy trots to first base, Williams announces in the dugout, "We know what we have to do."

This is another one of Williams' themes: A team plays together. A team sticks up for one another. One for all, and all for one. All those clichés that are taped to the wall in every high school locker room in the country—Williams believes in every one of them.

Lonborg doesn't have to be told twice. In the bottom of the inning Lonborg throws at Tillotson, hitting him in the shoulder. Tillotson shouts at Lonborg. Lonborg shouts back. Foy, who knows Tillotson intentionally threw at him, starts walking in from third base, telling Tillotson that if he wants to fight he should fight him, not Lonborg. Both benches empty, but nothing happens. Joe Pepitone starts arguing, first with Foy, then with Petrocelli. Then he charges Petrocelli. The Red Sox rush to defend Petrocelli, Scott grabbing Pepitone and throwing him to the ground. Like spontaneous combustion, a brawl starts on the grass between home plate and the pitcher's mound. It lasts for five minutes, spilling over to what seems like the entire field. It eventually takes 12 stadium guards to break it up. Ironically, one of them is Dave Petrocelli, one of Rico's older brothers who works security at Yankee Stadium and is always stationed in the visiting team dugout when the Red Sox are in town.

But it isn't over.

In the top of the third Tillotson throws at Lonborg, and both benches empty again and rush out on the field. This time it's just shoving and shouting. In the bottom of the inning Lonborg brushes back Charley Smith and hits pinch hitter Dick Howser in the back. Again the benches empty. The umpires stop the game and summon Williams and Yankee manager Ralph Houk to home plate, telling both of them that the throwing at people has to stop.

But Lonborg has proved to Williams he's not going to be just another pitcher with talent. He's going to be a scary kid with talent. Just by pitching inside.

There is perhaps no one who seems more miscast as a pitcher who throws inside on people than Jim Lonborg, "Gentleman Jim" himself. He'd grown up in San Luis Obispo on the coast of California, a large agricultural area halfway between Los Angeles and San Francisco where his father was a professor of agriculture at Cal-Poly. His family stressed academics. Summers he worked on nearby farms. Sports was just something you did on the side.

He had a very traditional childhood. He played Little League, on a team called the Red Sox. One year his team won the championship and one of the prizes was an autograph from a Red Sox player. His had been from Mel Parnell, the star pitcher. He played Babe Ruth League, then high school baseball. He also played basketball, at the time considered his best sport. He was about six foot three, but thin, gangly. He was a decent high school pitcher, nothing exceptional, while his best friend Mel Queen was considered an outstanding prospect, good enough to sign an $80,000 contract with the Cincinnati Reds. So while his best friend went off to professional baseball, Lonborg went off to Stanford, three hours north, planning to major in premed. He'd been admitted to Stanford because he was a straight A student and the president of his class, not because of his athletic ability. It was 1960. Nor was he a recruited athlete at Stanford, just a student who "walked on" to the baseball team. He had good control and good mechanics as a high school pitcher, but he was tall, thin, couldn't overpower anyone. It wasn't until he was 20 that he began to mature physically. As he did, he began to grow into his ability.

During the summers he played in the Basin League, a collegiate league the Orioles had established in Everett, Washington, north of Seattle. In the same league was a team from nearby Fort Lewis, a team that because of the Berlin crisis had a few major league and Triple A players on it. One of them was Tony Kubek of the Yankees, who'd been the American League Rookie of the Year in 1957. Lonborg had just completed his sophomore year at Stanford, and here he was having success against some professional players. For the first time he began to think he might be able to play professional baseball. Before that, being a major-leaguer had been just some Little League fantasy. He never had had any real confidence in himself as a pitcher. Now he was getting some.

There was no baseball draft at the time, and it was assumed the Orioles were going to sign him. But the following summer Bobby Doerr, then a Red Sox scout, came to Winner, South Dakota, where he was playing in a summer league and offered $30,000. Lonborg's father wanted Jim to stay in school and become a doctor. Lonborg wanted to give professional baseball a try. So he signed with the Red Sox not only because they ultimately made a better offer than the Orioles did, but also because he figured the Sox were in more desperate need of pitching and he might get to the big leagues sooner.

The next spring he packed his car and set off for Florida

and spring training. He never had been east of Colorado before, and he considered it the beginning of a great adventure, driving across the country, his first spring training, all of it. He knew he was different from the average rookie in professional baseball. He was older, had been to college for three years. He also was quiet, controlled, and soon came to realize that his school experience was a real advantage in baseball. He felt he was given a degree of respect by the veteran players, though it was a time when the gap between rookies and veterans in spring training was a wide one.

He was sent to Winston-Salem, spent the summer riding buses through the small nowhere towns of the South. The next year he went to Seattle, then the Sox's Triple A franchise. At the end of the year he was told he would be pitching in Boston in the spring, but first he had to do six months' active duty in the Reserves, at Fort Leonard Wood in Missouri. With him was Petrocelli, and the two spent the winter giving each other positive reinforcement. He also carried flash cards with him. They said, "I have a major league fastball . . . I can strike out any batter I want to . . . I can win in the big leagues."

Before he got to Boston, though, he remembered the team stopping to play an exhibition game in Las Vegas on the way from spring training in Scottsdale, Arizona, to Boston, of walking through hotel lobbies in his uniform and with flip-flops on his feet and how bizarre it all seemed. The first time he saw Boston was at night. The team flew into Logan Airport and he went to the Kenmore Hotel, a foul ball from Fenway Park. It was 1965, a transition time for the Red Sox. Players like Radatz, Frank Malzone, and Eddie Bressoud were finishing. The organization, now under O'Connell, was looking to the future, committed to younger players. Lonborg felt a part of it. His first year he went 9-17. He was a sinkerball pitcher, and the infield was porous. In the next two years it would be completely revamped with the arrival of Scott, Andrews, Petrocelli, Foy. But it wasn't until the summer of 1966 that Lonborg began to think he belonged in the big leagues. At one stretch, pitching poorly, he was routed in the first game of a doubleheader against the Tigers in Detroit. He thought he was going to be sent down. As fate would have it, he was sent to the bullpen for the next game, and was spending it sitting there, devastated, wondering where his career was going, when Billy Herman called him into the game in the ninth inning. The Sox had the lead. There were two outs, but the Tigers were threatening. Dick McAuliffe, a good contact hitter, was at the plate.

"Keep the ball low on this guy McAuliffe," Herman said when Lonborg got to the mound. "Make him hit it on the ground so we can get the hell out of here and go home."

Lonborg threw two pitches. The second was slapped to Petrocelli at shortstop ending the game. Lonborg went into the clubhouse, sat down in front of his locker and cried, catharsis after all the emotion. Herman's faith in him had restored his faith in himself. He finished the season 10-10, then went to play winter ball in Venezuela. He also vowed to stop listening to all the advice everyone was forever giving him, and to just go out and pitch his game.

But it had all happened fast, and there are still times when being a major league pitcher seems unreal to him, as if watching a movie about someone else. His family still can't believe he's a major league pitcher. His father, a quiet, academic man, is especially thrilled. He always had stressed education to his son, and now, in one of life's small ironies, his son is a major league pitcher.

He also has learned to throw inside.

After the game with the Yankees that was marked by so many hit batters, he's asked if he'd thrown at Tillotson.

He hesitates a moment, knows it's a loaded question.

"What do you think?" he says finally. "I have to protect my players."

It's his ninth win of the season against two defeats, and he now leads the American League in strikeouts. It's also the 10th batter he's hit this year. After each one, he makes a notation on the back of his glove, like a gunfighter who keeps track of those foolish enough to step out into the middle of a dusty street to challenge him.

song of the summer, "Light My Fire." The group is named after Aldous Huxley's book about the value of taking psychedelic drugs, *The Doors of Perception*, and overnight lead singer Jim Morrison becomes one of rock's superstars. He also will die a drug-induced death in 1971.

And the Beatles release *Sgt. Pepper's Lonely Hearts Club Band*. It's the most expensive rock album ever made, and follows the last Beatle album, *Revolver*, by 10 months. In January, the Beatles had released a single, "Penny Lane" and "Strawberry Fields Forever," and the group appears now on the *Sgt. Pepper* record sleeve with their new mustaches. No other album represents the summer of 1967 and the emerging counterculture more. The cover picture of the Beatles in hippie garb undoubtedly does more to legitimize the new trends than anything else.

The album is structured as a musical trip. The Beatles play the part of Sgt. Pepper's Lonely Hearts Club Band, an old-time musical group that is to serve as the tour guide through the history of music. That is the framework, but what the album also does is create a surreal, hallucinogenic world of "marmalade skies," "tangerine trees," and "looking glass ties," a world so different from "She Loves You." Four of the songs have overt drug references, including Lennon singing "I'd love to turn you on" in "A Day in the Life." And if Lennon later says he got the idea for "Lucy in the Sky with Diamonds" from a children's book, the perception remains that the song title is a rather obvious reference to LSD.

All of the Beatles have been using LSD, starting two years earlier when their host had slipped a cube into the coffees of both Lennon and George Harrison after a London dinner party. Not surprising. LSD had become part of the English pop scene, with big names like Donovan, the Yardbirds, the Animals, and the Rolling Stones all writing lyrics influenced by acid culture. Paul McCartney even tells *Life* magazine, "LSD opened my eyes. It made me a better, more honest, more tolerant member of society," adding that if world leaders were to take LSD even once they would be ready to "banish war, poverty, and famine."

The Beatles' personal odyssey becomes a generation's.

Not only have the Beatles been the most popular musical group in the world for over three years now, the one true supergroup, they have the power to influence the culture. These aren't the Rolling Stones, full of sneers and pouty rebellion, rock versions of Peck's Bad Boys. They aren't some San Francisco hippie band, some group that seems to have sprung from nowhere with their drug references and Eastern mysticism. These are the Beatles, cuddly, non-threatening, as familiar as house pets, the same group that first had burst into American prominence singing about how they wanted to hold your hand. Pictures of them hang in every teenager's room in America, their songs embedded in the culture. And now they are seemingly embarking on a strange new trip, about to take America's youth along with them.

The album is quickly denounced.

The John Birch society, the bastion of extreme right-wing politics, says the album exhibits "an understanding of the principles of brainwashing," and suggests the Beatles are part of an international conspiracy. Spiro Agnew, the governor of Maryland, wants to ban one of the songs on the album, "With a Little Help from My Friends," because it deals with getting high.

In the summer of '67, rock 'n' roll is the thread tying many disparate styles together, nirvana to a built-in audience of American adolescents searching for their own identity. It is wild, uninhibited, hinting at some unexplored world of the id, some place that exists where parents and teachers can't reach. It is the *basis* of youth culture, to the point that it now influences fashion, films, books, television, language, and fads. Rock music is the music of a generation, and the Red Sox players are not exempt. Athletes tend to be insular by nature, focused on themselves and their careers, often oblivious to the larger forces going on around them, and the Red Sox are no exception. But they listen to the same radio stations. And the younger players go to clubs where the music plays, whether it's home in Boston, or on the road.

Two of the clubs are in Kenmore Square, Mother's and Smoky Joe's. One of the owners of both of them is Lonborg's roommate, Neil McNerny, and Lonborg is a frequent visitor. So is Dennis Bennett, who also lives with them at the Charles River Park apartments, and some of the other single guys on the team, namely Conigliaro and Ryan. It is all one big singles supermarket, and to be single and a Red Sox player is to be in social demand. Despite his swinging, girl-chasing image, Conigliaro rarely drinks, though. Maybe just an occasional beer. He and Lonborg also don't like to be in the same club at the same time because they seem to be attracted to the same girls.

Lonborg has adopted a personal rule: He owes the ballclub two good nights' sleep before he pitches. It's something Sandy Koufax had told him, and he tries to follow it. Since he pitches every fourth day, that leaves two nights for partying and good times, two nights for making sure he gets his rest.

The radio is always on in the Sox clubhouse; there's no escaping it. The Top 10 singles, played endlessly on the radio, are "Windy," by the Association; "Little Bit of Soul," by the Music Explosion; the Four Seasons' "Can't Take My Eyes Off of You"; "Don't Sleep in the Subway," by Petula Clark, rated the number one female vocalist in the world; "Come On Down to My Boat, Baby," by Every Mother's Son; "Up, Up and Away," by the Fifth Dimension; the Grass Roots' "Let's Live for Today"; "Groovin'," by the Young Rascals; "Tracks of My Tears," by Johnny Rivers; and "If You're Going to San Francisco (Be Sure to Wear Some Flowers in Your Hair)," the Scott McKenzie song that's a tribute to the ongoing scene in Haight-Ashbury, one that's already starting to be chronicled on the nightly news, America's freak show coming into the living room.

Once again, the key news for the Red Sox happens off the field. On June 24, the Sox sell Dennis Bennett to the Mets for cash and a minor league outfielder, Bennett leaving with a 4-3 record, and an ERA just under four. The club also options Billy Rohr to Toronto. He'd just returned from two weeks of military service, but in his last six starts had an ERA of 4.63, with no complete games. So different from the afternoon game in Yankee Stadium back in April when the season was young and Rohr had pitched himself into New England's heart. The next day the Sox beat the Indians in a steamy Fenway, drawing over 83,000 fans for the three-game series with Cleveland. The winning pitcher is Bell, who's captured his tenth win. The losing pitcher is Luis Tiant, who a few years later will become the darling of the Fenway fans.

The Sox then go on a nondescript road trip to Minnesota and Kansas City. Before June ends, however, Yastrzemski and Petrocelli are selected to the American League All-Star team, in a vote of the players. Hank Bauer of the Orioles is the manager. The leading vote-getter in the league is Al Kaline, getting 242 out of 247 votes.

But it's not a good time for Kaline, now 33. He had been signed right off the Baltimore sandlots of his youth by Detroit, and never played an inning in the minor leagues, making it to the majors in 1953. When he first came up there had been doubts about his power, but Ted Williams told him he could improve his hand strength over the winter by squeezing baseballs as hard as he could. The next year, his second full one, he came back with a super season, hitting 27 home runs and beating out the immortal Ty Cobb as the youngest American League batting champ in history. He's been an All-Star ever since, long has been the one name most associated with the Tigers. But the Tigers have now lost 14 out of their last 19, and after striking out against the Indians' Sam McDowell, Kaline is so upset he slams his bat into the bat rack, breaking a finger. Kaline has become obsessed with winning. He has won awards. He has made money. He is famous. Now he wants the one thing he's never had, a World Series ring. He is so embarrassed he won't come into the clubhouse for several days. When he comes back he finds a telegram taped to his locker.

"Nice going, stupid," it says. It's signed by Harmon Killebrew and Bob Allison of the Twins.

For Rico Petrocelli, the first Red Sox shortstop to make the All-Star team since Johnny Pesky in 1946, being named to the All-Star team is very significant. "It's a real big happening for me," Petrocelli says. "It's something a kid looks forward to, or thinks about, and he doesn't know if he'll ever make it."

On the surface, this seems like an obligatory quote from a young player just named to the All-Star team for the first time. But it's more than that for Petrocelli. It's also his personal validation as a major-leaguer, one that's come in his third full season. He grew up in Brooklyn, the youngest of seven kids, 10 years between him and the rest of his brothers. Both his parents had been born in Italy, were Old World, complete with Old World values. His father ground tools in the garment industry, viewed hard work as the passport to success in this new country, not playing some silly game called baseball. His parents also were appreciably older, so Rico was essentially raised by his brothers and sisters. In a sense, he became his brothers' beneficiary. They had had to quit school to go to work. He didn't have to. He was allowed to play sports, to have the chance at life his brothers never had. His older brothers were his heroes, and he always felt indebted to them, always knew that in some way his athletic success became their success, the success they hadn't been allowed the opportunity to seek.

As a young kid he went to P.S. 52 in the Bedford-Stuyvesant section of Brooklyn, the only white kid in his class. Later, the family moved to Sheepshead Bay, out near Coney Island, where Petrocelli became a high school basketball star. In the summers he played for a baseball team called the Cadets in a Brooklyn sandlot league, the same league that also produced Sandy Koufax and the Torre brothers. He was signed in 1961 by Bots Nekola, the same scout who'd signed Yastrzemski. Petrocelli was 17.

That first summer after he signed he was sent to Johnstown, Pennsylvania, for two weeks, not to play, but rather to get a little preview of life in professional baseball. He went to the Red Sox developmental camp in Ocala, Florida, the next spring, then was assigned to Winston-Salem in the Carolina League. He had been an outfielder-pitcher in high school. Now he was a shortstop. He ended the season hitting .280, but he thought it was terrible, that he was a failure. He had

had expectations for himself, rigid, inflexible standards. He also had a temper, something that often got in the way when things didn't go right. By his own admission, there was a lot of anger in him, the residue of his childhood, anger that had caused him to get into many childhood fights. Some of that too was the way of life in the Brooklyn streets; fight first, negotiate later. By the time the family moved from Bedford-Stuyvesant fighting had become the norm.

But he had doubts too. Was he good enough? Would he ever get to the major leagues? Those doubts would remain with him for years, through minor league stops at Reading, Pennsylvania, and Seattle, and even when he broke in with the Red Sox in 1965. The major leagues were overwhelming to him. He was just a kid, plagued by doubts and insecurities, still trying to sort out his own personal demons, and here he was facing older, more experienced pitchers, men who knew how to set hitters up, how to take advantage of a young hitter's impulsiveness, his inexperience, knew things a young hitter couldn't begin to know. He often struggled at the plate those first two years, and there were times he thought he would never make it, felt no different than a kid who sneaked into the ballpark knowing it's only a matter of time before someone discovers who he is and sends him home. Most of all he worried. He worried if he was good enough to play in the big leagues. He had a young family and he worried about whether he would be able to support them. It's not until this season that he begins to feel he truly belongs.

A few days before his All-Star selection, Petrocelli had been hit on the wrist by George Culver of the Indians, suffering a deep bone bruise. At the time, he'd fallen to the ground in obvious pain, amid speculation the wrist was broken. It's only a deep bruise, and he's expected back within a couple of weeks. He's been replaced at shortstop by Adair, who's become the Red Sox's version of Mr. Fix-it, filling in around the infield when he's needed, doing just what O'Connell and Williams envisioned when they'd traded for him.

June ends. The standings look like this:

Chicago	42-28	.600	—
Detroit	38-33	.535	4½
Boston	37-34	.521	5½
Minnesota	36-34	.514	6
Cleveland	37-35	.514	6
California	38-38	.500	7
New York	33-38	.465	9½
Baltimore	33-38	.465	9½
Kansas City	34-41	.453	10½
Washington	32-41	.438	11½

The top 10 hitters in the American League are Yastrzemski, Frank Robinson, Kaline, Conigliaro, Carew, Paul Blair of the Orioles, Don Mincher, Bill Freehan of Detroit, Petrocelli, and Jim Northrup of Detroit. The top five in the National League are Roberto Clemente, Rusty Staub, Tim McCarver, Orlando Cepeda, and Pete Rose. Yaz is third in home runs with 17, behind Killebrew's 22, and his 51 RBI's place him fourth behind Frank Robinson's 58.

George Scott is hitting .289. Mike Andrews and Joe Foy are at .259 and .248. Williams' troika of catchers—Mike Ryan, Russ Gibson, and Bob Tillman—all are mired below .240. Rookie Reggie Smith continues to struggle at the plate, and is now at .204. José Tartabull and Dalton Jones give some spark off the bench, both hitting in the .250 range.

At the close of this third month of the season, the big news in baseball is happening in Chicago where the Cubs, under manager Leo Durocher, are fighting the Cardinals for first place in the National League. The preliminary talk is of a Chicago World Series, since the White Sox are starting to be the consensus choice to win in the American League.

Williams thinks Chicago is the team to beat. "But I don't think they'll run away and hide," he says. "They have fabulous pitching, but I don't think their defense is all that good and their offense is nil."

Conigliaro gets the news in Kansas City that Bauer has

named him to the All-Star team. It's the biggest thrill of his life. Like Yastrzemski, Conigliaro seems to be maturing into a leader. He is still single, and is still good-time Tony, but he also is starting to take baseball, and his career, more seriously.

"He is much more baseball-minded this year," says catcher Mike Ryan, Conigliaro's roommate on the road and closest friend on the team. "He talks a lot of baseball, which he didn't used to do, and personally I think he's one of the best competitors in the league when he's up at the plate."

JUNE STATS

BATTING	AB	R	H	HR	RBI	AVG.
Santiago	12	2	4	1	3	.333
Yastrzemski	253	47	84	18	53	.331
Conigliaro	195	32	60	11	43	.308
Petrocelli	223	29	66	8	32	.296
Scott	256	31	74	10	37	.289
Andrews	224	33	58	2	14	.259
Fischer	8		2		1	.250
Foy	230	41	57	10	24	.248
Tartabull	142	15	35		5	.246
Ryan	101	9	24	1	12	.238
Gibson	95	6	22	1	10	.232
Jones	78	10	18	2	7	.231
Adair	153	13	35	1	14	.229
Tillman	54	4	12	1	4	.222
Smith	235	29	48	4	22	.204
Thomas	32	6	6		3	.188
Osinski	6		1			.167
Waslewski	6		1			.167
Brandon	26	1	4			.154
Stange	15	2	2			.134

BATTING	AB	R	H	HR	RBI	AVG.
Bell	34	3	4		1	.118
Lonborg	45	1	5		3	.111
Wyatt	7					.000
Cisco	3					.000

PITCHING	IP	H	BB	SO	W	L	ERA
Waslewski	18	13	9	9	1	0	1.00
Osinski	31⅓	26	17	20	2	1	1.72
Cisco	19⅔	16	6	8	0	1	2.84
Lonborg	124	102	41	120	10	3	2.96
Wyatt	41⅔	27	18	34	4	3	3.06
Bell	107⅔	88	34	67	4	3	3.06
Stange	59⅔	62	12	41	2	5	3.77
Santiago	56⅓	54	18	46	4	3	4.18
Brandon	91⅓	79	36	59	2	7	4.24
Landis	7	7	6	8	0	0	9.00

Tony's younger brother Billy, the Red Sox's top draft choice earlier in the year, recently hit his first home run with Greenville in the Western Carolina League. It has become the dream of the Conigliaro family to one day have Tony and Billy both in the Red Sox outfield. There also are stories that youngest brother Richie, now only 12, is a great prospect, and the ultimate family fantasy is that all three will be alongside each other in the Sox outfield. But for now, Ed Kenney, who oversees the Red Sox farm system, says, "Some people in our organization think Billy runs and throws better than Tony."

Bauer also names Lonborg to the All-Star team, and Conigliaro and Lonborg quickly celebrate by being the stars of a 10–2 win over the Athletics on a muggy night in Kansas City. It is Saturday, the first of July. Conigliaro hits his 11th homer; Lonborg gets his 10th win. He now leads the league in both wins and strikeouts. The Sox win again the next day on Foy's homer in the eighth, and afterward the slumping A's send three young players back to the minors for more seasoning. The three are Reggie Jackson, Dave Duncan, and a pitcher named John "Blue Moon" Odom. The Red Sox are now tied for second with the Tigers and the Twins, four and a half games in back of the league-leading White Sox.

Mickey Mantle, who has missed the past two All-Star games with injuries, is also named to the All-Star team by Bauer. He is 36 now, near the end of a great career. He had come to the Yankees in 1951, billed as the next Yankee superstar, and the following year had replaced the legendary Joe DiMaggio in center field. Four years later he lived up to all the hype, winning the Triple Crown, becoming the greatest switch-hitter in the game's history. Once, Kaline was taunted by a young kid who said, "You're not half as good as Mickey Mantle."

"Son," Kaline supposedly said, "nobody is half as good as Mickey Mantle."

In addition to Mantle, the American League All-Star team includes Don Mincher and Jim Fregosi of the Angels, Dick McAuliffe of the Tigers, third baseman Max Alvis of the Indians, Tommie Agee of the White Sox, and Paul Casanova, the Senators' catcher. They will join starters Yastrzemski, Petrocelli, Brooks Robinson of the Orioles, Killebrew, Carew, and Tony Oliva of the Twins, and Bill Freehan of the Tigers. Dean Chance of the Twins is scheduled to be the starting pitcher. The most notable omission is Frank Robinson, but he's on the disabled list with a concussion, the chief reason the Orioles are nine and a half games back, sinking like a stone in the American League race.

The starters for the National League, also selected by a vote of the players, are Orlando Cepeda at first, Bill Mazeroski at second, Gene Alley at short, and Richie Allen at third. The outfield is Lou Brock, Hank Aaron, and Roberto Clemente. Joe Torre is the catcher. Juan Marichal is the pitcher.

On July 4, as the Red Sox are losing in Anaheim, LBJ makes an announcement from his Texas ranch, telling the American people to "remember the cannons flaring across the seas as they watch fireworks."

A new movie also opens in Boston, *Barefoot in the Park,* starring two young performers, Robert Redford and Jane Fonda. The Red Sox aren't there to see it. They're in Detroit for a four-game series, the last before the All-Star break. It's July 6. They've been on the road for two weeks, to Minnesota, Kansas City, and Anaheim. So far, they're 5-4 on the trip, all their losses coming by one run. Their last nine losses have come by one run, a sure sign that the Sox are playing very good baseball.

Their bad luck continues in Detroit. They lose the first game by one run again, this time in extra innings, when Freehan doubles home the winning run in the bottom of the 11th against Wyatt. Then they are shut out by Denny McLain for their fourth straight loss, 2–0. McLain, the flamboyant young pitcher who is the son-in-law of former Red Sox manager Lou Boudreau, is in his fifth year in the majors. Already he's one of the best pitchers in the league. Last year he won 20 games. He is cocky and confident, known to occasionally wear a white mink coat, and claims to drink as many as 20 Cokes a day.

It is Sunday, July 9, a hot, muggy day, and after the Sox lose big in the first game of a doubleheader, it's Lonborg's turn. Before the game, he feels more pressure than at any time this year. He knows he's the stopper, and realizes everyone is depending on him to stop the slide. By the sixth inning he is so drained that when he bends down to take a deep breath, he blacks out. He goes on to pitch the seventh inning, but Williams knows Lonborg is through when he becomes incoherent in the dugout.

"I was out of it," Lonborg says afterward. "It was so hot I couldn't concentrate, and everything was hazy."

But through seven innings, Lonborg had shut out the Tigers. Wyatt comes in to finish it off for him, saving Lonborg's 11th win.

It's just one of many times the veteran Wyatt has bailed out the Red Sox. He has become another of the team's unsung heroes, and maybe no one deserves this season more than he, for no one has paid more dues on a long and circuitous journey to the major leagues, one that began back in the Negro Leagues, and even, for a while, took him to the Mexican League.

"It was bad down there," he says. "Bad baseball. Bad lights. Bad everything. It was as bad as when I was playing in the Negro Leagues, playing as much as three games a day. The ball had raised seams, and one day my finger blistered and began to bleed. When I told the manager I couldn't continue he took a poke at me. Just as I pulled my fist back to let him have it, nine Mexican guys stood up. 'Cool it, man,' they said. I cooled it."

In 1964, his fourth year in the majors, in Kansas City, he was picked for the All-Star team. Two years later he was traded to the Red Sox. Now he calls himself "Old John," shrugs off the Vaseline rumors with wide-eyed innocence, and just goes about his business. He long ago learned to get along by going along, pitching his ball and keeping his mouth shut. He claims the charge that Vaseline is a large part of his pitching repertoire began with former White Sox manager Al Lopez.

"In a doubleheader they beat me in the first game and I saved the second," he says. "That's when Al Lopez claimed I was doctoring the ball. 'How come you didn't say that in the first game?' I asked him. It's only when I win that anyone accuses me of anything illegal. The only time I ever threw a spitter was against Yaz. He hit it off the scoreboard. I never threw another spitter."

He's also known for the nicknames he bestows on people and things. When he was in Kansas City owner Charles O. Finley was the "Green Goose." Money is "hogs." Kaline was "Line," as in "the Line took me deep." Killebrew was "the Brew." Yaz was "Skie." Who else? he's asked. Wyatt shrugs. "I grew out of names," he says.

Williams believes it's the most important game of the year. Not only does it stop the losing streak, it closes the first half of the season on a positive note. The Red Sox are 41-39, in fifth place, six games out. "If we had lost, a lot of our good work would have gone down the drain," he says. "So we get a little pepped up again, and a couple of days to get refreshed."

The team, with the exception of Yastrzemski, Petrocelli, Conigliaro, and Lonborg, flies back to Boston that night. The other four go to Anaheim in preparation for the All-Star game to be played Tuesday night, a game in which the National League will be going for their fifth in a row.

Out in Anaheim, the National League wins 2–1 in the 15th inning on a home run by Tony Perez off the A's Catfish Hunter. Yaz gets three hits. Petrocelli fails to get a hit in his only plate appearance. Conigliaro fails to get a hit in six trips, but makes two great catches in right field. Lonborg, who pitched those grueling seven innings in the Detroit heat just two days before, does not get in the game.

The Sox come back on Thursday, July 13, in a day-night doubleheader at Fenway against the Orioles. It's their first game in Fenway Park in 18 days. They draw a combined 42,000 for the day, split the doubleheader. The day is significant in that it marks the first Red Sox appearance of relief pitcher Sparky Lyle, up from Toronto, by way of Reynoldsville, Pennsylvania, a town so small it didn't even have a high school baseball team. He's a free spirit, someone who later in the season will immortalize himself in the eyes of his teammates by his habit of sitting on many of the cakes that people send to the Sox clubhouse.

The game also marks the third time Gary Bell fails, after being billed as the best thing to come to Boston since the Prudential Center.

But it's the next day that begins the streak that catapults the Red Sox into the thick of the pennant chase, delivering on the promise they've shown since the season started. It begins innocently enough. It is a Friday, another big crowd, nearly 28,000. The Red Sox bats, silent for much of the past three weeks, come alive. Conigliaro hits a massive home run over the screen in left, Yastrzemski hits his 20th. Lonborg wins his 12th game, and says afterward that at the

All-Star game he talked with Gary Peters of the White Sox, who told him he shouldn't think so much about strikeouts the second half of the season, for the simple reason that as the season progresses and your arm gets worn out it gets increasingly more difficult to strike people out.

Coincidentally, the streak starts at the same time one of the most important events of the summer occurs, the riots in Newark. They started with the arrest of a black cab driver for tailgating and driving the wrong way on a one-way street. The cab driver began arguing with the two white policemen who arrested him. They, in turn, beat him for resisting arrest. Blacks from a nearby housing project saw him being led into the precinct police station, located in the crowded ghetto. Soon, the word went out that a white policeman had beaten a black cab driver, creating a furor, and people began assembling on the streets. Civil rights workers arrived at the police station to protest police brutality, but soon groups of blacks began throwing rocks, bottles, and Molotov cocktails at the police station, amid cries of "You ain't seen nothing yet."

There were soon thousands of people in the streets, and in the beginning it was like a mad celebration. People looted without fear, ripping iron bars off stores and taking what they wanted, as if all the old rules no longer applied. They loaded their arms with records and liquor, with clothes and appliances. There was no sense of guilt, rather it was the feeling that the store owners had been ripping them off for years, and now it was their turn. One of the people in the streets that first night was Tom Hayden, then a young radical. He'd grown up in Michigan, been radicalized at the state university in Ann Arbor, and been one of the founders of SDS, Students for a Democratic Society. Its credo, which came to be known as the Port Huron Statement, called for a leftist vision of the future, one largely based on Hayden's readings of Camus, Marx, John Dewey, and C. Wright Mills. Hayden also had spent some time in the civil rights movement in the South in the early '60s before coming to Newark in 1964 as a community organizer, part of a migration of young, idealistic students into the impoverished parts of America. Now, on this first night of the Newark riots, he and some of the other young white community organizers find the rioting almost like a "festival of the oppressed," an attack against the system and indifferent politicians, against the society that promised so much and delivered so little.

The incident aside, the racial situation in Newark is highly volatile. Since 1950 the city's black population has gone from 17 to 50 percent, the largest percentage of blacks in any city north of Washington. Many of them are a spillover from nearby New York City. Most are poor, uneducated. The ghetto is old, bleak, crumbling. There also is strong tension between blacks and the overwhelmingly white police department, most of them either Italian or Irish, the ethnic makeup that had dominated Newark politics for generations.

After the second night Governor Richard J. Hughes, calling Newark a "city in open rebellion," orders in 4,000 virtually all-white National Guard troops and 500 state police. The city now resembles a war zone, with convoys of military jeeps and trucks cruising empty streets, the silence occasionally broken by the sound of sniper fire. The city looks like Dresden, broken windows, boarded-up stores, littered streets patrolled by thousands of troops with fixed bayonets and nightsticks. They dodge rocks and sniper's bullets from rooftops. The rioting subsides after four days, with 23 dead and nearly 1,000 injured, and another 1,000 arrested. The only stores that have not been gutted have "Soul Brother" written on them, an attempt to tell rioters the store is owned by blacks. It doesn't always work. Poet LeRoi Jones, a Newark native, is arrested and charged with having two guns in his car. His arrest results in 25 artists, both black and white, writing letters to both Hughes and Newark mayor Hugh Addonizio, saying Jones was jailed because of his outspoken attacks on the city's administration.

It is not the only racial violence. Nearby Plainfield, New Jersey, has three nights of rioting, including the death of a policeman. So do New Jersey cities New Brunswick and Elizabeth. Bands of blacks and white teenagers fight in Miami after a rhythm and blues concert. Fresno, California, has two nights of rioting. Seventeen people are arrested in Des Moines. There are other racial disturbances in Cincinnati, Buffalo, and Tampa. So far this summer there have been racial outbreaks in some 30 cities.

But the Newark riot has far-reaching ramifications. Shortly afterward a conference of many civil rights groups is held in Newark. It's billed as the largest and most diverse group of civil rights activists ever to assemble in the United States. It's also billed as a "black power" conference, one of the first times the phrase is used in mainstream newspapers, and the language is volatile, inflamed. Martin Luther King, Roy Wilkins, and Whitney Young, the three most well-known black leaders, don't attend, sending representatives instead. Only fitting. It's increasingly apparent a schism now exists in the black community, which is split over the riots, the issue of violence, strategy, the blueprint for the future. This conference belongs to the younger, more militant leaders, men who call themselves "black," not "Negro." Ron Karenga, a self-described black nationalist, says, "Everyone knows Whitey's a devil." Then there is 23-year-old H. Rap Brown, supposedly called "Rap" for his telling blacks to "rap it to them, baby." He is the national chairman of the Student Nonviolent Coordinating Committee (SNCC), and he escalates the rhetoric.

"Wage guerrilla war on the white man," he tells the conference. He also says he loves violence, somewhat ironic because SNCC started out espousing nonviolence. "It's as American as cherry pie. If you give me a gun and tell me to shoot my enemy I might shoot Lady Bird."

On July 16 the Sox get their third win in a row by beating Detroit in front of a large and enthusiastic Sunday afternoon crown in Fenway. Again, both Yaz and Tony C. homer. The day started with the Red Sox's annual father-son game being called because the field was wet. Both Yastrzemski and Conigliaro are on tears at the plate. Yaz credits Ted Williams for getting him to pull the ball more in spring training. The year before Ted had been trying to get Yaz to do so in hopes that this would give him more power, but Yastrzemski had been reluctant. He had had a good year at the plate in '65 and wasn't keen to change things. But he had struggled last year, thus was more willing to take a chance. Conigliaro is giving every indication he will have a great career. He is fourth in the league in hitting, now starting to hit for average as well as power. Eddie Popowski is not surprised. He says he liked Conigliaro ever since he first saw him in the Instructional League because he was always eager to improve.

The Sox get veteran Norm Siebern from the San Francisco Giants, another bat off the bench, more insurance for a pennant race. He is an 11-year veteran who has also played with the Yankees, Kansas City, Baltimore, and California. In return, the Sox send reserve infielder George Smith, who's been out all year following knee surgery. He will be sent to the Giants' farm team in Phoenix. The Sox also send pitcher Galen Cisco to Toronto. Cisco has only appeared in 11 games.

"I think Siebern can help us," Williams says. "I've played with him and I like his hustle and effort."

"The club has a winning attitude," says Yastrzemski. "We believe we can win. We didn't think that in other years. Now you never see any lack of hustle."

Yastrzemski has become the Sox's unofficial spokesman. Where once he was considered a tough interview, full of one-word answers and offering little, now he often stands in front of his locker after games, commenting on what happened. It's one more visible example of his maturity, one more example of his leadership, not only on the field, but off it.

The Sox make it four in a row the next night, also against the Tigers, this time before a crowd of 29,000, huge for a Monday night. Yastrzemski homers again, his 22nd. Lee Stange pitches a complete game, moves to 5-6. Stange is 31, grew up outside Chicago where one of his childhood friends was Green Bay Packers linebacker Ray Nitschke. He later went to Drake University in Iowa for a while, but signed a Class D contract with the Washington Senators for $200 a month, then began the long climb through the bushes.

"The feeling then was that you had to be 26 or 27 to pitch in the big leagues," he says. "That if you won 20 games in the minors everyone waited to see if you could do it again."

Stange is not overpowering. Even as a kid he never really was strong enough to simply rear back and blow the ball by hitters. He has come to learn that in the major leagues if you keep giving batters fastballs eventually they're going to hit them. Until 1962 he essentially was a two-pitch pitcher, fastball and curve. Then one day when he was with the Twins, he was warming up on the sidelines with Hal Naragon. Naragon taught him to throw a slider. The next year Stange went 12-5 with the Twins, for his best year in the majors. Now, catcher Mike Ryan considers Stange the smartest pitcher on the staff. Lonborg and Bell both possess the great stuff, but Stange has become a master at keeping hitters off balance, nibbling at the corners, making batters hit his pitch. He came to the Red Sox last June in the trade that sent Dick Radatz to the Indians.

The Sox move into sole possession of third place, three and a half games back. It's Detroit's seventh loss in a row. The next night it's number five for the Red Sox, this time in Baltimore's Memorial Stadium, the ballpark that originally had been built in the late '40s for the city's International League team and was enlarged when the Browns moved from St. Louis in 1954 and became the Orioles. Lonborg chalks up his 13th win, and the Sox pick up a full game on first-place Chicago. The next night it's the sixth straight as they ride a three-run Mike Andrews home run for another victory. Andrews is another of the young players who often gets overlooked. Signed by Joe Stephenson, the Red Sox's West Coast scout, he is tall and rangy, adequate in the field, with occasional power.

Eddie Stanky announces he's not afraid of the Red Sox, saying, "I don't see all this excitement about Boston. This is just normal for a team to go on a hot streak. Nobody got excited when we won 10 in a row. Why should I get excited about them?"

But everyone else is. Pennant fever grips New England. There are stories on page one of newspapers, radio updates. The region hasn't had a pennant race to get excited about in nearly two decades, and it's embracing this one with all the ardor of first love. Two nights later the Sox are at Municipal Stadium in Cleveland, where Darrell Brandon pitches his second complete game of the year, Foy hits his 14th homer, and the Sox coast to their seventh win in a row. Stange comes back the next day and shuts out the Indians for the team's eighth consecutive victory, his first shutout of the year. Last year he'd pitched well in the second half of the season, had been named "Boston's Unsung Hero" by the Boston baseball writers. Now he's got his fifth victory in his last seven starts after being slow to get into the rotation. Yastrzemski adds his 23rd homer, and Joe Foy continues his hot bat.

On a team with so many promising young players Foy often gets overlooked. Williams sometimes gets on him about his weight and a propensity for making mental mistakes. Though some players can motivate themselves, with only an occasional reminder needed from the manager, Williams believes Foy must constantly be motivated. Unlike many of the players, he hadn't grown up obsessed with the game, hadn't been a true fan as a kid, even though he grew up in the Bronx, in the shadow of Yankee Stadium. Baseball was just something he was good at. Often he would look at the people in the stands and wonder why they were there. Didn't they have better things to do? For he knew that if he was not being paid to be a baseball player, he never would go to a game.

But no one questions his talent, since two years earlier he was the International League's player of the year. He was first signed by the Twins, then drafted by the Red Sox after the '62 season. Last year he started slowly at the plate, but came on strong and eventually ended the season with 15 homers and 63 RBI's to go along with a .262 average. This year has been more of the same. He's spent time in Williams' doghouse. He's had times when he's struggled at the plate. Plus, he knows that Dalton Jones, the Louisiana native who originally signed with the Red Sox for a reported $60,000, is always looking over his shoulder. Jones can hit, and only supposed defensive liabilities and lack of power keep him from being an everyday player. Williams often uses his presence to keep Foy focused, to the point that one day Foy, who's not feeling particularly well, tells Popowski he's going to play anyway because if Jones gets a chance to play and gets hot with the bat he might never be able to get Jones out of the lineup. Popowski tells him it's a good idea. Foy has gotten the message.

The next day is a Sunday, July 23, a doubleheader. In the game Lonborg wins his fifth in a row, striking out 11. It's his 14th win. The Sox waste no time in jumping all over the Indians, the big blast being Conigliaro's two-run homer in the first off John O'Donoghue. It's the 100th of his career, and at 22 it makes him the youngest player in baseball history to reach 100 homers. In the next inning Foy hits a grand slam and is met at home plate by the entire team, yet one more visible sign of how focused, how unified, this team has become.

After the game, Yastrzemski and Andrews meet everyone at the door of the clubhouse, offering congratulations, exhorting the players to keep on track. Yaz goes around the room shaking everyone's hand. About 20 minutes later the second game begins. Gary Bell, who'd been struggling of late after his quick start since joining the Red Sox, five-hits the Tribe and the Red Sox have done it again.

It's their 10th win in a row, the first time they have done that in a decade. It's also been 10 games of superlative baseball, games in which everyone has done his part. Conigliaro, Yastrzemski, and Foy have provided the lumber. Adair fills in where he's needed, always the old pro, getting a key hit to keep a rally going, making the big defensive play, already one of the season's quiet heroes. The starting pitching has been superb, so different from the year before when no Red Sox starter had been over .500 and the staff's ERA of 3.92 was the worst in the league. Now Lonborg is 14-3. Bell is 6-4 for the Red Sox, after beginning the season 1-5 with Cleveland. Stange is coming on. The defense has been solid, the Red Sox now having gone 67 innings without making an error.

Last year at this time the Sox were 24½ games from the top of the league. Now they are in the middle of a pennant race. Williams is still publicly cautious. This latest stretch has convinced him that in this wild and wacky year in the American League his team can win it as well as anyone else can, but he refuses to say it, as if saying it will only put a hex on everything. Once again he reverts to the ''we will win more than we will lose'' line he's been using since spring training, the automatic pilot he clicks on whenever he's asked where he thinks the Sox will finish. But if Williams won't say that he too is a victim of pennant fever, everyone else isn't so reticent.

On the airplane ride back from Cleveland to Boston, the pilot comes over the loudspeaker and announces something unusual is going on at the airport. At first, no one seems to know what he's talking about. But thousands of people have come to Logan to welcome the team home, crowding into the terminal, causing a major traffic jam in the Callahan Tunnel that leads from downtown Boston to the airport in East Boston. The crowd is so huge that hundreds of people have spilled out onto the runway, making it impossible for the plane to come to its destination at the United gate. Airport officials decide the players should disembark at an adjoining terminal, where they are then to be bused over to the United gate. But hundreds of people are on the runway. They surround the bus, start shaking it. Police have to form a blockade to get the players into the terminal where they are mobbed by adoring crowds, as if the players were the Beatles here to start another American tour. To a player like Petrocelli, who'd been in Boston when fan apathy seemed a part of the roster, it's an unbelievable sight, one of those scenes so indelibly stamped in his mind that he'll never forget it. To the rest of the players it's an affirmation that the fans of New England believe in them, that the people of New England already have surrendered their hearts to this gritty team of overachievers.

It's already become the best Red Sox season in 17 years, one that's brought baseball alive again in New England. And the success of the Red Sox, this feeling that the team really is one of destiny, couldn't be happening at a better time. Not only has New England been hungering for a winner, there is the feeling that beyond Fenway Park nothing else seems to be going right. There is a horrible uncertainty—a fear of what tomorrow may bring.

It's also a time when conventional heroes no longer seem able to fill their roles. Even celluloid heroes like John Wayne seem rooted in some gone-forever time, back when the good guys wore the white hats and everything seemed less complicated. It is all shades of gray now, the legacy of war and a growing segment of society that questions the most basic assumptions underlying American culture. The new film heroes such as Paul Newman and Steve McQueen are not heroic in any traditional way, but instead tend to portray loners, men alienated from their culture, living by some private code. Since the death of John Kennedy there have been no political heroes, as if the president's death left a void no one can fill. From the beginning Johnson had suffered by comparison, a throwback to some other era, when politicians seemed old and staid, grandfatherly. He is an authority figure in an age when authority figures are being questioned. The only larger-than-life figures in the American landscape seem to be rock stars and other counterculture figures, but all that's still new and not easily understood, even by the people who see them as icons. Everything is changing.

Except for baseball. The game has become balm, a respite from the awful realities of the summer. Within the confines of the game everything still makes sense; the world is as orderly as it ever was. It's still the same game, as timeless as a memory of childhood. And here in Boston it comes complete with its own song, "The Impossible Dream," a stirring anthem from the hit Broadway musical *Man of La Mancha*. It's sung by Jack Jones, and was released the summer before when it was on the charts for four weeks. It becomes the unofficial soundtrack to this Red Sox season, complete with such lyrics as "to beat the unbeatable foe," and "this is my quest, to follow that star, no matter how hopeless, no matter how far." It's Don Quixote's song, all about striving after lost causes, and tilting at windmills, and in Boston it's all over the radio. "The Impossible Dream." The Red Sox's quest for the American League pennant.

Baseball in Boston also comes complete with old-fashioned mother, flag, and apple pie heroes. Lonborg. Tony C. The Boomer. Rico. And, of course, Yaz.

Who is more heroic than Yastrzemski? He seems to have stepped out of the pages of adolescent fiction. He gets the big hit. He makes the big play in the field. He says the right things afterward. In this age of youthful rebellion, he is a clean-cut athlete, a throwback to a simpler era. And when we appear to be losing in Vietnam, when for the first time there are doubts about the country's ability to get things done, Yaz always delivers. He's become a traditional hero in every sense of the word, has become almost mythic. Like all mythic figures he only seems to exist on the field. We know little about his life off the field. We know little about his innermost thoughts. We don't know what he thinks about hippies, or *Sgt. Pepper's Lonely Hearts Club Band*, or the war, or riots in the cities, or any of the things that confuse the rest of us. He seems to come alive only on the field, this place where he continues to do heroic things.

Because he does, the Red Sox are in the middle of a pennant race, and there's no underestimating this. An entire generation of New Englanders has grown up never knowing what a pennant race is. Others, old enough to possess memories of past failures and too many seasons where spring promises had died long before the dog days of summer ever arrived, have long ago learned the Red Sox always break your heart. So Red Sox seasons of the past were made up of small moments, little frames of success that became part of the larger mosaic of failure. In the '50s it had largely been the individual brilliance of Ted Williams, though there were others who, for a brief time, managed to transcend the mediocrity around them. Infielder Billy Goodman won a batting title in 1950, one of five times he hit over .300. Jackie Jensen drove in over 100 runs five out of his seven years with the Red Sox, and was the league's MVP in 1958. Tom Brewer won 19 games in 1956. Bill Monbouquette won at least 14 games for four straight years in the early '60s. Pete Runnels, who arrived from the Washington Senators, won two American League batting titles with the Red Sox in '60 and '62. Later, it was a young pitcher Don Schwall, the rookie of the year in 1961 before slumping the following year and being traded to the Pirates for slugger Dick Stuart. Mike Fornieles led the league in saves in '60, and made the All-Star team the following year. Then it was Radatz, who for a few short seasons was the most dominating relief pitcher in the game. Or else it was the promise of a young Yastrzemski, or Conigliaro.

This is different. And not just for the fans. For the players, too. Take Petrocelli, for example. As a kid he dreamed about being a major-leaguer. Like any kid, all he saw was the glory, the home run, the big hit, the World Series, the spoils of victory. But the reality of being a professional ballplayer, especially in those early years of losing, had given him a different perspective. "Then you find out about the heartaches,'' he says. ''The bad days. The losing. Things happen at home and you have to leave anyway. The kids are growing up without you and you miss your wife something fierce. You hang around hotel lobbies all day long, hours of your life wasted. I would ask myself, 'What am I doing here?' and I didn't have any good answers.''

Now everything seems heightened. As if reality is finally living up to all those childhood fantasies. Every game is important. There are big, enthusiastic crowds. There are teammates who support you, root for you. There is the same feeling about the game that you once had as a kid. Everyone feels it.

There's also the feeling the team's success has helped quiet the pressures in the city. Tim Horgan, a writer for the *Boston Herald*, believes it's cooled off racial tensions in Boston, has arrived like some godsend. The entire city is caught up in it.

''The amazing thing,'' he says, ''is it's not just baseball fans. It's everywhere you go. Every porch you walk by someone has the ballgame on.''

Horgan is 40, went to Tufts University in the greater Boston area, and has been writing sports in Boston ever since he graduated twenty years ago. He's covered the Red Sox for years, and long ago came to know that the team is not particularly easy to cover, that the underlying tension between the Red Sox and the press always has been there. The most obvious example had been Ted Williams' ongoing feud with the Boston media, particularly Dave Egan, the acerbic columnist of the *Record* who was called ''the Colonel.'' Egan verbally chastised Williams every chance he got, a personal picador whose target always was Williams. Not too many days went by without the Colonel blasting Williams for not hitting in the clutch. The bitter relationship between Williams and many of the Boston beat writers who covered the Red Sox had its roots back in 1942, when Williams, only 24, and coming off hitting .406, one of the all-time great baseball accomplishments, applied for a military deferment. He claimed he was the sole support of his mother, a Salvation Army worker in his native San Diego. The press criticized him. Williams never forgot. Depending on his mood, Williams would sometimes carry his resentment to any sportswriter who came near him. One of his favorite tricks was to come into the dugout before a game, see a sportswriter sitting there, and put his nose in the air, sniff as though he were some hound picking up a scent, and say, ''I smell something. There must be a sportswriter around here someplace.'' Although Williams is gone now, and Egan is too, the friction continues, an unfortunate legacy. Horgan believes it comes from the top of the organization, trickles down.

Horgan, however, is one of the few Boston sportswriters who have any kind of relationship with Yawkey, and that happened by accident. For a while he didn't even know what Yawkey looked like, a not uncommon situation, since for years Yawkey was never photographed and the Boston newspapers kept running the same file photo of him, one taken when he was both younger and heavier. One day Horgan saw someone walking through the clubhouse in a blue windbreaker and an old pair of pants, looking like some old, wizened clubhouse guy coming back for a reunion. Who's that? he asked. Mr. Yawkey, he was told. Even so, Horgan had never dealt with him.

That had changed last year when Williams had been inducted into the Baseball Hall of Fame in Cooperstown. Just before the ceremony was to begin, with Williams already at the podium, someone yelled, ''What would Dave Egan say?''

''Fuck Dave Egan,'' Williams allegedly said.

''No one could believe he said it,'' remembers Horgan, ''and there was some confusion about it. I was sitting with the Red Sox people and some other writers and even some of them weren't too sure about what had happened. As it turned out I was the only one who wrote it, and three days later I was summoned to Yawkey's office. He was sitting there with Dick O'Connell and Haywood Sullivan and he called me every name in the book. Afterward, he was apologetic. He told me Ted had wanted to handle it himself, but that he was Ted's friend and had told Ted he would take care of it. Then he said he'd never mention the incident again. And he never did. After that we just sort of got along.''

Though there's a sense of unreality about baseball in Boston, its power to distract is sorely tested by the specter of a society about to ignite.

JULY STATS

BATTING	AB	R	H	HR	RBI	AVG.
Yastrzemski	357	63	115	26	75	.322
Conigliaro	294	53	89	19	61	.303
Scott	350	49	101	13	51	.289
Petrocelli	272	32	73	9	39	.267
Andrews	324	55	83	5	24	.266
Smith	342	43	86	6	33	.251
Fischer	8		2		1	.250
Osinski	6		2			.250
Lyle	4		1			.250
Foy	352	57	87	17	45	.247
Tartabull	151	16	37		5	.245
Jones	87	11	21	2	9	.241
Ryan	160	15	37	1	18	.231
Adair	219	20	50	1	21	.228
Santiago	18	2	4	1	3	.222
Gibson	114	6	24	1	12	.211
Tillman	64	4	12	1	4	.188
Brandon	33	3	6			.188
Thomas	49	7	9	1	5	.184
Lonborg	59	3	7		5	.119
Bell	46	4	5		1	.109
Stange	31	2	2			.065
Wyatt	9					.000
Landis	1	1				.000

PITCHING	IP	H	BB	SO	W	L	ERA
Lyle	16	13	4	20	1	0	1.68
Wyatt	55	36	25	47	5	4	2.45
Osinski	47	47	17	27	2	1	2.54
Stange	113⅓	97	18	61	7	6	2.78
Lonborg	167	133	49	152	14	4	3.34
Bell	141⅓	123	46	87	7	9	3.62
Brandon	118⅓	111	45	75	4	8	4.33
Santiago	77⅔	83	23	60	6	4	4.40
Landis	17	16	7	12	1	0	6.35

A new outbreak of racial trouble had begun two nights earlier in Detroit, the nation's fifth largest city. Its population is 1.7 million, one-third black, with high unemployment and deficient housing. Once again, the rioting starts after what appears on the surface to be an isolated incident. This time it's a raid on an after-hours club in the middle of the ghetto, a club rumored to be one of the city's centers for black power meetings. On the second day of rioting President Johnson orders federal troops into Detroit. Some think it's a reaction to recent criticism by Republican leaders who claim LBJ has failed to cope with the "national crisis of race riots" and have called for a congressional investigation of the summer's disorders. Eventually, the number of federal troops will swell to 4,700. Before the riots are over 43 people will die, most of them blacks gunned down in the streets by police or National Guard. Entire neighborhoods are looted and burned. In terms of lives lost and property damage, it's the worst uprising in the United States in this century. From Grand River Avenue to Gratiot Avenue six miles to the east, the skies are alive with flames, illuminating the skeletons of gutted homes and shops.

On August 3 Johnson says we have "endured a week such as no nation should live through." Robert Kennedy calls racial strife the greatest domestic crisis since the Civil War. No one knows where it will end, if it will end.

A week earlier black power advocate H. Rap Brown had been arrested at Washington's National Airport and charged with inciting a riot in Cambridge, Maryland. Maryland governor Spiro Agnew claimed it was Brown's speech that set off the riot there.

"Black folks built America," said Brown, as he was led away. "If America doesn't come around we're going to burn America down. We're going to burn it if we don't get our share of it. We stand on the eve of a black revolution. Our people are on the move, responding to counterrevolutionary violence with revolutionary violence, an eye for an eye, a tooth for a tooth, a life for a life. These rebellions are but a dress rehearsal for the real revolution."

There is the sense that America is splintering, coming apart in pieces like shattered wood. Meanwhile the television news and magazines continue to focus on the exploding Haight-Ashbury scene, the advance guard for the strange new counterculture that seems to have sprung from some other planet. The war in Vietnam grinds on with no end in sight. Senator William J. Fulbright, chairman of the Senate Foreign Relations Committee and the most vocal congressman against the war, tells the American Bar Association that America is a "sick society," involved in a morally incompatible role both at home and abroad. "We are truly fighting a two-front war and doing badly in each," he says. "Each war feeds off the other, and although the President assures us that we have the resources to win both wars, we find we are not winning either."

Though the real world and the world of baseball often seem poles apart during this summer of 1967, they can—and sometimes do—collide. The Tigers announce their series with the Orioles, scheduled for Tiger Stadium, will be moved to Baltimore. The riots in the cities have even reached baseball.

Boston has unconditionally fallen in love with the Red Sox.

A nightclub called the Tender Trap on Lansdowne Street, the street that runs behind the left-field screen, has a sign in the window. It says the club will now start taking World Series reservations. Tonight is Tuesday, July 25, and Fenway is festive. The day before there had been long lines at the ticket windows on Jersey Street. Ironically, though, the park is not filled tonight. Seems there were rumors that the game was sold out, rumors so strong that many fans stayed away. Even so, the Red Sox are going for their 11th straight win, and expectation seems to hover over Fenway like coastal fog. For a while it looks as though the Sox are going to prolong the streak, keep the fantasy alive, but eventually they lose, 6–4, to the Angels.

The Sox come back the next night before over 32,000, the largest crowd of the season so far. The narrow streets around the ballpark are jammed before the game. People spill out of the subway station in Kenmore Square, walk past the bars and the souvenir stands, past Lansdowne Street and the back of the Green Monster, to the front gates on Jersey Street. This is Red Sox baseball out of some fairy tale, a large crowd on a night in August, here to watch a game that means something. In the seventh inning the old ballpark starts to rock 'n' roll with noise, spurring the Sox on, adding to the feeling that this is once again a team with destiny in the dugout. It's a wild night in Fenway, climaxed by umpire Bill Haller tossing Angels' manager Bill Rigney and pitcher Jack Hamilton after they keep riding Haller. Rigney is particularly incensed, claiming Haller is doing this for the home fans. It's one more demonstration that success breeds success, that big crowds not only make money for the front office and pump up the home team, they also tend to magnify the game. That's what is happening now in Fenway Park, and everyone is aware of it. The Red Sox players. The fans. The other team. Everybody. Unlike many other cities, where games are played before sections of empty seats, each game in Fenway is big, an event, a festive occasion.

It's the mood that carries over to the next afternoon. It's a day game, also against the Angels, a beautiful summer afternoon where Fenway resembles a picture postcard, a cathedral in varying shades of green, colors that compete for attention with a blue sky. It's also the biggest crowd in nine years, unheard of for an afternoon game in the middle of the week. The Sox trail 5–2 going into the bottom of the ninth, curtailed all afternoon by Jim McGlothlin, off to one of the best starts in the league.

But Foy hits a two-run homer to bring the Sox to within one, then Conigliaro takes Angels' reliever Bill Kelso's pitch into the screen and the game is tied. The Sox finally win in the bottom of the 10th, after another great Yastrzemski catch in the top of the inning. Although not particularly fast, Yaz has turned playing the Wall into an art form. To Yaz, the left-field corner, with its strange bounces and odd angles, has become his personal playpen. Within its confines he's become a great defensive outfielder. Today, he's done it again, as once again this Red Sox team has proved it has character, determination, grit, heart, and all those other intangibles Red Sox teams never had before. There is togetherness, a common focus. Once again the Sox celebrate on the field, as if they've just won the pennant, and Fenway is a hurricane of noise, another love-in at this old ballpark off Kenmore Square.

On the same day, at the Peekskill, New York, training camp of the New York Jets, quarterback Joe Namath, the most visible and well-known football player in the American Football League, refuses to cut his hair. By Haight-Ashbury standards Namath looks like an accountant. But his hair is longish, falling over his forehead, creeping over his ears. Coupled with long sideburns, Namath looks more like a rock singer than a professional athlete, and has become the first athlete to adopt both the look and the life-style of a rock star, one of the first times the line between the two previously separated spheres has been blurred. Until then athletes and rock stars had been polar opposites, athletes regarded as All-American boys, with short hair and traditional values, the opposite of countercultural. Now here is Namath looking like he hangs out backstage at the Fillmore with Gracie Slick.

"Some image," mutters Jets coach Weeb Ewbank, who sports a crew cut.

Less than two weeks later Namath once again will be in the news, this time when a sports editor for *Time* magazine claims Namath and two other men assaulted him in an Upper East Side nightspot in Manhattan because of Namath's general disdain for the press. Namath is no stranger to controversy. In this age where professional athletes often seem to disappear as soon as they leave the clubhouse, with little known about their private lives, Namath is an exception. Ever since he came out of the University of Alabama and signed with the AFL in 1965 for $400,000, huge money for the time, he's been swimming in the center of a media fishbowl. Everyone knows of his plush New York penthouse apartment with the white llama rugs, his swinging life-style, his low-cut white football shoes, his penchant for trendy East Side discotheques, and his famous remark that he'd rather go fight the Vietcong than be married. No one knows it now, but Namath, and the larger-than-life aura that surrounds him, is a sneak preview of the future, a time when athletes will become public property much more than they are now.

At this time they seem to exist in a cloistered world— cardboard cutouts who play games, then disappear until they return to the ballpark to play more games. It is still two years before *Ball Four*, the Jim Bouton book that will talk about womanizing and pep pills and coming to the ballpark hung over. It's still a time when sportswriters write about hits, runs, and errors, and pretty much forget about everything else. Namath is different. Along with Muhammad Ali, he's come to represent the new breed of athlete.

The closest anyone on the Red Sox comes is Tony Conigliaro. He's young and handsome and single and loves everything about being a baseball star, not to mention the attention. He seems to seek the spotlight like a moth. George Thomas thinks the difference between Yastrzemski and Conigliaro is that, while they both want to drive in the big run, Yastrzemski wants to do it to help the team, but Conigliaro wants to do it to see his name in headlines the next day. But unlike Namath or Ali, he doesn't challenge authority and the existing order of things. He doesn't particularly like Dick Williams, but it's about personality, not values.

No one else on the Red Sox can be classified as anything close to a rebel. Lonborg is single, good-looking, and receives lots of fan mail, but he too revels in his newfound success and the thrill of being a major-leaguer. Yastrzemski has become a great baseball player, but has no interest in being a celebrity. He wants to come to the ballpark, then go home to his family in Lynnfield. He's rented a beach home for the summer, but unlike in Lynnfield where his neighbors respect his privacy, he's been hounded by people wanting autographs.

The White Sox have made a move to bolster their anemic hitting, picking up veterans Ken Boyer and Rocky Colavito. Boyer arrived from the Mets two weeks ago. Colavito, now 34, has come over from the Cleveland Indians for Jim King, some cash, and the proverbial player to be named later, after a series of disagreements with manager Joe Adcock over Adcock's strategy of platooning him. Born Rocco Domenico Colavito, he first arrived with the Indians in the mid '50s and quickly became their most popular player, a handsome home run hitter, a sort of precursor to Conigliaro. In 1960, the year after he had hit 42 home runs tying Killebrew for the American League lead, he was traded to Detroit for batting champ Harvey Kuenn, one of the most controversial trades of the era. Two years ago new Indian general manager Gabe Paul brought him back to Cleveland, but Adcock had been platooning him with Leon "Daddy Wags" Wagner.

Stanky downplays any talk of Colavito's problems with Adcock, telling sportswriters he likes players who fight with their managers. He still touts his team, and again expresses annoyance that no one seems to take the White Sox seriously, the thinking being that even their great pitching can't compensate for their popsicle stick offense over an entire season. Stanky realizes it too, thus his willingness to take a chance on Colavito. It quickly pays dividends. One of the first things Colavito does is hit a two-run homer in the 10th to give the White Sox a dramatic win over the Indians. But

Yankee manager Ralph Houk warns that the addition of the two veterans doesn't necessarily assure a pennant for the White Sox.

"You never know when you deal for veterans," he cautions. "It depends on how much baseball they have left. Pitching is still Chicago's strong point. They're deep in starters and in the bullpen. Boston's got the runs, and Detroit and Minnesota are also in the picture. The American League's the strongest it's been in years from top to bottom."

As July comes to a close, the Red Sox are still in search of more pitching especially now that Lonborg has left on the 29th to begin two weeks of Reserve duty in Georgia. Waslewski has been sent back to Toronto in favor of Dave Morehead, the onetime promising Sox right-hander who's had shoulder trouble. Morehead was only 19 when he shut out the Senators in his major league debut in 1963. Two years later he pitched a no-hitter against Cleveland. Extremely effective this year in Toronto, he's now getting another chance.

The month ends, and the standings look like this:

Chicago	58-42	.580	—
Boston	56-44	.560	2
Detroit	53-45	.541	4
Minnesota	53-47	.530	5
California	55-49	.529	5
Washington	51-53	.490	9
Baltimore	45-54	.455	12½
Cleveland	46-56	.451	13
New York	44-56	.440	14
Kansas City	44-59	.427	15½

Batting Leaders

F. Robinson, Baltimore	.331
Kaline, Detroit	.325

Yastrzemski, Boston		.322
Carew, Minnesota		.303
Conigliaro, Boston		.299
Blair, Baltimore		.289
G. Scott, Boston		.289
T. Horton, Cleveland		.287
Fregosi, California		.282
Tovar, Minnesota		.280

Home Runs

Killebrew, Minnesota	32
Howard, Washington	28
Yastrzemski, Boston	26
F. Robinson, Baltimore	21
Conigliaro, Boston	19

RBI's

Yastrzemski, Boston	75
Killebrew, Minnesota	75
Howard, Washington	67
Conigliaro, Boston	61
F. Robinson, Baltimore	59

Pitching

McGlothlin, California	9-2	.818
Horlen, Chicago	13-3	.813
Lonborg, Boston	14-4	.778
Sparma, Detroit	10-4	.714
Merritt, Minnesota	7-3	.700

As August comes to Boston, so do three new movies: *To Sir with Love*, starring Sidney Poitier as a black teacher in a white classroom in working-class London; *Up the Down Staircase*, starring Sandy Dennis as a young white teacher in an inner-city high school; and *Two for the Road*, with Albert Finney and Audrey Hepburn. In less than two weeks the *Dirty Dozen* will open, with Lee Marvin, Charles Bronson, Telly Savalas, and Jim Brown, the great Cleveland Browns running back who's announced he's given up professional football for a movie career.

Arlo Guthrie, son of famed folksinger Woody Guthrie, whose songs and activism were a part of the '30s, gets noticed at the Newport Jazz Festival with a song called "Alice's Restaurant." The song is about Arlo's trip to the induction center, his subsequent arrest, and a woman named Alice who runs a restaurant. It soon becomes one of the counterculture anthems, and Guthrie, with his long hair and hippie garb, becomes an overnight star. "You can get anything you want, at Alice's Restaurant." In a sense those lyrics become a demarcation line, a secret code for the new culture. As though, if you have to ask what they mean you just don't get it anyway.

On August 1 Lonborg gets up at 5 A.M. in his army barracks in Georgia, and flies to Boston where he gets his 15th victory, salvaging a split against Kansas City. "I took a workout with the Atlanta Braves on a day off," he said. "About what I would have done here. Some pepper. Some shagging. Some throwing. I was in a baseball atmosphere. But I didn't get in here tonight until right before the game."

A couple of weeks before, Lonborg had been visited by Bill Craig, a Boston area freelance writer doing a story on him for the *Saturday Evening Post*. The headline of the story eventually would read "Don't Dig In on Gentleman Jim," and carry the accompanying copy, "He likes Beethoven and quotes Aristotle, but Jim Lonborg, star pitcher for the exciting young Red Sox, will dust off any overconfident batter."

Craig's intent had been to explore the seemingly inherent contradiction between the young, urbane man who sometimes attends the Boston Symphony and takes dates to outdoor concerts along the Esplanade by the Charles River, and the pitcher who now leads the American League in hit batters.

Lonborg told Craig about the personal crisis he had faced, back when he wanted to try professional baseball and his father wanted him to pursue his premed studies.

"I am a physical person," he said. "The things that move me are physical things, like striking out a guy, seeing beautiful scenery, or maybe a beautiful woman. I wanted to give baseball three or more years to see if I could make it."

He also talked of his evolution as a pitcher.

"Billy Herman told me last year that I had to be more aggressive against the hitters, that I had to start knocking them down to protect myself. All I had to do was do it once or twice to each team and it would get around the league. I want the hitter to know, in the back of his mind, that I might knock him down."

He was asked about the earlier incident in Yankee Stadium.

"When you pick up a baseball and deliberately throw it at a batter it's a very serious matter," he said slowly. "But you have to sometimes. You know, Aristotle once said, 'Passion dulls the reason of all mankind.' A reasonable man would not do such a thing. But when passion enters into it, it overrides everything else."

One of the nights Craig visited, Lonborg was scheduled to pitch against the Orioles in Fenway Park. As was his usual custom, Lonborg had gone to the movies that afternoon, a practice he'd first started on the road. This particular afternoon it had been *Blow-Up*, the Antonioni film about deception in London's hip art community. He came into the clubhouse about 5:30 for the night game, took batting practice, then went into trainer Buddy LeRoux's office. Several of the players were sitting in front of their lockers beginning to get dressed. Conigliaro was listening to one of his own records. The training room was a bit of a sanctuary, away from reporters and their questions. Lonborg fell asleep on one of the tables.

He pitched into the seventh inning that night as the Red Sox won easily, but one incident stood out. In the top of the fourth inning, the Orioles' Paul Blair was the batter. The day before, Blair had homered. Without changing expression, Lonborg threw a pitch inside that sent Blair sprawling into the dirt. Blair then made an easy out.

The next night, a couple of hours before another game, Craig and Lonborg were sitting in the stands along the first base side. It was raining, a tarpaulin covered the infield. The organist was playing "Hello Dolly."

"You said that you wouldn't allow them to stand in against you," Craig said. "Is that what happened to Blair?"

Lonborg nodded.

"How many have you hit this year, Jim?"

"Eleven," Lonborg answered. "No, twelve."

"But you're not wild?"

"No," Lonborg said. "I'm not."

If that seemed a little cold-blooded, maybe something Lonborg had told Craig earlier sheds some light on the turmoil he must have felt. Asked how he viewed life after baseball, he said, "I'd like to work with people who need help. I don't want to be involved where I have to outthink other people. I don't want to compete with other people, where they get hurt, or I get hurt."

On August 3 the Sox get Elston Howard from the Yankees for cash and two players to be named later. The great Yankee catcher has played in nine World Series, been named to eight American League All-Star teams. In 1963 he was the league's MVP. But he is 38 now, and his career is in the past tense. He's only hitting .196 and spends most games on the bench. On a bad Yankee team that's trying to look into the future, Howard is all about the past. But the thought of leaving the Yankees after all the years, and all the great moments, is unsettling. At first, Howard balks.

He was the first black Yankee, and had been selected—as Branch Rickey had once selected Jackie Robinson to be the first Dodger—as much for his temperament and his character as for his ability. There'd been other black players in the Yankee farm system before Howard. One was Vic Power, a flashy first baseman who'd torn up the minors. But he was excitable, and there had been some sentiment within the organization that he didn't possess the necessary patience and personal discipline that were considered prerequisites to be the first player to integrate the Yankees. Consequently, he was traded to Kansas City. Howard was quiet, gentlemanly, not considered aggressive on issues of race. Instead he internalized racial slights, hiding behind a calm, assured demeanor. The Yankees had wanted their first black player to possess certain attributes; they couldn't have found any better racial pioneer than Ellie Howard.

He'd grown up in St. Louis. Coming out of high school he signed to play with the Kansas City Monarchs in the Negro Leagues, because the major leagues already had started to scout the Negro Leagues and he figured he'd get to the major leagues quicker. He once said the happiest day of his life was when he heard Jackie Robinson had been signed by the Dodgers. He first got to New York in 1955. He already was 26, after having spent two years in the military. Even then the Yankees had legendary Yogi Berra behind the plate so Howard played a lot of right field and first base in his early years with the club. It wasn't until 1961 that he caught more than 100 games for the Yankees.

Though he went on to become a great Yankee star, he always understood that his color imposed certain limitations. His first home in metropolitan New York had been in an integrated neighborhood in Teaneck, New Jersey. Things had been fine at first, and the Yankees even had for him an Elston Howard Day. But when he eventually tried to buy a bigger home in a different area, it no longer mattered he was a Yankee. He was just a black man trying to live in a neighborhood that didn't want him. The builder, who was white, had to buy the house for him, and when he and his family moved in they found "nigger" written all over the house.

Howard has always been a Yankee, and the thought of going somewhere else at the tail end of his career is traumatic. Particularly when he has to explain it to his three kids. "They took it hard," he says. "Especially my oldest boy. He's 14. He was only a baby when the Yankees brought me up. He doesn't know any other club but the Yankees."

There are pictures in the New York newspapers of Howard cleaning out his locker in Yankee Stadium for the last time, saying goodbye to teammates, pictures of him walking arm in arm with Ralph Houk against the backdrop of the towering and empty Yankee Stadium stands.

"I talked this over with my business associates and Tom Yawkey before deciding to come to Boston," he says. "I'm glad the Red Sox want me, and I'm going to try and help them as much as I can."

Williams agrees.

"He's a professional both on offense and defense," he says. "He'll see a lot of action. With his knowledge and experience of playing under pressure he'll be invaluable."

Mike Ryan, who's been doing the bulk of the catching, is not so thrilled. "I think I'm the better catcher, judging by the numbers," he says. Ryan also feels this is one more indication that Williams doesn't particularly like him, a feeling he first got two years ago when the Red Sox sent him down to Toronto for a short while and he first encountered Williams. It was not anything he could pinpoint, just the feeling that the two somehow didn't click. He feels Williams likes Russ Gibson more, because Gibson played for him last year in Toronto and hit well. Ryan can understand how the Red Sox might think Howard's experience could be beneficial in a pennant race, yet he still feels slighted. He's been the catcher, the team is winning, and why break up a good thing?

It's already been an emotional summer for Ryan. His younger brother Steve is in Vietnam, and never far from Ryan's thoughts. Often he thinks that if not for the vagaries of fate and circumstance he would be in Vietnam, not his brother. But there is the thrill of playing for the Red Sox in a pennant race, the culmination of all his baseball fantasies, the local kid playing for the hometown team. Ryan is from Haverhill, an old mill town along the Merrimack River, about 30 miles north of Fenway Park. One of his uncles had played semipro ball for a while, his father had played a lot of baseball as a kid, so Ryan had grown up with baseball as the first dream. He's the oldest of six, has four brothers, and they all played sports. But he went to St. James, a small Catholic high school in Haverhill, the school all the Ryans had gone to, and by the time he was there the school had dropped baseball. He was frustrated. All his friends, the ones he'd grown up with and played ball in the summers with, were playing baseball at Haverhill High School and here he was, at a small school that didn't have a team. The irony was that by this time baseball had become everything. He didn't have either the grades or the inclination to go to college.

"I hated going to St. James because they didn't have a team," he remembers, "but I just kept playing baseball every chance I got."

As fate would have it, the Hearst newspapers sponsored a national baseball tournament back then, and when Ryan was a senior in high school he went to Fenway Park for a regional tryout. He was one of three kids selected to the team, one that later played a game in Yankee Stadium. He spent a year at a prep school in Boston, nothing more than killing time while he waited for an offer, and eventually signed with the Red Sox for $5,000.

The next year, 1961, found him with Olean in the New York–Penn League. Then in the fall of '64, his season over, he was back home in Haverhill, just drinking beer and hanging out, letting the season unwind, when one night he came home and his father said the Red Sox had called and they wanted him at Fenway Park the next day. He didn't know what to think. He didn't sleep a lot that night. He was too excited. The next morning he got into his '64 Plymouth and drove to Boston, his stomach doing flips the entire way. He walked into the clubhouse and it seemed like some foreign country. Since he'd never gone to spring training with the Red Sox he knew very few of the players. He was told he would be catching that day, and was introduced to pitcher Bill Monbouquette, who was to be his battery mate.

"It all happened so quickly," he says. "You spend your whole life thinking about it, and then it happens just like that. I was just a kid right out of nowhere."

Now, three years later, he is right in the middle of all his dreams. Sometimes after night games he will stay in Lonborg's apartment at Charles River Park, a new complex across the Charles River near Massachusetts General Hospital, but mostly he still lives at home in Haverhill. Since he does, he's come to know firsthand the amazing interest this season has generated. He can't go anywhere without people wishing him luck, telling him the Sox are going to win. Friends constantly call his house asking for tickets. There is no more privacy, no more anonymity. He's beginning to get some insight into what it must mean to be a Beatle.

He looks at Howard's arrival and knows it means reduced time for him. But Yastrzemski quickly acts to downplay any acrimony.

"I'm happy Elston Howard is coming," he says. "He calls a game better than anyone I ever saw. I know he can help Mike Ryan. He's been under the present pressure before, many times. I'm not always sold on average for hitters if they are hitters, and I've always regarded Howard a good tough hitter in the years I played against him."

Ryan is not the only one less than thrilled with Howard's arrival. So is Leonard Koppett, a New York sportswriter. Koppett, 44, grew up in the Bronx a block away from Yankee Stadium, and has been writing sports in New York for nearly two decades. He calls the kind of deals that brought Howard to the Red Sox and Boyer and Colavito to the White Sox "disgraceful," a violation of the rule that says no major trades can be made after June 15 to bolster a contender.

Koppett links the two deals together, but there's a difference in how the White Sox and the Red Sox view the rest of the season. With the White Sox everything is geared to winning now. They've been in first place the entire way, and feel the only thing they need is more offense. Boyer and Colavito have been added for that reason. Everything is geared to the present tense. It's a little different with the Red Sox. The addition of Howard is one more visible sign the front office is serious, but their overall philosophy still remains long-range. The Red Sox are a young team whose best years together promise to be in the future. The last thing O'Connell wants is to hurt the confidence of the young players by bringing in veterans for the pennant race. So it's become more of a balancing act, the idea of bringing in veterans to *augment* the younger players, not replace them.

Howard joins the team the next night in Bloomington, Minnesota. He's immediately surrounded by the media in the visitors' clubhouse at Metropolitan Stadium. He's tall and erect with a receding hairline, an impassive face, an almost stoic demeanor. He admits he'd been initially reluctant to join the Sox, and credits Yawkey's calling him as being decisive in his changing his mind.

"When you have somebody like Mr. Yawkey telling you they want you, and see something in you, it makes you feel good," he says. He also says a player has to expect things like trades to happen, that when you put on the uniform anything can happen. "Especially when you get connected with a corporation," he added, a reference to the Yankees now being owned by CBS.

He sees a couple of comparisons between the Red Sox and the great Yankee teams he's played for, namely, the will to win, and the fact that most of the key players were developed within the organization.

August 7 is an off-day in Kansas City, a day for relaxing around the hotel pool, a brief respite from the pennant race. Yet the pennant race is on everyone's mind, especially Dick Williams'.

"We are playing the Twins two times on the last weekend of the season in Boston," he says. "I believe the race will go down to those two days, and that the Twins and the Red Sox will be fighting it out for the pennant."

It's the first time Williams has talked about the pennant, the first time he's ventured from his party line of "we will win more than we will lose," the prediction he first made in spring training. In fact, just a few days before he had made a point of avoiding a reference to the Sox as a contender. After Elston Howard's wife had said her husband was happy to be coming to a contender, Williams said "*She* said that." He also says it will take between 90 and 95 victories, and he believes the Red Sox will have at least 90. They currently are 58-49.

Since the 10 straight the Sox are only six for their last 15.

Left to right: **Carl Yastrzemski, Reggie Smith, and Tony Conigliaro.** (Boston Red Sox)

Slugging shortstop Rico Petrocelli. (Boston Red Sox)

First baseman George Scott, aka "the Boomer." (Boston Red Sox)

Super-sub Jerry Adair. (Boston Red Sox)

Red Sox Manager Dick Williams (*left*) **and Chicago White Sox manager Eddie Stanky in Fenway Park, April 12, 1967—Opening Day.**
(AP/Wide World)

Owner Tom Yawkey and star outfielder Carl Yastrzemski in Boston's clubhouse, September 27, 1967.
(AP/Wide World)

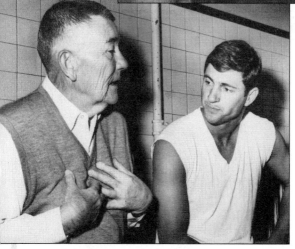

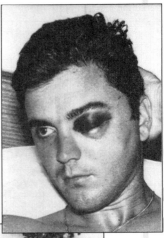

Tony Conigliaro shortly after being hit by a Jack Hamilton fastball—August 1967. (AP/Wide World)

Conigliaro reading one of the thousands of get-well letters—September 6, 1967. (*Providence Journal Bulletin*)

Conigliaro's replacement in the Red Sox outfield, Ken Harrelson.
(Providence Journal Bulletin)

Red Sox ace Jim Lonborg being carried off the field after the Sox win the pennant, October 1, 1967.
(AP/Wide World)

Lonborg triumphant.
(*Providence Journal Bulletin*)

**Fans Joanne, Betsy, and Judy Fay
of Roslindale, Massachusetts.**
(*Boston Herald*)

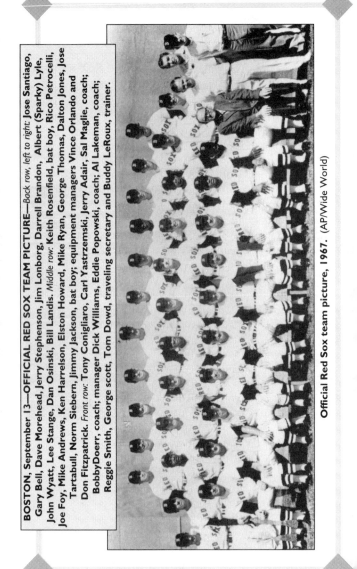

BOSTON, September 13—OFFICIAL RED SOX TEAM PICTURE—*Back row, left to right:* Jose Santiago, Gary Bell, Dave Morehead, Jerry Stephenson, Jim Lonborg, Darrell Brandon, Albert (Sparky) Lyle, John Wyatt, Lee Stange, Dan Osinski, Bill Landis. *Middle row:* Keith Rosenfield, bat boy, Rico Petrocelli, Joe Foy, Mike Andrews, Ken Harrelson, Elston Howard, Mike Ryan, George Thomas, Dalton Jones, Jose Tartabull, Norm Siebern, Jimmy Jackson, bat boy; equipment managers Vince Orlando and Don Fitzpatrick. *Front row:* Tony Conigliaro, Carl Yastrzemski, Jerry Adair, Sal Maglie, coach; BobbyDoerr, coach; manager Dick Williams, Eddie Popowski, coach; Al Lakeman, coach; Reggie Smith, George scott, Tom Dowd, traveling secretary and Buddy LeRoux, trainer.

Official Red Sox team picture, 1967. (AP/Wide World)

Twelve of those games were at home, where only Lonborg
and Stange pitched complete games. The pitching was good
in the recent three-game series in Minnesota, except for
Darrell Brandon, who once again had a bad outing as a
starter. But though they dropped two out of three to the
Twins they only lost a half game in the standings because
the White Sox were losing to the Orioles in Baltimore.

"We were lucky," Williams says.

"When will Brandon pitch again?" Williams is asked.

"When he comes out of the bullpen," he says. "That's
where he's going. Into the pen. I'm not an authority on
pitching, but I can see results, and the results haven't been
too good." Brandon has now lost his ninth game in 13
decisions. He will be replaced in the starting rotation by
José Santiago.

The Sox get a split in Kansas City on the first night of the
series, although Williams again shakes up his lineup in the
second game after the Sox drop the first. He benches Reggie
Smith, moving Yastrzemski into center field, and again
benches Foy. Siebern plays left, and Jerry Adair, who has
been invaluable, gets the nod at third. Williams is not one to
let things slide nor one to take any loss lightly, and his
players have come to know this. So Smith's and Foy's being
benched for the second game is not as potentially disruptive
as it might be with a different manager. Not that they like it.
Players hate to be shown up, and nothing shows them up
more than putting them on the bench.

There's some speculation that Williams has two sets of
rules, one for Yastrzemski, Conigliaro, and Lonborg, and
another for the rest. But there's no doubt that everyone, at
one time or another, has felt the sting of Williams' wrath,
the caustic side of his personality. Some managers might
relax a bit now that the team has obviously overachieved.
Not Williams. Even though the team played a doubleheader
the night before, he calls a special workout for Scott, Smith,
Foy, Howard, and Dalton Jones at 10 the next morning.

Lonborg gets his 16th win that night, once again flying in
from Georgia, and the Sox now trail the White Sox by only
a game and a half. Detroit, riding former Red Sox pitcher

Earl Wilson's 15th win, is now two games back. The Twins are two and a half behind and the California Angels are only three back. The Red Sox also make another roster move, sending Bob Tillman to the Yankees and activating Hank Fischer. Tillman, 30, who has been with the Sox since 1962, is only hitting .188, and the addition of Howard to go along with Ryan and Gibson has made him expendable. Fischer is 27, a journeyman right-hander who's already been with the Braves and the Reds. He's been on the disabled list since May.

The Sox keep heading west on this road trip, to the edge of the country, Anaheim Stadium. It was built the year before, just for baseball, a modern three-level stadium 36 miles from downtown Los Angeles, called the "Big A." It gets its name from the massive left-field scoreboard that is supported by a tall Angels logo, a letter A with a halo. One of the players' more popular places while playing here is the Whiskey-A-Go-Go, a trendy spot in Hollywood full of starlets and other pretenders. It's one of Conigliaro's favorites.

After the Red Sox's first trip of the season here Williams had expressed displeasure about "extracurricular activities" and a lack of focus, maybe the thing that most infuriated him. So Williams is afraid of this trip. Maybe that's why, when he sees Scott eating a banana split, he orders him on the scales. Williams has been on Scott for his tendency to gain weight ever since spring training, has told him not to be over 215. For Scott, that's probably a tougher task than laying off the low-and-away curveball. Once in Baltimore, after curfew, he called up Keith Rosenfeld, one of the Sox batboys who was making the trip.

"I'm hungry," Scott said. "I'll give you $20 and you can keep the change if you go out and get me a grinder."

"I'll be right up," Rosenfeld said.

"Don't stop, or you'll get eaten," Scott said.

Williams feels that when Scott gets heavier he's slower with the bat. Now Scott is over 215, and Williams says he won't play again until he loses weight. No matter that the Sox are in a pennant race. Or that Williams might be, as the old adage goes, cutting off his nose to spite his face.

"It's the way I've operated all season and I'm not going to change now just because we're in a race," Williams says. The Sox have just lost 1–0, the only run coming on a wild pitch by Stange in the fourth inning. Jim McGlothlin of the Angels silences the Sox bats on only three hits.

The next day they lose again to California, this time 2–1, dropping to fourth in this incredibly tight American League race, two games off the pace. Scott is again kept out of the lineup because of his weight, while Foy escapes a similar fate by sweating off five pounds in a steam bath. Then the Sox lose again the following day, also by one run. Now they're fifth, two and a half back. But this time they're chasing the Twins, who beat the White Sox and move into the lead.

It hasn't been a good trip, but once again the Sox have played star-crossed baseball, losing four times on the nine-game trip by only one run. Although they've gone two of nine on the trip, they've only lost a half game in the standings, since the five teams in contention continue to beat one another up.

And they're coming home.

They arrive back in Boston at 8:30 A.M. after an all-night plane ride from the West Coast. It's an off-day, a much-needed one. Except for Scott. He's ordered to work out with Popowski in Fenway, punishment for being overweight.

The next day everyone is in the clubhouse by four o'clock, three and a half hours before the game, the result of a Dick Williams decree. His reasoning? Thrown together, people might start thinking about baseball again. This is Williams' way of announcing he's still unhappy with the recent trip to Anaheim.

Maybe the strategy works, because the Sox beat the Tigers 4–0, behind shutout pitching by Dave Morehead and home runs by Yastrzemski, Scott, and Reggie Smith. Scott is in the lineup because he's made his weight. He's made his weight because it's Popowski's job to weigh him, and realizing both Williams' stubbornness and the Sox's need for Scott in the lineup, Popowski assures Williams that Scott is ready to play. When the game ends Morehead is given a standing ovation.

"I couldn't throw hardly at all this time last year," says Morehead. "I needed something like this. When I was recalled I was so tense, excited, and nervous, I didn't pitch my game. Tonight I did."

Scott is another center of attention in the Sox clubhouse.

"I haven't intentionally been overeating," he says, his high-pitched words all but tumbling over themselves. "But sometimes it's hard for me to pass up fried chicken. I was raised on that." Scott contends Anaheim was his Waterloo in his battle to stay away from food. "It was the day off there that killed me. There was no colored people to visit like in the other cities. So I hung around the room all day and ate too much. I just look at food and I gain weight."

But the news in the American League centers around the Baltimore Orioles. The Birds are denying rumors manager Hank Bauer is about to be fired. The world champions are ninth, and have witnessed both the collapse of their pitching staff and prolonged slumps by Boog Powell and Brooks Robinson. They've also been hampered by the injury to Frank Robinson, who was the most dominant hitter in the league when he went out, with even better stats than Yastrzemski. He's 32. Once Robinson had been the leader of the Cincinnati Reds and one of the most commanding players in baseball. He'd been traded to the Orioles after the '65 season, Reds general manager Bill DeWitt calling him an "old 30." He went to the Orioles in exchange for pitcher Milt Pappas, Jack Baldschun, and Dick Simpson. But last year he'd been the first Triple Crown winner since Mantle in 1956, and only the 14th in baseball history.

Anyone who really knows Robinson isn't surprised. He grew up in Oakland, in a tough section where blacks and Mexicans battled for turf, went to McClymonds High School, the same school that produced basketball great Bill Russell, Vada Pinson, and Curt Flood. Soon after he left high school he signed with the Reds for $3,500 and was immediately shipped to Ogden, Utah, a long way from the Oakland of his childhood.

"The only other Negro on the team was named Chico Terry," says Robinson. "Chico couldn't speak English and he couldn't hit a curveball."

Robinson focused on baseball, and the next two years were spent in Columbia, South Carolina, where the team played throughout the South. It was the mid '50s, and Robinson soon learned that when he went to the movies he sat in the balcony, and sometimes he had to eat on the bus while his teammates were in the restaurant.

On August 16 the Sox beat the Tigers 8–3 and take over third place. José Tartabull is recalled from Pittsfield and starts in right field in place of Conigliaro, who has to attend a Reserve meeting. Tartabull quickly proves Dick Williams made the right choice, getting two hits and taking two home runs away from Detroit hitters in right field. Backup catcher Russ Gibson replaces Tartabull in Pittsfield, leaving the Red Sox with only Howard and Ryan as catchers. Also called up from Toronto is pitcher Jerry Stephenson, who's been hot lately, Hank Fischer going down to the farm club. Stephenson is the son of the Red Sox's West Coast scout Joe Stephenson, a former major league catcher who's been scouting for the Red Sox since 1950 and who signed Mike Andrews and former pitcher Earl Wilson. Williams is playing musical chairs, playing for today. It is all very simple: Those who produce play; those who don't go right to his doghouse. Sometimes the doghouse even stretches to the minor leagues. The doghouse is even physical now; some inmates at a Massachusetts prison have made one and sent it to Williams. Williams likes it.

But the star of that August 16 game is Scott. He tattoos two Denny McLain pitches for his 15th and 16th homers, and there's no question that a Scott home run is an event. Despite Dick Williams' constant refrain that Scott shouldn't always think home run, that he must learn to forget the Wall and stop trying to pull everything; and despite Scott's professed understanding of this, all you have to do is watch him dig into that batter's box to realize everything gets forgotten. He scowls at the pitcher, menacingly. He wiggles his bat. He almost comes unglued every time he swings, a Ruthian swing that leaves no doubt that Scott would undoubtedly sacrifice everything for one of his precious taters.

He now supposedly weighs 213 pounds, two less than Williams' limit for him. The *Boston Globe*'s Ray Fitzgerald proclaims Scott a vision, "a walking ad for rye crisp and zwieback toast."

"I feel great and I've got to say that Dick Williams certainly knows something," Scott says, happy again. "I'm quicker when I'm lighter. But I never thought I was getting heavy. I'm a guy who takes a sip of soda and a few potato chips and it stays on me. But I'm sticking to this diet of steak and eggs twice a day, and nothing else."

Scott's response is typical. Though he sometimes gets down when he feels Williams is picking on him, it's not his nature to stay down very long. He's gregarious, outgoing, never met a microphone he didn't like. Before many games he'll talk to his bats. He'll pick up one in the clubhouse. "You got any hits in you today?" he'll ask, staring accusingly at the bat. "Nah," he'll say disgustedly, throwing it back down on the ground. "You don't got any hits in you today."

There's nothing too complicated about his moods. When he's hitting he likes everyone; when he's not, he doesn't like anybody.

There's another sense in which Scott lives in two different worlds. There's the white world of Fenway Park and baseball, and there's the black world of Roxbury where he socializes. Not that Scott is not liked by his teammates. It's impossible not to like Scott. But the world of professional baseball in Boston is overwhelmingly white, and the black players learn early not to be outspoken, to try and make the most of an imperfect world. Elston Howard tells Scott not to swear so much, not to make waves. It's not easy being a black athlete in this summer where there's so much hate and violence, this summer of black power and an emerging black consciousness.

In the middle of the month there's more evidence of the shifting philosophy in the civil rights movement. Speaking at the 10th anniversary of the Southern Christian Leadership Conference at the Ebenezer Baptist Church in Atlanta, Martin Luther King, Jr., says the SCLC will start conducting strikes and massive sit-ins in Northern cities. It's a major philosophical shift for a movement that previously had concerned itself almost exclusively with the rural South. There will also be simultaneous school boycotts, sit-ins at factories, and a "camp-in" in Washington, D.C., for unemployed youth. King blames the summer's violence on the policymakers of white society, adding that the riots are a "Negro response that such inequality will now be resisted to the death." It's his most militant speech yet on urban rioting.

King has come to believe that the tactics of nonviolence, effective for blacks in the South, are unsuitable in big cities where everyone is absorbed in the hectic pace of urban life. His new strategy is to "dis-locate the functioning of a city without destroying it. This can be more effective than a riot. . . . Armed insurrection will not achieve the goal."

The same day folk singer Joan Baez says there's huge opposition to the Vietnam War. She's 26, first achieved fame as a "protest singer," in the early '60s. Bob Dylan had been the king of the protest singers, one of the most effective in articulating the social conscience of a generation. Baez was the movement's diva. Now she runs a pacifist school near her home in Carmel, California, and believes marijuana will soon be legalized. She recently staged a free concert on the grounds of the Washington Monument before 30,000 people, and shrugged off reports that opposing the war makes her a bad citizen. "I'd rather be a decent person than a good citizen."

The lead sports story on Thursday, August 17, is Muhammad Ali is taking out a marriage license in Chicago to marry Belinda Boyd, 17, of Blue Island, Illinois, the daughter of a Muslim minister. It's been a busy time for Ali. A couple of weeks earlier he'd been denied permission by a Houston judge to box in Japan. The judge had ruled then that Ali seemed on the verge of taking part in "antigovernment, antiwar activities." Ali countered by vowing to keep preaching. He told reporters he would follow the law of the country, as long as they didn't interfere with his religion. He also reiterated his refusal to enter the armed forces.

"I think it would be cowardly to leave the country, to

leave 22 million Negroes, and to leave my mother and father, to go to a country where I don't even speak the language,'' he said.

It's not as dramatic as his earlier statement that ''no Vietcong ever called me nigger,'' but it shows Ali is steadfast in his belief to oppose induction. It's also one of the first times in a long while that sports have become politicized. Not only is Ali the most visible and well-known sports figure in the world, he's also a black athlete refusing to play by the rules instituted by the sports establishment. He's not someone who can be put in a nice little tidy package and labeled ''a credit to his race,'' like Joe Louis was, not someone who's acting like the white sports establishment wants black athletes to act, thankful and respectful, all the while well aware of the status quo. Instead, he's coming to symbolize an emerging black consciousness, one that's not only mysterious to most of white America, but also threatening. Ever since he first came into the national spotlight, winning a gold medal at the Olympics in Rome in 1960, then beating Sonny Liston to become the heavyweight champ, he's been the most visible black athlete in the country. He makes rhymes, says funny things, seems born for the role of larger-than-life celebrity. Now it's becoming a lot more complicated.

In Fenway, the Sox go over the million mark in attendance for the first time in seven years, but lose to the Tigers in the 10th inning. They're now in fourth place, three and a half games in back of the Twins.

It's Friday night, August 18. There are 31,027 people in Fenway Park to see the Red Sox play the California Angels, another big, noisy, boisterous crowd in the middle of a pennant race. The pitchers are Gary Bell and Jack Hamilton. Hamilton is 29, a journeyman, in his sixth season in the major leagues. He broke in with the Phillies, then spent time with both the Tigers and the Mets before coming over to the Angels. On the recent Sox road trip to Anaheim Mike Andrews had complained to the home plate umpire that Hamilton was throwing spitballs, something Hamilton has a reputation for. Tonight's game is scoreless for three and a half innings. In the bottom of the fourth Scott is thrown out trying to stretch a single to left into a double. Someone then throws a smoke bomb on the field, and the game is held up for 10 minutes. The game resumes. Reggie Smith is the batter. He flies to deep center for the second out.

Up steps Tony Conigliaro.

His father called him "Choo," and he'd grown up in Revere, not far from Suffolk Downs and Logan Airport, in a working-class area where hard work and sports were two of the things that were most respected. Tony was the oldest of three boys. His father, Sal, had worked at many jobs, everything from selling Christmas trees on the corner with his brother to investing in the raising of chickens. Tony's uncle on his mother's side, Vinnie Martelli, was one of the first people to get him interested in baseball. He coached a Little League team in East Boston that Tony played on.

Tony went to high school at St. Mary's, a Catholic school in nearby Lynn, where right from the beginning he was a great athlete and indifferent student. He was first seen by Red Sox scouts in his sophomore year, almost by accident. They were there to look at Danny Murphy, a pitcher from St. John's of Danvers, then one of the most highly touted players in Massachusetts. Murphy only gave up four hits that day. Three of them were by Conigliaro, a tall, rangy kid with magic in his swing. Soon after, Murphy signed a professional contract with the Chicago Cubs in the vicinity of $100,000, one of the first times Conigliaro became aware that he one day might get some bonus money too.

There's not a whole lot of emphasis on high school baseball in Massachusetts. The season is short, the weather often cold and damp, the competition uneven. But by his junior year scouts started coming regularly to his games. One was Milt Bolling, a former Red Sox shortstop. Sometimes the scouts would take Conigliaro out to dinner, telling him how much he was going to like playing in such places as Detroit and Baltimore, places that seemed very far away. He would close his eyes and see himself playing in Fenway Park, for the hometown team, the team he'd grown up rooting for all his life. The summer after his senior year the Red Sox brought him into Fenway for a tryout. Another kid was there too. His name was Tony Horton and he'd flown in from California. Conigliaro was six foot three, thin, about 170. Horton was appreciably more muscular. Under the watchful eye of Neil Mahoney, the chief Red Sox scout, Horton was to throw batting practice to Conigliaro, then the two would reverse roles. Conigliaro sprayed line drives all over the park, was pleased. Horton hit the first pitch to him into the center-field bleachers. He then hit a few into the screen in left, and suddenly the workout was over. Conigliaro couldn't believe it. He hadn't even begun to sweat yet. Soon after he read in the Boston newspapers that the Sox had signed Horton for $125,000. That September, Sal Conigliaro announced Tony would sign. Scouts were scheduled to come to the Conigliaro house throughout the day. The first scout offered $8,000. Tony couldn't believe it. Hadn't he said $80,000? No. $8,000. The Red Sox were the next-to-last team to visit. Mahoney and Bolling offered $20,000, the same as the Orioles did a while later in the day. Sal Conigliaro told the Orioles that for another $5,000 they could have his son. The Orioles said no, and Tony Conigliaro signed with the hometown team, the one he'd wanted to sign with all along. But not before Mahoney told Sal Conigliaro that Tony didn't have any power.

The next month he went to the Instructional League in

Bradenton, Florida, where he underwent all the trauma and disappointments most young players go through, away from home for the first time, and seeing *professional* pitching, not some kid from the next town. He returned home that winter convinced he had to get stronger. He bought some weights and a lead bat and worked endlessly in the basement of his parents' home. Then he went to spring training, and was assigned to Wellsville, New York, in the New York–Penn League. It was 1963. He was 18 years old.

"I was staying in a cottage with a couple of guys and we took him in," remembers Mario Pagano, a pitcher, who'd also grown up in New England. "Even then, Tony had a certain charisma about him. He had a lot of confidence in himself. Some people took it the wrong way, but he would give you the shirt off his back. And he was a great natural hitter. He tore the cover off the ball that summer."

Wellsville is a sleepy little town in the western part of New York. The only nightspot was the Hotel Wellsville. The players often hung out there after games, drinking beer, looking for girls, killing time in a small town far from home. Sometimes Conigliaro would sing with the band.

"Tony was always dragging me up to sing with him," Pagano remembers. "He loved to sing that song that went 'I'm in love and Ruby is her name.' That and 'Alley Oop.' And that song 'Where or When.' Remember that one. The one that went 'we looked at each other in the same way then, but I can't remember where or when'? Tony loved that one."

They became fast friends. Both from New England. Both of Italian heritage, raised in families that viewed the world the same way. Both young and chasing the baseball dream. They played together that fall in the Instructional League in Sarasota, Florida, along with Scott and Foy. They lived at the Sarasota Terrace Hotel, and one afternoon, sitting around the pool, they heard that President Kennedy had been shot in Dallas. It was November 1963, the first time a generation came to learn that inexplicable events happen, and that they change things forever.

Afterward, when Conigliaro had gone on to live in the

middle of an adolescent fantasy, and Pagano was back home, his career over, Pagano often still thought about Conigliaro. But not the Tony C. who'd hit a home run in his first time at bat in Fenway Park, or the Tony C. who became the youngest player in baseball history to hit 100 home runs. When Pagano thinks about Tony Conigliaro he thinks about when they both were back in Wellsville, both kids, everything still ahead of them, and how Tony C. loved to get up on stage and sing "Where or When."

Sometimes, on the ride back to his parents' new home in suburban Swampscott about a dozen miles away, driving on the highway through Revere and Lynn, the two places where he'd grown up, Conigliaro could see both the house in Revere where he was born, and the first baseball field he'd ever played on. Sometimes, if he was in a reflective mood, he'd think about his childhood, of how far he'd come from that small field in Revere.

He's come very far. In his world he's rich and famous with a great distinctive nickname to boot. Tony C. The *Record-American*—the Hearst tabloid that splashes sports across the back of the paper in big, black type—loves it. Or else he's "Conig," another newspaper creation. All this, and the teenyboppers love him too. In a sense he's like a kid in a candy store, complete with the Corvette and the records and the frequent trips to the Kenmore Square clubs where he's the center of attention, although he seldom drinks. When he first came up there'd been some resentment from the older players. But now the team has changed. It's younger, more his team. He and Yastrzemski never have been particularly close, with few common interests, and opposite life-styles. But they follow each other in the lineup, and talk about pitchers, and what they're throwing in certain situations. His best friend on the team is Mike Ryan. He's friendly with Petrocelli. Often, on the road, the three of them and Lonborg hang out together. He likes to joke with Scott. Everyone respects his talent, and that, for all his notoriety, he plays hard, always competes.

Maybe they also realize that he's the local hero with the predictable perks, and that's just the way it is. About the only cloud on this dream life is Dick Williams, a dislike that goes back years. But even that's usually on some distant burner. Williams believes that without discipline Conigliaro will inevitably end up like so many of the spoiled stars of Red Sox seasons past. But he also knows that, between the white lines, Conigliaro battles. So the two coexist like two neighbors who don't necessarily like each other, but have come to realize that they both benefit by not letting the animosity escalate. Williams essentially leaves Conigliaro alone, using Scott, Foy, and pitchers who don't throw strikes as the main vents for his frustration. Conigliaro, in turn, has responded with the best year of his career. On this night of August 18 he already has 20 home runs and 68 RBI's, despite missing two weeks in the Reserves.

He'd singled off a curveball his first time up against Jack Hamilton, so he goes to the plate expecting fastballs. He steps into the batter's box, wide stance, crowding the plate, aggressive, just like always, for he knows no other way. He is wearing a batting helmet, but not one that has a flap coming down over part of the left side of his face, because flaps are relatively new and not many players use them. He wonders if the 10-minute delay for the smoke bomb in the left field might have caused Hamilton's arm to stiffen. It's his last thought before the ball hits him.

"You never go up to the plate expecting to be hit," he'll say later, "then in a fraction of a second you know it's going to happen. When the ball was about four feet from my head I knew it was going to hit me. And I knew it was going to hurt. I was frightened. I threw my hands up in front of my face and saw the ball follow me back and hit me squarely on the left side of the face. Just before everything went dark I saw the ball bounce straight down on home plate. It was the last thing I saw for several days."

He's not unconscious. He can't see, nor can he breathe, but he feels the swelling in his mouth, feels the fluid. He prays to God to keep him alive, feels that it's some show-down between him and God, and he's afraid he might die, right here at home plate in Fenway Park.

Petrocelli is in the batter's box. He's the first one to reach him. "Take it easy, Tony," he tells him. "You're going to be all right."

Conigliaro lies on the ground, surrounded by his teammates, coaches, and trainers. Ryan holds an ice bag to his face, the spot where the ball has made an indentation. Fenway is eerily silent. He is carried off the field on a stretcher, and taken into the clubhouse. He's placed on one of the trainer's tables and Dr. Thomas Tierney, the Red Sox physician, attends to him. His father is in the room with him. Eventually, he's taken to Sancta Maria hospital, across the Charles River in Cambridge, where both his parents and two brothers come in the room with him.

The next morning there's a picture of Conigliaro in all the morning newspapers. He's lying in his hospital bed, his left eye deeply bruised and swollen shut. He looks very young. "If he had been hit two inches higher he would have died," Dr. Tierney is quoted as saying.

That day Ryan climbs the fire escape and sneaks into the hospital. Conigliaro is lying in bed when he hears a familiar voice.

"Is that you, Mike?" he calls out.

"Hey, roomie, you in there?" Ryan asks. "Hey, come on out. I got the babes and some beer waiting downstairs in the car. Let's go."

"No, I'm dying, Mike," Conigliaro says, too sick to even laugh. "Some other time."

"Come on, Sister," Ryan says to a nearby nun. "See, he needs me."

Ryan's visit helps Conigliaro's spirit. The two players had first met in the fall of '62 at Logan Airport, about to fly to Florida and the Instructional League—two Massachusetts kids, both with it all ahead of them. Soon after they boarded the plane, Ryan, scared of flying, threw up all over Conigliaro. It was the start of a beautiful friendship.

The next morning when he wakes up Conigliaro can see for the first time. The room is full of flowers and sacks of mail. Yawkey comes to see him. He learns that Hamilton had come to see him the day before, but hadn't been allowed into his room. In the days that follow several of his teammates will come to visit him—Ryan, Petrocelli, Scott. Dick Williams never does, and Conigliaro will never forget it. While he knows they've never really gotten along, he believes Williams owes him this, that he's played hard for him, and that in this toughest moment of his life, Williams should have done something, a card, a note, a visit, something. So he lies here in his bed at Sancta Maria Hospital, his vision blurry in his left eye, and he feels terribly cheated. For the Red Sox are in the midst of this incredible season, and now, for the time being at least, he's no longer a part of it.

It is the dog days of August in this incredible summer, and nothing seems changed. New Haven, Connecticut, is put under curfew as racial violence erupts. A report says that poverty is still prevalent in Appalachia despite billions in aid that were supposed to turn this region of the country into a "woodsy suburb" of LBJ's "Great Society." There's speculation that Johnson's support in the Senate has eroded so much that he would be hard-pressed to get a majority to back his policies in Southeast Asia. While military leaders, led by General Westmoreland, continue to remain highly optimistic about the war, there is growing skepticism in the Senate, a marked difference to just a few short months ago. More and more it seems Johnson is caught in the middle, criticized on the left for our involvement in the war in the first place, criticized on the right for not pursuing a more aggressive war strategy.

In Chicago, Teamsters president Jimmy Hoffa is denied another trial on his charge that the government used illegal wiretaps to convict him of conspiracy and mail fraud. He's ordered back to federal prison in Lewisburg, Pennsylvania, where he's serving a five-year sentence. Twiggy, one of the most famous models in the world, arrives at Kennedy Airport in New York for the start of a U.S. tour. She's dressed as an Indian. She's not the only one making news in New York City. At the New York Stock Exchange, two men who haven't been in the news before begin throwing money from the visitors' gallery. It seems such a bizarre act, so symbolic of the jingle-jangle times, that the New York media descends on the scene. The names of the two are Abbie Hoffman and Jerry Rubin. They've met in the planning of the giant mobilization march against the war, scheduled for October in Washington.

In baseball, Alvin Dark, on the verge of signing a new two-year contract with the Kansas City Athletics, is fired as manager by owner Charlie Finley. Dark was the Rookie of the Year with the Boston Braves in 1948, and had started the rally in the famous 1951 playoff game between the Giants and the Dodgers, which was won by Bobby Thomson's memorable home run. Finley is 49, has owned the A's since 1960. Already, he's emerged as one of the most controversial owners in the game, known for such publicity ploys as the mule that's paraded around at games draped in the green and yellow of the Athletics. Finley had started as a player-manager on a semipro team in Indiana, then gone on to build an insurance empire. When he bought the A's they were known as a glorified farm club to the Yankees, continually sending young players to New York in exchange for old journeymen long past their prime. Finley stopped that. He also emerged as an owner who wasn't going to be content to exist in the shadows. He's averaged one manager a year for the past seven years. The roots of Dark's dismissal go back a few days to when Finley suspended pitcher Lew Krausse for an alleged disturbance on a team flight. The players then held a meeting, issuing a statement accusing Finley of undermining the morale of the team and using informers to spy on players.

"We players feel that if Mr. Finley would give his fine coaching staff and excellent manager the authority they deserve, these problems would not exist," the statement said.

Visibly shaken, Finley retaliates by claiming Dark has lost control of the team and fires him. The players counter with another statement, one that says they feel a deep personal loss at the firing of Dark. Finley wants the players to rescind their statement criticizing him. The players refuse. Finley retaliates by giving Ken Harrelson, one of the most vocal critics of the Dark firing, his unconditional release. Harrelson has called Finley a "menace to baseball." Now Harrelson feels Finley will blackball him, but he's immediately contacted by several major league clubs, plus the Tokyo Giants, who reach him through an interpreter.

"You're always shocked when you lose your job," he says. "I'm sorry the whole thing had to come about. The situation is explosive, and something's going to happen. I think he made a great mistake in firing Alvin Dark."

Meanwhile, the Sox sign veteran outfielder Jim Landis, who'd been released by the Tigers. He's 33, has been with four American League clubs, and one in the National League, and in his prime with the White Sox had been an excellent defensive outfielder. He's been added to try to plug the hole left by Conigliaro's absence, but everyone knows that if Conigliaro is going to be out awhile the Red Sox are going to need more than Landis. Conigliaro has been placed on the 21-day disabled list, but no one has any clue to when he'll come back. What everyone does know is that Conigliaro's loss is potentially devastating. In addition to the right fielder's own production, his presence in the lineup following Yastrzemski prevents pitchers from pitching around Yaz.

It's August 22, a Tuesday, in Fenway Park. It's also Yastrzemski's birthday, and at one point everyone in the stands in left field starts singing "Happy Birthday" as he comes out to left field between innings. Two of them are 23-year-old guys from Providence, Rhode Island, Mickey Klitzner and Ron Kart. They're both ardent Red Sox fans, best of friends, and they've made the hour-long trip to Fenway about a dozen times already. Klitzner has grown up with the Red Sox, in a house where the games were always on the radio, and remembers sitting in the garage in some lost year in the '50s listening to Mel Parnell pitch a no-hitter. He's married, so has a deferment that keeps him out of the military, but there have been riots earlier in the summer in Providence and there still is an 8 P.M. curfew. Where he lives adjoins the ghetto, and occasionally he can still hear gunfire, like the sound of firecrackers off in the distance. The Red Sox have become his passion this summer, something that blocks out everything else. He listens to the games on the radio. He gets up the next morning and reads about them in the *Providence Journal*. He knows which team they're playing next, and how they're doing.

"They have gotten me through the summer," he says, "because they are ongoing. Anything else, you go out at night, then the night ends and it's over. But the Red Sox never end."

Now he and Kart find themselves sitting in a jammed left-field section of the Fenway grandstand, a part that hugs the foul line. Much of the game the crowd is swaying back and forth, chanting. Klitzner's never been in such a festive atmosphere before, and he thinks that it's a reaction to the negativity that surrounds so much of the summer. Fenway Park has become a magical place where you check your troubles at the door, reality gets put on hold, and you join some incredible celebration, something infinitely larger than yourself. Here there's no specter of Vietnam, no sound of gunshots, no evidence of a changing world. Here it's all timeless, as innocent as childhood.

Later that night he and Kart go to a nightclub in Newport, Rhode Island, a summer resort almost two hours from Fenway Park. The performer is a regional singer called Sully who travels around the Boston and Cape Cod circuit doing sing-alongs. At one point Sully asks all Red Sox fans to get up on the tables. Klitzner and Kart do, of course, along with most everyone else in the room, and suddenly they're all singing and waving and cheering for the Red Sox, this incredible team that's helping everyone forget, at least for a while, the terrible headlines the morning newspaper brings.

Conigliaro is released from Sancta Maria hospital on the 24th, goes for a short vacation with his family, as the pennant race continues. One of the key Red Sox performers has become Jerry Adair. He's had two game-winning hits and has started two game-winning rallies in the past 10 days. He's made the key fielding plays in two games, one of which he won with a homer. Since joining the Red Sox in early June, he's hit .298 in 55 games, a great addition.

"He's been there every time we've needed him," Williams says. "He either gets the big hit, or makes the big play. He's exactly what we needed."

Adair sits on his folding chair in front of his locker after every game. He has close-cropped sandy hair and a face right out of the *Grapes of Wrath*. He often has a chaw of Red Man stuck in one cheek. He doesn't volunteer information. His answers are short, and delivered in a low voice. He seems like the embodiment of the baseball mercenary, professional, emotionless, with no allegiance to anything around him. Many of the writers covering the team think he's sullen. No one questions his toughness, though. Once in 1964 he was hit in the mouth by a wild throw in the first game of a doubleheader, received 11 stitches, then returned for the second game. He was signed by Baltimore in 1958 out of Oklahoma State, where he also had been a basketball star, and became the Orioles' regular second baseman three years later. Last year he was shipped to the White Sox in a deal that brought pitcher Eddie Fisher to Baltimore.

"I guess I've always been quiet," he says. "But I get along with the players. The age difference doesn't bother me."

He pauses.

"This is a different ballclub. Not just younger, but more enthusiastic. It's looser than most clubs. In Chicago, Eddie Stanky wanted everybody thinking and talking baseball. You couldn't make any remarks in the dugout that weren't baseball. It's much looser here."

He pauses.

"I think we have a helluva chance to win. I didn't think so when I joined it. I didn't think they were that good. I didn't think the pitching would hold up the way it has. And I didn't think it had the power the way it has."

It's August 25, and the Red Sox are in Chicago tonight for the start of a five-game series. Forty thousand are expected at Comiskey Park, the old park at 35th and South

Shields on the city's South Side that was built in 1910. In its early years it was dubbed the "Baseball Capitol of the World." It also was the site of the first All-Star game in 1933, and for years it was the annual site of the Negro Leagues' annual all-star game. This series has been called the biggest for the Red Sox since the last weekend of the 1949 season when the Sox lost two games to the Yankees, losing the pennant in the process.

Once again, as he's done so many times throughout this summer, Eddie Stanky defends his ballclub. "They call us the dullest club in baseball, but they don't write about the guts and determination of the White Sox. Everybody is waiting for the White Sox to collapse so they can say 'I told you so.' But no bottom is going to fall out."

Informed that 12 writers will be traveling with the Red Sox, Stanky snorts. "So the 12 writers are coming in for the kill. Well, the Red Sox over the past five years had the best young players in baseball. It's about time they came to life." He goes on to say, his voice laced with sarcasm, that it's obvious his White Sox don't belong on the same field as the "hairy-chested Red Sox" and their "new breed" of a manager.

It's vintage Stanky, and as the season now starts to get serious, he's more and more combative, a jockey who knows he has to whip his horse if the horse is ever going to win. Eddie Stanky, still the Brat after all the years.

Before the game it's announced the Red Sox have signed Ken Harrelson, outbidding the White Sox. He's hitting close to .300 and is considered a necessity with the uncertainty surrounding Conigliaro's status. Harrelson had met with O'Connell and Haywood Sullivan for five hours before coming to terms, but the bidding process had commenced when White Sox general manager Bob Short called Harrelson and said he and Stanky had agreed they wanted Harrelson to play in Chicago, and were offering him $100,000 for the rest of this season, and next year—an outlandish amount of money. Harrelson *had* been making $12,000 a year.

"He said he didn't want to get into a bidding war and he was only going to make one offer," Harrelson says. "I'm dumb, but when I heard bidding war I knew I wasn't going to accept right then. I wasn't that dumb.''

The Red Sox were the next team to make a definitive offer, Haywood Sullivan calling and saying he wanted to fly down to Baltimore, where Harrelson was with the Athletics, and talk. "We met at the airport in Baltimore and he offered $118,000," Harrelson says. "I tell him I think we have a deal. But the next morning I fly back home to Kansas City and the phone rings. It's Paul Richards of the Braves, and an old golfing buddy. He asks how much have I been offered and I tell him $118,000 by the Red Sox. He says, 'I'll give you $125,000.' You got me, I say. So I call Haywood back and tell him that I'm going to the Braves, that it's a great opportunity for an old Georgia boy like me and, besides, he's giving me $125,000. Haywood doesn't say much, and I call Paul back and tell him he's got a deal. The next morning the phone rings. 'Ken, this is Dick O'Connell, we want you to play for the Red Sox.' I tell him Paul Richards has made me a great offer to play for the Braves, and that I'm from Georgia and everything and he says, 'What will it take?' No small talk. No sales pitch. Just, 'How much will it take?' I say $150,000 and he says fine. So I call up Paul and tell him I want to go to Boston, that Fenway Park is made for me. He says he can get me $200,000, but I tell him, Paul, please, let me go to Boston.''

Tonight is a doubleheader, and the Red Sox win the first game behind Lonborg. It's his first complete game in roughly a month. But the White Sox come back to win the second game, and the two teams remain tied for second, a half game behind Minnesota.

The Red Sox take the lead the next day, beating the White Sox while the Twins lose to Cleveland. It's a big game for the Red Sox because they chase the White Sox ace Joel Horlen and get a win from youngster Jerry Stephenson. "I was nervous going out there," Stephenson says, "but Dick told me to throw as hard as I could for as long as I could. 'We don't want a complete game, Jerry,' he told me. 'We want you to go out there and do the best you can for as long as you can. Don't pace yourself.' ''

It's the first time in 18 years that the Red Sox have been in first place this late in the season, and Stanky is almost beside himself. He claims the Red Sox lost the second game of the doubleheader the day before because Williams had managed timidly, and had done so because he'd been in first place and didn't know how to handle it. He criticizes Adair—who'd said Stanky ordered Tommy John to throw at him—implying that the White Sox pitchers had been less than thrilled with Adair playing behind them. No one is safe. Stanky has seen his lead lost, and he strikes out at everybody, part frustration and part gamesmanship. Give no quarter. Take no prisoners. Like Williams, Stanky is always looking for an edge, something to give him an advantage. Everyone around the league believes he keeps the infield grass long in Comiskey Park so that his speedy, Punch-and-Judy hitters will have an advantage in beating out ground balls. Anything to get that edge. He can't run, he can't throw, and he can't hit, all he does is beat you. And if he can't do that, he lashes out at you.

The next morning Red Smith writes a syndicated column about the Boston Red Sox. There can be no clearer evidence that the Red Sox have gone national, have made the transformation from a regional story to one that's captured the entire sporting world. Smith is 61, the preeminent sportswriter of his generation, syndicated in nearly 500 newspapers across the country. He worked for the *Milwaukee Sentinel* as a news reporter in 1927 after graduating from Notre Dame, then moved to the *St. Louis Star* where he began writing about sports. In 1945 he moved to the *New York Herald-Tribune*. Last year the *Herald-Tribune* folded, but Smith continues to write his column and sell it for syndication.

Actually, the focus of Smith's column is Ted Williams, the most famous Red Sox player of them all. Williams is officially listed as a Red Sox vice-president, but he has no duties. While he makes an annual visit to spring training, he is rarely seen in Fenway Park, if ever. Instead, he spends summers fishing in Nova Scotia, winters fishing in the Florida Keys. It's a ceremonial title, and this year he's been distanced from the team more than in other years, because of the friction that had existed in spring training between him and Dick Williams. Ted had looked at the pitchers playing volleyball and shook his head. Dick had looked at Ted shaking his head and undoubtedly wanted to wring Ted's neck. Eventually, Ted had sensed this and left. The friction was probably unavoidable. It had been Dick Williams' first spring training, and as he urgently tried to establish his own imprint on the team, the last thing he needed was Ted's large and sometimes intimidating presence.

But now Ted has nothing but praise for this Red Sox team. He likens Dick Williams to Joe McCarthy, the former Yankee manager who eventually managed the Red Sox, because they both run a baseball team as a business for two and a half hours a day. He credits Petrocelli's emergence as an outstanding player with Rico's seeming to have transcended the personal problems that plagued him his first two years. "I know how hard that is," he tells Red Smith. "It's like playing with a piano on your back." Ted also calls Reggie Smith the greatest prospect the Red Sox have ever had.

Though Smith is acknowledged to have great potential—a rocket arm and a powerful bat—he's struggled at the plate most of the year, his average hovering as low as .200 through May. He's in the big leagues, but even so, it's been difficult for him. He and his wife spent the winter in Puerto Rico where he played winter ball, but afterward he went to spring training and she went back to California to try to save some money before she joined him in Boston in the summer. All through spring training they'd telephoned twice a week, but even that proved too expensive and they resorted to writing every day.

Smith is not the only Red Sox player who spent part of the season without his wife for financial reasons. Joe Foy has done it all season. His wife, Sadie, and year-old daughter, Stephanie, have been staying in the Bronx throughout the summer while Foy has leased former Red Sox pitcher Earl Wilson's apartment in Jamaica Plain. This is the side of being a professional athlete the public doesn't see. Foy's wife says, "It's bad for Stephanie. She's only a little girl and she calls for her daddy and he's not here. I try and explain where he is, but she always calls for him.''

Smith blames his poor start on his wife's absence, though he admits he also got off to a poor start the year before in Toronto. Yastrzemski thinks Smith is too prone to let a bad plate appearance affect him, especially early in a game.

"Some days when Reggie gets fooled his first time at bat he gets down on himself and gives away his next two times up," he says. "You can't do that in this game. You have to ignore what happened to you the last time and concentrate on the next time."

Smith is also prone to showing up late at the park, a quirk that Williams isn't so sure how to deal with. He often goes to O'Connell asking for advice. What to do with Smith? He's so awesomely talented, has so many physical gifts, yet there also sometimes seems to be a wall around him, some personal moat that keeps everyone away. He's comfortable around Foy and Yastrzemski. Virtually everyone else is kept at a distance, and no one seems to know just what to do about it. George Thomas, who's good at reading his teammates, sees Smith as a very fragile personality.

"He really admires Carl," he says, "and it's like he follows him around and wants to do everything he does. To the point where if I throw extra batting practice to Carl I also have to throw it to Reggie too."

Smith is a new breed of black player, proud, sensitive, wanting to be treated with respect, not just as a piece of meat. So Red Sox management, sensitive to their being the last team in the major leagues to integrate, walk carefully around Reggie Smith. In a few years he'll say Boston is a racist town, that the Red Sox don't promote their black players, pointing to how few endorsements he gets. He'll be called a cancer in the clubhouse, have public battles with both Carlton Fisk and Billy Conigliaro, and suffer so much abuse from the fans in Fenway Park that he'll take to wearing a batting helmet in center field. By the early '70s he'll lament that he was once said to have the potential of a Willie Mays or a Henry Aaron, simply saying that all he ever wanted to be was Reggie Smith, no one else. But in this summer of '67, that is all ahead of him. He's still all about the future, the young kid with all the talent.

Once again, the feud that's simmered all summer between the Red Sox and the White Sox adds another chapter in today's doubleheader when Scott claims White Sox pitcher Fred Klages intentionally hit him after Yastrzemski had homered in the fifth. Throughout the game several of the Boston hitters had been brushed back. All believed it was on orders from Stanky. "I heard him yell from the dugout," Scott says.

Stanky denies it.

"He's got it all wrong. If he heard me order Klages to hit him, then the umpire would have heard it and I would have been tossed out of the game. I don't know what they're talking about. I don't play the game that way. Now that you mention guys being hit by pitchers, doesn't that guy named Jim Lonborg, who pitches for Boston, lead the league in hit batsmen? And aren't they paying dearly for it? You know Tony Conigliaro is not playing because he was hit by a pitch. That was the result of them hitting someone else."

The teams split the doubleheader, but the first game contains one of those moments that live on long after so many others are forgotten. This one comes in the bottom of the ninth. The Red Sox are leading 4–3, courtesy of Yaz's 33rd and 34th home runs. But the Chisox come to life in the ninth, the speedy Ken Berry on third with only one out. Gary Bell is the pitcher, but is tiring, and Williams pulls him in favor of John Wyatt. The batter is Duane Josephson. Wyatt throws a fastball on the first pitch and Josephson hits a medium line drive to right field, where Tartabull is playing. As he runs in and makes a one-handed catch, Berry tags up from third. It is the essence of White Sox baseball, Eddie Stanky baseball, aggressive, running, taking the initiative, forcing the action. Tartabull, known for his weak arm, throws to the plate. Berry is racing to the plate, the crowd roaring.

The other two key performers in this minidrama are Elston Howard and umpire Marty Springstead, in his second year as a major league umpire. The throw is high. But Howard, blocking the plate with one foot, reaches up to make the catch as Berry begins his slide. Howard's foot initially forces Berry off the plate, so that Berry knows he must touch home plate with his hand as he slides by. But Howard, making the catch one-handed, instantly reaches down in one motion to tag Berry. Springstead makes the out sign, and Stanky bolts from the dugout, berserk at the call. He stomps his feet, kicks sand. He puts his face into Springstead's and jaws with him. He's enraged, a portrait in frustration. But the play stands, the Red Sox win, and Tartabull's clutch throw and Howard's great play become an integral part of this summer pageant, this Red Sox season that's already sprinkled with pixie dust.

Back in Boston, Dick O'Connell tries to calm the furor Yawkey had caused earlier in the summer when he said that if a new stadium wasn't built he might take the Red Sox out of Boston. "There is no plan for anybody to leave Boston," O'Connell says. "But change in ownership, which will take place sometime in the future, could mean extremely different circumstances."

He adds that the team has a market value of $10 to $12 million, and that the Red Sox have no preference as to whether the new stadium should be downtown, or in the suburbs. They aren't in favor, though, of a domed stadium. A week ago a new five-tiered, multipurpose stadium officially opened in San Diego, one that cost $27 million to build, a fact O'Connell uses to put more pressure on the city of Boston.

Controversy of a different sort is predicted as plans go forward for a massive antiwar demonstration in Washington in October, sponsored by the National Mobilization Committee to End the War in Vietnam. It was announced by a group whose stated policy is to embrace blacks, women, students, hippies, draft resisters, and political organizers, virtually anyone who feels estranged from the system. H. Rap Brown is asked by the media if he will be one of the participants. He recently was released on bail on a federal charge of carrying a weapon on an airline flight between

New York and New Orleans, while additional charges are still pending against him for inciting a riot in Cambridge, Maryland. "It would be unwise to say I'm going there with a gun because you all took my gun last time," he says. "I may bring a bomb, sucker."

Brown subsequently told a crowd of 3,000 blacks in Detroit that they did a good job in the recent riots, and that the city's riots will look like a picnic when blacks unite.

It is not the only news that makes newspaper headlines. George Lincoln Rockwell, the head of the noisy and hate-filled American Nazi Party, is assassinated by a colleague in an Arlington, Virginia, shopping mall. And Brian Epstein, the Beatles' manager who some think is the marketing genius behind the group's incredible popularity, dies in Liverpool after a night of drinking and pill-popping.

The Sox have won three out of five in Chicago and arrive in New York on August 28 as a headline says, "Even Blasé New Yorkers Decide Red Sox Are for Real." Back in Boston, in the largest parade in the city's history, 20,000 Legionnaires march in support of the war led by Massachusetts governor John Volpe, the honorary marshal. It's an obvious response to the growing antiwar sentiment.

At Yankee Stadium, in the dugout before the game, Dick Williams is telling a group of sportswriters that it's been known for a long time the Red Sox have good young talent and that they should have been winning more in the past.

"That's not putting the knock on anybody," he says.

He's asked to enumerate some of the intangible reasons for the club's success.

"There's more fun in winning than losing. I think that's one point we've gotten across to the players this season. Another thing is togetherness. Everybody on this club pulls for everybody else."

It's Carl Yastrzemski Night at the Stadium—a bid by Yankee management to draw a few more fans—so naturally Williams is asked about him. "He is the best player in the American League this season, and I've never seen a player, or been on a team with one, who's played any better over a full season. Yaz has never stopped trying. He gets some fly balls you don't think he can catch. He hustles all the time. I never played with Willie Mays, but watching Yaz, day in and day out, I don't think Willie could do it any better. Over a career I'd have to take Mays. Over a season Yaz is my man.''

"Why is he doing so well?"

"Well, for years he was on losers, and with losers you have to look to your own batting average or yourself. But on a winner it's exciting, and a good player wants to be a part of that. You think of the club and the other stuff takes care of itself. You know, for years Yaz was in the shadow of a fellow named Williams. Now this kid has an awful lot to do to ever crack a dent in Williams' popularity. He tried hard, and nothing happened. Maybe he got discouraged.''

Williams also says he's told his pitchers that, with only a few exceptions, what Elston Howard calls for, they throw.

"I'll be responsible for that," he says. "Not Ellie. Me.''

This follows a recent game where Sparky Lyle shook off a sign from Howard. The veteran catcher had wanted a fastball. The 24-year-old pitcher shook him off, threw a slider instead. He walked the batter. The next two guys got hits, and Lyle was gone. Afterward, Howard expressed his displeasure to Lyle, and the young pitcher argued back before Yastrzemski told Lyle he'd only been in the big leagues a short time while Howard has been in the bigs for 13 years. Dick Williams was not thrilled. "I had a nice talk with him after that," Williams says. "I told him that when Elston calls something you throw it. You can shake, but it will cost you $50.''

Before the game, in a ceremony attended by his father, wife Carol, and children Mary Ann and Mike, Yaz is honored. Foy presents him with a television set, courtesy of the Red Sox players. He's also given a convertible. Yaz thanks Yawkey for the way he's been treated in Boston.

Things are not going so well for Conigliaro. He's back at his parents' house in suburban Swampscott. He still has blurry vision in his left eye, in fact has seen little progress since he left the hospital. He's also been told that he might have a cyst on his eye, which essentially causes a blind spot. The doctor uses words and medical terminology he doesn't understand, but he knows enough to know a blind spot in one eye is serious business when you're a major league hitter whose career depends on trying to discern what a 90-mile-an-hour pitch is going to do. He asks the doctor if he's ever going to be able to play baseball again. "I don't know," the doctor says.

One day he goes out in the yard with his younger brother Richie. They start to play catch. Tony quickly discovers he has to concentrate to even catch the ball. He's so embarrassed that he tries to nonchalant it, sticking his glove out at the last minute, so if he drops one it will look like he's only fooling around. They then play a little pepper, and sometimes he misses the ball altogether, something he's never done in his life. It's a graphic reminder of how far away he is from the pennant race.

Ken Harrelson has arrived, and the Boston Red Sox may never be the same.

He was raised in Savannah, Georgia, an only child. His father left when he was eight years old, and he grew up a "mama's boy," with his mother, Jessie, as his best friend and number one supporter. She was a secretary in a meat-packing plant, making $56 a week.

"Nobody ever had a better relationship with his mother than I had," he says. "She raised me and the sun rose and set on her son."

He was such a great athlete in junior high school that he was recruited by three high schools in the city. One was Benedictine Military Academy. They arranged for him to have a job that paid $40 a week, plus there were several benefactors slipping him money. One guy gave him $20 after every football game. Another gave him a dollar for every single, increasing it by a dollar for every extra base. Soon he was making more money as an athlete at Benedictine than his mother as a secretary. It was probably money well spent. As a sophomore he was six foot two, 195 pounds—an old-fashioned three-letter man in football, basketball, and baseball. As a high school quarterback he was considered one of the best in the South, recruited by many schools. In basketball, his favorite sport, he was All-State as a sophomore. As a baseball player, he was good enough to have scouts crawling all over him. He was such a great athlete that he was already a well-defined local celebrity. When his high school team traveled to other towns to play there were often signs calling him a mama's boy, signs making fun of his rather large and distinctive nose. It never bothered him. At a young age Ken Harrelson was comfortable with his celebrity.

Years after he graduated in 1959 he found a picture of himself and several of his friends, taken when he was at Benedictine. He was the only one with sunglasses and long hair, the only one who looked different. Maybe that's because he *was* different. He liked to shoot pool and arm wrestle for money. He liked automobile racing. When he was 16 an American Legion coach took him and a couple of teammates to play golf. Six weeks later he shot a 72.

He signed with the Kansas City Athletics for $30,000 shortly after his high school graduation, turning his back on all the college scholarship offers. To a mother and son who'd never had any money, $30,000 was all the money in the world. The Dodgers had offered more money, but the Kansas City scout had convinced his mother that because the Dodgers had so many minor league teams the odds were her son would have to spend a lot of years in the minors, working his way through the organization.

By the time he was 21 he was in the major leagues. Already he was called "Hawk." He'd gotten the nickname his first year in winter ball. Also playing winter ball was Dick Howser, later to become manager of both the Yankees and Kansas City Royals. After watching young Harrelson continually fail to make contact at the plate, Howser said sarcastically, "You look like Henrietta Hawk," a reference to a cartoon character.

Harrelson didn't like it. His high school nickname had been "Spider," and here was Howser disparagingly calling him Henrietta Hawk.

Howser kept it up, calling him "bonus baby," and generally being tough on him. Harrelson kept taking Howser's abuse, because his mother had taught him not to talk back to his elders, just to keep working hard.

"Dick," Harrelson said one day, "when are you going to let up on me?"

"When you get a couple of hits," Howser answered.

That day he did.

"Okay," Howser said. "I'll drop the Henrietta."

Hawk it became.

Throughout his minor league career Harrelson was forever telling PA announcers that he wasn't Ken Harrelson. He was Hawk Harrelson.

He also learned a valuable lesson in building an image. It had happened in one of his early years in Kansas City. He'd had a big day and was anxious to get to a post-game party, but there was a large group of people at the gate who wanted his autograph. He was brushing his way through the crowd, trying to get out of there as quickly as possible, when he felt someone grab him. It was Rocky Colavito, a teammate, who'd been one of Harrelson's heroes when he was a kid, and his mother's favorite player.

"Come with me," Colavito said. They went into the clubhouse where Colavito told him, in no uncertain terms, that if he ever was as inconsiderate around fans again, Colavito was going to kick his ass. "You have a responsibility, especially to the kids," Colavito said. "The fans are who pay our salaries."

Harrelson went back outside and began signing autographs. He also never forgot the lesson.

He is very happy to be in Boston. He's always liked the ballpark, not only the short wall, but also the close proximity of the fans, enjoying kidding with them. He also had idolized Ted Williams as a kid. Mantle had been his favorite player, but he'd always wanted to emulate Williams.

And he is colorful. He goes through money like a fish goes through water. His light hair is longish, especially in the context of athletes. He wears Nehru jackets and love beads. The first thing he does in Boston is rent a splashy apartment with a large waterbed that virtually covers every inch of the bedroom. Then he puts a black silk bedspread over it.

He's also a plus in the clubhouse. He likes the banter with the press, and the press likes him, so he takes some of the pressure off the other players. It's all new to him, a different world from the one he left behind in Kansas City, where there might only be a couple of writers in the clubhouse after games. Here there's a gang of them, and they're here every day. He loves it. Isn't this what the major leagues is supposed to be? Sportswriters and newspaper stories and the feeling everything is important? Not like Kansas City where the season was winding down as slowly as sand through an hour glass, the suspense long over, the players merely waiting for the end, the only true excitement coming on the first and 15th of every month, the day the checks arrive. This is a pennant race, every game important, and though there's a level of anxiety that goes along with that, it's also the essence of what made him love the game in the first place.

He talks, has opinions on anything and everything, is a sportswriter's dream. Yastrzemski, in particular, likes this, because he's never been comfortable with the horde of sportswriters who wait by his locker after every game, angling for quotes, insight, anything. He knows feeding the quote machine is part of his job, part of being the leader, but he still likes it when the writers go off in another direction, because that means it's fewer of them he has to deal with.

Harrelson quickly realizes that, despite Yastrzemski's performance at the plate and Lonborg's on the mound, the key to the team's success is Williams. The day Harrelson joined the Sox he went to Williams' hotel room. The last time Harrelson had been to Fenway Park with the Athletics he'd done well, hitting a home run when Lonborg hung a slider in one game, knocking a John Wyatt spitter off the wall in center in another. Williams had been incensed, standing at the top of the dugout steps yelling at Harrelson, calling him "bush" and a "jerk" and just about anything else derogatory he could think of. Harrelson hadn't liked it.

"Can we forget about that?" Williams asked, as Harrelson came into the room.

"Yes, sir," Harrelson said, though he was still angry at Williams.

Harrelson soon learns it doesn't matter if he's angry at Williams, or even if Williams is angry at him. He realizes that all Williams cares about is winning. Harrelson believes you can make a judgment about a manager about as quickly as you can about a player. When he'd been in the minors he'd played against Earl Weaver and had thought then that Weaver was a major league manager just waiting to happen. Now playing for the Sox he realizes that Dick Williams has great baseball instincts, and the courage to utilize them. Harrelson has been around managers who talked tough, but didn't back it up—managers who inevitably went by the book to shield themselves from criticism, both from the press and the players. Williams doesn't care about being second-guessed. He's secure enough to follow his instincts, and if they fail him, so be it. Harrelson quickly decides that the only thing that matters is if Williams puts his name in the lineup. It doesn't matter if Williams rarely speaks to him, or doesn't seem to like his life-style. With Williams, that's all irrelevant. If you produce, you're in the lineup; if you don't, you're in the doghouse.

"Dick Williams is the reason the Red Sox are in the pennant race," he says. "He is the strongest personality on the club, and it's not even close."

Harrelson also quickly learns to respect Yastrzemski, not only for his great performance, but for his leadership. It's not leadership in the traditional sense, nothing fiery or showy. It's subtle. If a player makes a glaring error, or fails to get a big hit, and the Sox lose, Harrelson notices that Yastrzemski will go out of his way to tell the writers that the error or strikeout wasn't what lost the game, but rather something he'd done. Harrelson is surprised. He too has heard Yaz is selfish, that he's arrogant, that he only cares about his stats—the baggage Yastrzemski has carried since he came into the league. But he sees Yastrzemski willing to take the blame for others' failures, sees him shepherding the young players like Smith and Foy, talking to them, counseling them, caring about them, and now views him differently.

The next year it will become even more pronounced to Harrelson when Yastrzemski gets off to a great start, then hurts his right wrist. As soon as he leaves the lineup, the Sox start to swoon, and one day Harrelson goes to Yaz and says he has to get himself back into the lineup, whatever it takes, if for no other reason than the emotional lift it will give everyone else. Yastrzemski agrees, goes to Williams and says his wrist is better, even though it isn't. He swears Harrelson to secrecy. So while his average quickly plummets, Yastrzemski never offers any excuses, never says that he's sacrificing his average for the team, and Harrelson's respect for him only grows.

But now it is the summer of 1967 and the Red Sox and Yankees are going at it in a doubleheader at the Stadium. Lonborg wins the first game, picking up his 18th win in the process. Afterward, Howard calls Lonborg the best pitcher in the American League, adding that Lonborg reminds him of Whitey Ford in his prime. But it's the second game that's memorable. It takes six hours to play, ends at 2 A.M., and the Yankees win in the 20th inning. It's a devastating loss, not only because of the game's length, but because Williams uses eight pitchers.

The next day is August 30, a day of firsts. Thurgood Marshall, the great-grandson of a slave and the son of a porter, receives Senate confirmation as a Supreme Court justice, the first black to be nominated. The presiding justice of the Supreme Court is Hugo Black, the former senator from Alabama who'd once belonged to the Ku Klux Klan before putting his personal past behind him and becoming a staunch defender of civil rights.

And in the Stadium the Sox beat the Yanks 2–1 in the 11th on Yastrzemski's 35th home run. They now lead the American League by one and a half games, as baseball looks toward September. Williams is asked how he feels.

"I don't know," he says. "I've never been here either."

PITCHING	IP	H	BB	SO	W	L	ERA
Stephenson	23	16	8	14	2	0	1.57
Lyle	34	27	10	35	1	2	1.68
Osinski	57⅔	54	13	36	3	1	2.37
Wyatt	79⅔	57	33	62	8	6	2.39
Stange	150⅔	133	25	83	8	8	2.64
Lonborg	218⅓	178	64	194	18	6	3.26
Bell	191	162	59	122	10	11	3.30
Santiago	110⅓	109	34	83	7	4	3.85
Landis	33⅓	22	11	31	1	0	4.09
Brandon	147	137	59	88	5	11	4.16
Morehead	33⅓	31	13	28	4	2	4.36

Eddie Stanky is sitting in the Fenway Park visitors' dugout in his uniform a couple of hours before his White Sox are set to play, holding court. It's only fitting. In the *Boston Globe*, writer Ray Fitzgerald is referring to Stanky as King Edward, setting the stage for another visit to Boston by Stanky, the designated villain. It's August 31, and the White Sox are in town for another big series. As he sits here, Stanky remembers the last time he was in Boston, back when people behind the visitors' dugout spent the better part of the series heckling him, throwing things at him.

"When Mary Poppins has a bad day nobody throws tomatoes at her," he says. "When I sit down at the table with my wife and six kids I don't want them to regard me as a villain. We're in the entertainment field and when a player makes a good play people should applaud. It shouldn't make any difference whether he's for the home team or the visiting team. The best place to play was Ebbets Field. There were real fans there. When you made a good play they applauded. It didn't matter what team you played for."

"Hey Stanky," yells a kid from the grandstand, a few rows back. "You're a bum."

"I won't even turn around," Stanky says to the group of writers with him. "But that kid's only nine years old. I can tell by the voice. Now he'll go back to his father and say 'I really gave it to Stanky good' and his father will say 'good boy.'"

"Hey Stanky, you stink," yells another voice.

"He's 11. I don't even have to turn around."

"Hey Stanky," comes another voice. "It's all over now."

"See what I mean," Stanky says. "That's all right. That's part of baseball, that kid hollering like that. He's doing what he's supposed to be doing, not throwing things."

Before the game starts both Stanky and Williams meet at home plate for the ceremonial exchanging of lineup cards. Also there is plate umpire Hank Soar, a large, burly man who was once a professional football player with the New York Giants, now in his 17th season as a major league umpire. He doesn't like the recent trend in the game toward brushing back hitters, and he knows the recent history of these two clubs.

"I'm warning you right now," he tells both of them, "that if there's throwing at the hitters you'll be the first to go and the pitchers will be next. You understand that, Dick?"

Williams nods.

"How about you, Eddie. You know what I mean?"

Stanky also nods.

"Hitting batters in the head doesn't belong in the game," Soar says. "I've been reading about this knockdown stuff in the papers and I don't like it. I've been around long enough to know when a manager tells a pitcher to hit a batter, and when a batter is hit by accident. That stuff wasn't in our league in the old days. That was strictly National League stuff. But now we're getting it over here."

The pitching matchups are Gary Bell against White Sox rookie Francisco Carlos.

In the top of the second inning a slow ground ball, foul, is hit to Popowski, the third base coach. He fields it cleanly. He rolls the ball across his shoulders and throws it back to Carlos over one shoulder, tricks he learned from his days traveling with the House of David. The crowd roars. So in the bottom of the inning when a similar ground ball is hit to Gunner Resinger, the White Sox third base coach, Stanky orders him to go through some gyrations and parody Popowski before throwing the ball back to Bell. Resinger makes some contortions, then throws the ball between his legs. It lands about 10 feet away from Bell. He has to walk to retrieve it as the crowd boos. Stanky loves it.

The White Sox are leading in the seventh inning when Stanky decides Carlos has had enough. Carlos had never seen Fenway before, and when he looked out at the Green Monster in left, a sight that's brought anxiety to the stomach of many a young pitcher, it reminded him of pitching in the minors at Asheville, North Carolina, where the fence in left was only 290 feet away from home plate, and the wind always seemed to be blowing out. He blocked out the Wall, and pitched well. But now Stanky wants veteran Don McMahon, traded by the Red Sox in June. When Stanky comes out of the dugout and crosses the infield to go to the mound to relieve Carlos he's booed. Yastrzemski is on third, Scott is on second.

"Are you tired?" Stanky asks Yaz as he passes.

It's a continuation of the mind games Stanky has been trying to play with Yastrzemski ever since he called him an "all-star from the neck down" earlier in the summer. There are some people in the Red Sox organization who think the best thing that happened to the team was Stanky's denigrating Yastrzemski early in the year, that that was one of the things that brought the club closer together. Stanky yells out to Scott that he's going to knock him down the next time he has a chance. Scott yells back. Stanky loves it. He finally gets to the mound. The crowd is howling at him, screaming. It's all wonderful theater, and Stanky is a master of it. A favorite trick of his is to fuel the crowd's passions by making a lot of body motions, both to umpires and other players, creating the impression he's really jawing at them, all the while saying relatively innocuous things. On the way back to the dugout he walks over to Popowski.

"Are you tired?" he asks.

"Us Poles never get tired," deadpans Popowski.

The White Sox win 4–2, and afterward Stanky is asked if he had any hesitation in taking Carlos out.

"I'd yank my own son under the same circumstances," Stanky barks. "I was looking for a strikeout."

So much for sentiment.

Tonight Stanky asks a Boston writer if he's upset the Red Sox lost. Before the writer can answer, Stanky snaps, "A reporter is supposed to be objective. Get the facts." The next day, after being heckled again in the late innings, he counters by saying, "It looked to me that about the end of the fifth inning all those civilized fans decided to go to the concession stands and the kooks took over."

He's not in the best of spirits since the Red Sox have beaten Gary Peters, one of the aces of Stanky's staff. Peters was Rookie of the Year in 1963. Last year he led the league in earned run average. Now, along with Horlen and Tommy John, he gives the White Sox the best starters in the league. But this has not been his day. His nemesis has been Harrelson, who's knocked in four runs with a double, triple, and home run. "I've never hit for the cycle before," he says afterward, "so if I got hit I was stopping at first base. But I've always liked this park." He admits he's been lunging at the ball recently, and some extra batting practice under the tutelage of Bobby Doerr and Dalton Jones has helped him regain his stroke.

Already Harrelson is very popular with the Boston fans, has that intangible star quality. It is welcome. Not only is Harrelson supposed to replace Conigliaro's bat, the Red Sox would also love him to fill some of the emotional void that's been left by Conigliaro's absence. For Conig was more than just a right-handed slugger with a swing made for Fenway. He's the team's heartthrob, the hometown kid who made it big, the embodiment of a region's fantasies, complete with the personality to be a star. No one else on the Red Sox has that. But now there is Harrelson, the larger-than-life Hawk, with his cowboy boots and his drawl and his desire to be right in the middle of the spotlight.

After every hit the fans in right field give him a standing

ovation as he comes out to the field at the start of the inning. When he came here with the Athletics earlier in the season he always bantered good-naturedly with the crowd and they remember. He's also starting to feel more comfortable playing right field. Before the game against the White Sox he'd taken extra practice shagging balls, and for the first time he was hoping someone would hit a ball in his direction. Not like the games in New York when he'd stood in right field and hoped the ball would go somewhere else, anywhere else but at him.

"He's a good ballplayer," says Santiago, who played with Harrelson in Kansas City. "I remember him the first day he reported at Olean in the New York–Penn League. I was the leading pitcher on the team and I won six games. So we got these two new players, Harrelson and this pitcher—I forget his name right now—but the next day Robby Robertson says he's shipping me to the rookie league to make room for these new guys. You don't forget an incident like that. It was a disaster."

It's Labor Day weekend, the symbolic end of the coldest and wettest New England summer in over 100 years. Boston celebrates with a free concert on Boston Common featuring singer Judy Garland. Over 10,000 people attend. Others head for Canobie Lake Park in Salem, New Hampshire, or Revere Beach, which bills itself as only 15 minutes from Boston by MBTA. A new movie opens, *In the Heat of the Night,* starring Rod Steiger as a sheriff in a small Southern town who must contend with Sidney Poitier as his assistant. Poitier is the most recognizable black actor in the country.

Yastrzemski is closing in on 40 homers, a total only three players in Red Sox history have matched. Jimmie Foxx did it twice. Ted Williams once had 43. Dick Stuart had 42 four years ago. Stuart, now playing in Japan, recently wrote Dick Williams a note. "Give my best to Yaz on his quest for the Triple Crown," it said. "Don't forget that I had a Triple Crown too. That is, for strikeouts, for errors, and for best quotes to the press." He's probably right about the latter. At a Boston baseball dinner one winter, he was at the podium when he spotted his manager Billy Herman in the audience. "Hope you're having a good winter, Billy," he said. "Because you had a horseshit summer."

"Personally, I would like to hit 40 homers," Yastrzemski says. "I know Ted hit 43, but I'm going to go for base hits."

Haywood Sullivan, a former Red Sox catcher who's now the franchise's director of player personnel, is asked to compare Ted Williams and Yaz. "Ted was a better overall hitter, but Carl has more speed and he's certainly great in the field. I was always a great supporter of Ted's, he's one of the game's greatest, but for one season I don't see how Yastrzemski's work can be improved upon."

The adulation has its downside though. Every morning now at Yastrzemski's house in Lynnfield there are a group of kids hanging around, waiting for him to come out and give them autographs. Some ride their bikes from as far as Peabody, 12–15 miles away, to wait outside his house. After a night game his ritual is to sleep until about 11:30, since he has trouble sleeping after games, watching late-night television as he unwinds, the emotion seeping out of him. When he does get up he goes out and gives the kids autographs, or else gives them to his daughter Mary Ann to take out to them. She is seven, old enough to know that it's her father's picture in the newspaper, old enough to like the idea of being a courier between her famous father and kids who wait on her lawn for autographs.

Yastrzemski is doing a column for the *Boston Globe*, reflections on the season that are ghost-written for him, and on this Labor Day weekend he writes that he needs a live-in maid, and that if anyone cares to apply they can call LI2-1482 and ask for his secretary. He's also doing some commercials. One is for Granger pipe tobacco and it shows Yastrzemski, complete with pipe, looking like a young Sherlock Holmes.

The White Sox come back to win the next two games of the series as the Bosox only score one run. On Sunday, September 4, the Red Sox are handcuffed by left-handed sinkerballer Tommy John, who throws 23 ground-ball outs. John is 24, led the league in shutouts last year. Now he's on his way to repeating that. This puts the Red Sox one half game behind the Twins, followed by the White Sox, who are a game out, and the Tigers at a game and a half. They're all pounding furiously down the stretch like four horses who can smell the finish line.

In Washington the Red Sox lose the first game of a Labor Day doubleheader with the lowly Senators. Williams is not thrilled.

"Check the lineup, men," he says loudly, as he goes back to his office with a sandwich.

Scott looks at it, sees Siebern is penciled in at first, takes some ice out of a cup of soda he is drinking, and throws it across the room. Then he picks up some bats and knocks them against the floor. Williams sits in his office, ignoring Scott's tirade.

"I have to do something," he says. "Scott is trying to hit everything out of the park, trying to pull every pitch, and he just can't do it."

Scott blames his recent slump at the plate to the loss of Conigliaro. "A pitcher can reach back and put everything he has on a pitch only so many times. When he has to do it to Tony he can't do it so many times to the rest of us. When Tony's in there I get better pitches to hit."

Foy is also slumping and is replaced at third base by Adair. During the Chicago series Williams had been critical of Foy, especially his work in the field, and thinks that once again he's too heavy. In the *Globe*, Ray Fitzgerald writes that Foy goes after ground balls like a man with "double lumbago" and picks up slowly hit balls with all the grace of a "three-toed sloth." It's no secret Foy has been Williams' biggest disappointment. There is strong sentiment within the organization that Foy is his own worst enemy, that he refuses to stay in shape, won't work on his weaknesses, and is moody to boot. The speculation is he'll be the organization's number one trade bait over the winter. In the beginning of the year one of Foy's excuses was that he was a slow starter. He said it so often that Williams finally said, "Maybe he should wait to report each year until July."

The Sox win the next two games in Washington, Yastrzemski

getting his 37th and 38th homers. Williams had asked Yastrzemski if he wanted a day off in Washington, but Yaz declined, reasoning that a day off now wasn't going to do him any good. Instead he hit two homers. But he appreciated the offer. He and Williams had begun the spring with their relationship under a microscope, and there's no telling what would have happened if Yastrzemski had resisted the new manager and his methods, if he'd turned Williams' first couple of months into a power struggle.

The club returns home to open a nine-game stand, all against second-division clubs: New York, Kansas City, and Baltimore. It's also the start of school in Boston, the first time that some black students will be bused to achieve racial balance in the Boston public schools. They're slated to be sent into such white ethnic areas as South Boston, East Boston, and the city's North End, all parochial, working-class neighborhoods where all outsiders are viewed with distrust, not just blacks. Four hundred and fifty black elementary schoolchildren are scheduled to be bused. Only a few show up, though, since a parents group in Roxbury believes these neighborhoods are hostile to their children.

Two days later a headline in the *Boston Record-American* says, "Sox to Finish Without Tony C." Yawkey tells columnist John Gillooly the organization will do nothing to jeopardize Conigliaro's career.

Conigliaro, in turn, is in limbo.

"It's hard," he says. "I sit here and think. I think of the ballclub all the time. I watch every game on television and I want to be back there. I like to think I could help. I'm rested. I've never been so rested in my life. People want to come and watch television with me, but I don't allow anybody but my family."

Yawkey also reaffirms the notion that the franchise will never leave Boston, regardless of the resolution of the stadium issue. "Stadium or no stadium, the Red Sox won't move one inch away from Boston, so long as the decision, if any, is mine." He says again the franchise has taken some financial losses in recent years, but "the people of Boston and New England have given this team wonderful support.

I'm convinced it's the best franchise in the American League.''

He is proud of his Red Sox, whether they ultimately win or not, and proud of Yastrzemski's maturation. ''His whole mental attitude is a lot better this year. He is a much happier boy. That makes a great difference. He is confident he can do the job. Ballplayers are people, just like you and me. I suppose it's an effort to come to the ballpark every day when you're eighth, ninth, or tenth. I can understand that. It's human nature.''

This team has renewed Yawkey's passion for his Red Sox. The love was always there, similar to the love a parent feels for a child, but there'd been so much frustration, so much heartbreak, so many times he'd seen his money and good intentions come back to haunt him. Surely there'd been times in the past few years when he had to question everything. He'd as much as demonstrated that earlier in the season when he'd publicly lobbied for a new stadium, adding that the team was losing money and only a fool keeps on losing money. Now the Sox have been reborn, and so, in a sense, has he. He's even considering traveling with the team, something he hasn't done in 17 years.

On September 7, against the Yankees at Fenway, Petrocelli hits his 14th home run and Lonborg fans 10 on his way to winning his 19th. Afterward, Lonborg is in the clubhouse, standing by his locker. He says how Williams had come to the mound in the first inning and told him to stop aiming the ball.

''I thought I was struggling,'' he says. ''I didn't have good stuff. I didn't seem to be mentally up for it. You come to the park and you have to talk to yourself, get yourself ready. Then I watched TV in Mr. Yawkey's office in the afternoon and, well, I don't know. Maybe I'm just physically tired. I'm doing so many things. I went to Wilmington [a town north of Boston] with Rico to an appearance at an automobile dealership. I thought I'd just sit around the lobby for a while, but right away there were about 200 kids in line, and they just kept on coming, thousands of them. I never saw so many kids. I must have signed 5,000 autographs in eight hours. I was tired from that. And my own pep talks didn't help much."

"What do you use on yourself in these talks?"

"Oh, nothing in particular. Just anything to get fired up. Sometimes I sit there on the bench and wish someone would come and hit me to get me awake."

The writers crowd around him.

"Excuse me," Lonborg says, motioning toward the trainer's room. "I have to get the ice. We'll talk in there."

He goes into the trainer's room, puts his arm into a bucket of ice water. Buddy LeRoux tapes an ice bag to his right shoulder. Lonborg's pitching philosophy is simple. If he feels he has good stuff he challenges hitters. If not, he tries to outfox them, tries to get his first two pitches over for strikes.

"Do you ever think of the pennant?"

"No, I try not to now. I just try and think of the vacation I'm going to get when the season's over."

But as it happens the Red Sox are not the biggest sports news in Boston on this day. They've been pushed into the background by a possible scandal. Bob Cousy, the former Celtic great and one of the most popular athletes in the city's history, admits he has a close personal relationship with a known gambler, but denies any wrongdoing. His denials follow a recent *Life* magazine story titled "7 Billion for Illegal Bets and a Blight on Sports." The story claims both Cousy and Patriots quarterback Vito "Babe" Parilli frequently visit a Revere, Massachusetts, store that allegedly is a hangout for gamblers. Parilli calls the story ridiculous, while Cousy, in tears, says in a 70-minute press conference at Boston College that, yes, he is friendly with known gambler Andrew Pradella. Cousy says he first met Pradella when Pradella's son attended his summer basketball camp in New Hampshire. Cousy is in his third year as the coach at Boston College, a job he began after retiring from the Celtics.

The Sox win two out of three from the Yankees, the loss coming at the hands of Bill Monbouquette, the former Red Sox star. Detroit, Minnesota, the Red Sox, and White Sox are all still bunched at the top, and Stanky proclaims, "The walking dead is walking again," after the Chisox sweep the Tigers and Joel Horlen pitches a no-hitter. Horlen is now using sleeping pills the night before he pitches, trying to calm his nerves.

It's mid September, and Conigliaro goes to Fenway for the first time since that August night when he'd been hit in the face and everything changed. As he will write in his autobiography "Seeing It Through" three years later, he had been staying away because he didn't think he could stand being in the clubhouse and not be able to play. Some guys are standing by their lockers. Reggie Smith is sitting in front of his, smoking a cigarette. Yastrzemski is lying on the trainer's table. Scott is inspecting a pile of bats. Conigliaro comes into the room and they all seem to see him at once.

"Hey, kid," Petrocelli says.

"What do ya say, roomie?" Ryan asks.

"TC . . . TC," says Scott, slapping palms with Conigliaro.

Conigliaro is nervous. Then Williams walks out of his office. Conigliaro doesn't know what to do. He wants to ask, "Where have you been? Why didn't you come to the hospital at least once?" But he doesn't. Williams sticks out his hand. Conigliaro shakes it. They exchange pleasantries, and that's it. Williams never mentions why he's never inquired about Conigliaro, and Conigliaro loses any respect he might have still had for Williams.

Seeing Williams is the toughest part about going back to the clubhouse. He feels like an outsider. It's been his baseball home for four years, and now he feels like it belongs to someone else. He can't play. He can't help his teammates. He's just a visitor, and he knows at that moment what all injured players come to know, that you're either a part of it, or you're not. He knows he has to get out of the clubhouse, or else he's going to explode.

"I got to go now," he tells his teammates. "This headache of mine keeps coming back. I can't stay for the game, but I'll watch you on television."

He goes home and doesn't watch the game.

The next time he goes to Fenway he suits up and shags

balls in the outfield during batting practice. But every time a ball comes toward him he sees two or three of them. So he nonchalants it again, like he did with his brother Richie. He lets the ball fall at his feet, then casually throws it back to the infield. The last thing he wants is for his teammates to feel sorry for him. He tells them everything is coming along fine.

Eventually, he takes batting practice for the first time. He arrives at a deserted Fenway Park, accompanied by his brother Billy. He steps into the batting cage wearing a protective flap for the first time. He takes about a dozen swings at pitches thrown by Billy, and the results are not encouraging. He fails to make contact on some of Billy's down-the-middle tosses.

"Not good," he says. "Not good at all."

He then shags some balls in the outfield, before going back into the batting cage. He tells Billy to throw all out, and this time it's not as bad. He even hits the Wall a couple of times.

"That was better," he says afterward. "But I know I'm not ready. I want to get back into action, but I'm not going into the lineup until the sight in my eye is perfect again."

He goes to see the doctor again, is told his eye has not improved and that there's no chance he can play the rest of the year. He goes home to his apartment in Kenmore Square, a short walk from Fenway Park. He lives on the 10th floor. His apartment overlooks Fenway, and it affords him a view of right field. He stands by himself on the balcony, looking out at the ballpark and tears begin to well up. That night, he stands there again and can see Harrelson playing right field, standing on the same grass that used to be his. He sees the lights and hears the hum of the crowd and for the first time he realizes how much he loves it, loves everything about it, his teammates, the competition, the roar of the crowd, the way the ballpark smells, all of it. He realizes he'd rather play baseball than do anything else, date the prettiest girl, own his own nightclub, anything. So he stands there on this baseball night in Boston, watching Harrelson play where he used to, and once again the tears come, tears for his lost season, his future, and for his world that always seemed so simple, but now has become so vastly different.

Lonborg gets his 20th win on September 12, over the A's and Catfish Hunter. It's a game in which he helps himself with a triple to right-center that gives the Sox the go-ahead run. The word is Yawkey is going to see that he makes at least $50,000 next year, a big jump from the $16,000 he makes now.

Not that his $16,000 salary is unusual. Young players usually don't make a lot of money. The general rule is still that the only players who make big money are the stars, the ones who already have had great success. Harrelson's huge contract has changed the equation, though, for it shows how much more a player can make if he is put up for bid. It's a sneak preview of free agency.

Lonborg's success this year represents only the fourth time since World War II that a Red Sox pitcher has won 20 games. Left-hander Mel Parnell did it in '49 and '53; Monbouquette accomplished it in '63.

"Twenty wins was one of my baseball goals," Lonborg says. "I had four—the All-Star team, which I achieved this season, a no-hitter, and pitching in a World Series were the others. There's still a chance for the last two, especially the World Series."

Yes, Yastrzemski and Lonborg have been the two most dominant players, but they've had help too. Throughout the summer there's always been the sense that others will step up when needed, every night a different hero. The next game it is Stange, who goes seven good innings, and Petrocelli, who knocks in three runs.

"The Sox have attitude," writes John Hanlon in the *Providence Journal-Bulletin*. "The Yankees used to have it, but they don't anymore. The White Sox almost have it and the Detroit Tigers have it now and then. Minnesota has a lot of it. Kansas City will never have it. And this season, at long last, the Red Sox have it in spades. It is an attitude, an approach to the game of baseball, and you can't measure it as you can a batting average. It is the mark of a good team, and there never has been a big winner without it. You know it when you see it. It's the chancy play that works. It's the brave move that pays off. It is a cockiness bordering on arrogance that practically shouts 'no sweat, all of this is going to come out all right.' "

It's the middle of the month, the country is back to school. The long, hot, explosive summer is over. But its legacy remains. In Springfield, Massachusetts, the six New England governors are meeting to discuss civil unrest. Julian Bond, a young Georgia state legislator who once was denied his seat because of his strong antiwar attitudes, predicts racial warfare will become so intense that police measures will turn ghettos into concentration camps. He's considered one of the new breed of moderate black leaders who still want to work within the system for social change, but he feels he'll soon be considered too tame in this time of rising black anger. Already he's been called an Uncle Tom by more militant blacks, a sign of the pressure on black leaders to be more militant. A week earlier Martin Luther King had again blamed whites for essentially being responsible for the summer's riots. King called slums the "handiwork of a vicious system of white society," and said that, while blacks live in the slums, that doesn't make them their home any more than a prisoner makes a prison his home. It's another example of how King's anger is increasing, how his stance is becoming more militant. He calls for massive public works programs, similar to what Franklin Roosevelt did in the '30s, as a way of uplifting blacks.

Pointing up the need for dramatic action is the tension in Milwaukee where open-housing demonstrators have been protesting since the beginning of the month. They're led by the Reverend James E. Groppi, a radical parish priest from St. Boniface Roman Catholic Church, one of the few white people in the country who seem to hold persuasive power over blacks. The white establishment in Milwaukee sees Groppi as a turncoat. The city council president calls him a "priest of Jesus Christ preaching hate instead of love." Groppi is not deterred. At one point he's asked by city leaders to "cool it," to reduce the tension in Milwaukee. "The words 'cool it' are no longer in our vocabulary," he says. His church is often used for black rallies. At one is comedian Dick Gregory, who tells the congregation, "I won't tell a brick thrower not to throw a brick."

There's news on a lighter side too. The President and Lady Bird Johnson announce that their daughter, Lynda Bird, 23, will marry Navy Captain Charles Robb in December. Robb is due to go to Vietnam in February. For the past two years Lynda Bird had been dating actor George Hamilton, best known for his year-round tan and portrayal of a rich preppie in the movie *Where the Boys Are* in 1960.

And the Beatles are scheduled to leave for India this week to visit with the Maharishi Mahesh Yogi, who's said to have worked in a factory before becoming a holy man. He wears flowing white robes and beads, and has organized something he calls the Spiritual Regeneration Movement. Toward his purpose of getting everyone to meditate, he's announced a plan to prepare one trainer for every 100,000 people. The Beatles and the Maharishi met for the first time in London three weeks ago. "Brian Epstein's death has been a shock and makes the Beatles' search for inner peace all the more important," a spokesman said.

On a Saturday night the nation watches *Jackie Gleason*, *The Dating Game*, *Lawrence Welk*, *Mannix*, *My Three Sons*, and *Get Smart* on television, all programs that represent the way the country used to be, before the summer changed everything. The hot new movie is *Bonnie and Clyde* with Warren Beatty and a new actress named Faye Dunaway, who attended Boston University on Commonwealth Avenue, around the corner from Fenway Park. In Las Vegas, reclusive billionaire Howard Hughes, 61, buys $100 million worth of real estate. David McCallum, one of the stars of the hit TV series *The Man from U.N.C.L.E.*, marries in a Long Island ceremony, and the newest rage in pop music is a 47-year-old Indian named Ravi Shankar, who plays a sitar. His popularity started last year when the Beatles' George Harrison played a sitar on some Beatle records and named Shankar as his personal mentor. Harrison eventually went to India, arriving with a bushy mustache as an apparent disguise. The disguise didn't work, and soon he was mobbed by adoring fans. Now that adoration has been somehow transferred to Shankar, who finds himself mobbed by American fans and profiled in American magazines, an unlikely star.

"I love hippies," he says, "not because they are admirers of my music, but because of their philosophy, their awareness. But one thing I do not approve: the use of drugs. I learned from my guru that true enlightenment comes from within, so I don't believe in smoking or drinking."

As LBJ's popularity declines, a victim of the summer, there's increased interest in potential Republican presidential nominees. Richard Nixon, the former vice-president who lost a very close race to Kennedy in 1960 and had told reporters two years later that "you won't have Richard Nixon to kick around anymore" after losing a bid to become governor of California, is considered the front-runner. He views California governor Ronald Reagan as his chief opponent, with Michigan governor George Romney and Illinois senator Charles Percy also contenders. The party's sentimental choice is New York governor Nelson Rockefeller. A recent poll shows he'd beat Johnson if the race was held today. But he's reported to be at peace with himself, with no more presidential aspirations.

The same can't be said of the four teams fighting for the American League pennant. They all have grand aspirations. There are only 14 games remaining, and the Red Sox, Twins, and Tigers all are tied at 84-64. The White Sox are one and a half back, and Stanky warns everyone to beware. He's taken to calling his team "zombies," a reference to their having crawled out of the grave everyone had put them in. "The zombies are walking and the teams in front of us better watch out," he says dramatically. He seems like a prophet when Joel Horlen three-hits the Twins, not giving up two of the hits until the ninth.

The Orioles are in Fenway for a three-game weekend series, and on the surface it seems like a wonderful opportunity for the Red Sox, a gift from the schedule maker. The Orioles' preseason plans never materialized and they have spent the second half of the season buried in the A.L. standings. They seem a perfect opponent for a team in the middle of a pennant race. The only player they have who's still playing for anything more than pride is Frank Robinson, now fighting Yastrzemski for the batting title. Both Robinson and Yastrzemski admit they're well aware of the other's statistics, to the point that Yaz tells the pitchers to bear down on Robinson. "Which one, Frank or Brooks?" becomes the team's private joke.

But the Sox lose the first game as Morehead shows wildness and the team plays bad baseball. Williams tries to rationalize the loss, saying that they were due for a bad game like this. Even the weather is a portent of Gothic horror, mist and fog enveloping the field. Then the Sox lose the next two, stirring up old fears that in the end the Red Sox will be nothing more than beautiful losers. Harold Kaese, a *Boston Globe* columnist, writes that it's very likely they won't win, that they're just not good enough.

They've only scored five runs against the Orioles in three games, in Fenway no less. Now they have to go on the road for three series, a potential death march through Detroit, Cleveland, and Baltimore. If the Sox are going to fold, this seems the ideal opportunity. They'd had a chance to control some of their destiny here in Fenway and they didn't do it. Everyone seems on edge. In his start against the Orioles, Lonborg was visibly upset when Maglie came out of the dugout to remove him in the seventh inning, the game tied 1–1. He'd been surprised to see Maglie even come out of the dugout, never mind actually remove him from the game, and afterward he hadn't been reluctant to tell the press of his feelings. Williams countered by telling the press Lonborg appeared to be laboring, already had thrown 163 pitches, and had just hit the Orioles' Curt Blefary on an oh and two pitch. He then added, "It doesn't make any difference who the pitcher is either," for effect. But Lonborg hadn't been happy.

The Red Sox seem to have hit some imaginary wall, as if there already have been too many big games, too many must wins, too many times when they've had to reach deep into their emotional grab-bag. They're feeling the pressure of being in a pennant race for the first time, a situation that changes everything. Petrocelli, for one, feels it will be good to get out of Fenway for a while, that there is too much pressure there, that the team is collectively tight.

Williams knows this, and once again he announces there will be changes. He wants more left-handed bats in the lineup, specifically Dalton Jones' bat. He knows Jones has a history of hitting well in Tiger Stadium, the Red Sox's next stop, and is willing to take a chance with him, even though Jones hasn't started a game since Labor Day. Tartabull will go to right field, Williams proclaims, in place of the suddenly slumping Harrelson, and Russ Gibson, recalled from Pittsfield at the start of the month when the Red Sox expanded their roster, will go behind the plate. The lineup needs a spark, and Williams is not reluctant to make changes. If that means bruising delicate egos, so be it. Williams doesn't care. He didn't care back in the spring. He cares less now.

The positive news is that even with this three-game slide the Sox still are only one game out. The weekend record for the four teams in contention is only 5-7, the race still there for any of the four.

It's September 18, a Monday, and in Detroit there's no escaping the turmoil of the summer. The Red Sox traveling party is ordered not to go into the city. Their world here revolves around the hotel, Tiger Stadium, and the bus that takes them back and forth. The evidence of the riots is everywhere, visible in the gutted buildings, the streets that are blocked off, the fixed stares on people's face. It's not surprising that attendance is down at Tiger Stadium this year. Many people are still afraid to come into the city; afraid to park around Tiger Stadium. The riot, coupled with an auto workers strike, has left the city dazed, like a once-proud fighter who's taken too many good punches. Also, Detroit doesn't believe in the Tigers. They haven't won a pennant since 1945, and there is skepticism about their chances this year, even though they now have a half-game lead over the White Sox, with the Red Sox and the Twins both a game back. Still, 42,674 turn out for the first game of the series, one of the Tigers' biggest crowds of the year. There are 63 newspapermen in the press box, representing 23 different papers. Despite everything, the pennant race has captured the country's attention.

It's become the Red Sox's fate to have a pitching staff that seems held together by masking tape. Williams keeps rolling his dice, trying to mix and match and somehow have it come out all right. Tonight's starter is Jerry Stephenson, who spent the better part of the summer at Toronto. Four years ago Stephenson and Morehead, both young pitchers, started a doubleheader in D.C. Stadium against the Senators. Morehead pitched well, and stayed with the big club. Stephenson was wild in the second inning, got yanked by Johnny Pesky, and eventually was sent back to the minors.

Today, Stephenson gives the Red Sox seven tough innings. But the game is tied 4–4 going into the bottom of the eighth. Wyatt is now pitching for the Sox, and he walks Kaline. Jim Northrup proceeds to double him home, and the Sox trail 5–4, about to stare into the abyss. They've just lost three in a row to the Orioles at home. Now they're about to lose to the Tigers in what is, to date, the biggest series of the season.

The Red Sox come to bat, trailing by one in the ninth. After Mike Andrews strikes out, Yastrzemski steps to the plate. The Detroit pitcher is Fred Lasher, who hasn't thrown a home run pitch all year, either in Detroit or Triple A Toledo.

In the press box, among the media horde, is *Boston Globe* writer Ray Fitzgerald.

"Right now," he says in a loud voice, "is when an MVP should hit a home run."

The day before, Fitzgerald had written that the Red Sox needed some spark, some special happening to once again infuse their season with magic. Now—as if scripted by Hollywood—Yastrzemski, who has carried this team all summer long, is at the plate. He's in the back of the batter's box, his stance a little closed. He stares out at Lasher, hands held high in what has now become a familiar pose throughout the summer, bat cocked, waiting, as all New England waits with him. A hero who has met his moment.

Lasher throws a fastball, and Yaz swings. His hips turn, and his wrists roll, his head steady as he meets the ball. The sound of bat on ball echoes through the stadium, the ball jumping off as if propelled by rocket fuel. Yastrzemski's swing turns him around, and as he drops the bat and starts running toward first base, he looks up and sees the ball heading toward the upper deck in right field, a small white dot in the night sky. It's his 40th home run, and the entire bench bursts from the dugout to greet him at home plate. Sure enough, the MVP has come through.

But the evening's heroics aren't over.

In the top of the 10th Dalton Jones, whose bat Williams knew he needed in the lineup, is at the plate. He's already had three singles, making Williams look good. The Tiger pitcher is Mike Marshall, who'd started out in the Phillies' organization as an infielder and eventually will end up setting relief appearance records in both leagues in addition to getting a doctorate in kinesiology from Michigan State. Marshall throws. Jones hits his own home run into the upper deck in right, and the Red Sox win 6–5. It's only the 18th home run of Jones' career, and it ties the Red Sox with Minnesota and Detroit for first, with the Chisox a game and a half in back.

Jones has had four hits. It's his fourth year with the Red Sox after being signed six years ago for a reported $60,000 bonus by scout George Digby in Baton Rouge, Louisiana. The joke on the team is that his wife won't let him pick up their infant child because his hands are so bad, the supposed reason he's not an everyday player.

"Is this the best night of your season?" he's asked.

"Of my career," he says simply.

Yastrzemski is asked to recount his home run in the ninth. He was in the on-deck circle when Detroit pitcher Fred Lasher struck out Mike Andrews.

"All I thought about was watching Lasher to see how he was releasing his pitch, to see if I could pick up when he threw his fastball and when he threw his slider."

"And could you?"

"No I couldn't. I just saw that he threw Mike three fastballs. I said to myself that he's got to throw me fastballs."

Yastrzemski would like to hit three home runs, a number that would match Ted Williams' 43, but not exceed it. "I think alongside of Ted would be a great thrill."

Dick Williams is asked how big the game has been. He was at the ballpark five hours before it started; it's been a long day. "Look at it this way," he says. "We had just lost three and we were losing this game. So it had to be the biggest of the year." He pauses a beat. "Until tomorrow."

He's right, of course. Every game now is the biggest of the season. Today quickly surrenders to tomorrow. The only thing that matters is the next game.

The next night is another page from the same dog-eared script the Sox have been using recently. They're down 2–1 in the ninth after a mammoth Willie Horton home run off Lee Stange, one that caused Stange to later shrug and say, "At least he didn't get one of those dinky little things in the stands out there." Mickey Lolich, the Tigers' portly left-hander, has had the Red Sox eating out of his hand most of the night, only giving up one hit in the first six innings, and striking out three in the eighth. Then comes the ninth.

In the top of the ninth, Scott singles home the tying run after missing two bunt attempts. There are Red Sox runners on first and second. Tiger manager Mayo Smith elects to lift Lolich in favor of Earl Wilson, the former Red Sox right-hander who is the Tigers' top pitcher. Last year he was traded to the Tigers for Don Demeter, a trade that's come back to haunt the Red Sox. Wilson, who'd been the Red Sox's first black player of any significance, already has won 21 games. This is his first relief appearance of the season. Reggie Smith quickly sacrifices the two Boston base runners over to second and third. Harrelson is up. Wilson intention-ally walks him, loading the bases. Petrocelli is the sched-uled batter. Williams pinch-hits Norm Siebern for Petrocelli. He wants Wilson to throw against a left-handed bat. Wilson's first pitch bounces to the backstop and Yastrzemski scores from third. After Siebern walks, Russ Gibson follows with a hit. The Sox are up 4–2.

In the bottom of the inning Santiago puts two men on base, and Williams brings in rookie left-hander Bill Landis to replace him. Landis has not pitched since the end of August, has only thrown 20 innings all year. Once again, Williams is playing the percentages, wanting a left-hander to face veteran slugger Eddie Mathews, a left-handed hitter. Mathews is 36, had begun his career back in the early '50s in the last year of the Boston Braves. He hit 25 home runs in his rookie season, and hit 190 in his first five seasons, a feat which at age 25 had him far ahead of Babe Ruth's pace. Eventually, he went on to become the third baseman of his generation, playing for the Braves in three different cities. He was let go by the Braves last fall, and was picked up by the Houston Astros before coming over to the Tigers in July to give them a boost down the stretch.

Landis has only seen Mathews once before in his life, and that was when he was 14 and his Boy Scout troop from California had come east to visit Valley Forge. One day he took a train into Philadelphia to see his idol, Warren Spahn, then pitching for the Milwaukee Braves, go against the Phillies. That day Mathews had hit a home run off Robin Roberts. Now it's 11 years later, and Landis is pitching against him in the most important moment of his career. Behind Landis is a makeshift infield, Scott at third, Andrews at short, Jones at second, Siebern at first. It's not a group to help a young pitcher's confidence.

Dick Williams comes out to the mound to visit Landis, tries to calm him down.

"Do you know what that oblong thing is right there?" he asks, pointing to the ground.

"That's the rubber," Landis says.

Williams thinks he's all right.

He is. He strikes out Mathews. Kaline, who's been on a tear in September, is due up, so Williams lifts Landis in favor of veteran Gary Bell. Kaline hits a screeching line drive that Reggie Smith runs down in center to end the game. Again, the entire Red Sox dugout runs out on the field in celebration as if the pennant had been won. Bell, whom his teammates call "Ding Dong" and who always seems to be quick with a quip, says dryly, "Oh well, tomorrow it will look like a pop-up."

The Red Sox, who just two days ago had lost three straight to the Orioles at home and seemed flatter than some old flapjack, have now won two on the road in Detroit. They are back tied with the Twins for first. Chicago is a half game out. The Tigers are one back.

Gibson is particularly happy. Howard's arrival in early August had made him expendable, and he'd been sent down to Pittsfield shortly afterward. He'd been recalled earlier in the month when the minor league season ended and the major league rosters were expanded. So this is his first real contribution in a while. "I was really under the gun," he says. "I haven't done much catching." In fact, nobody seemed to know he was around. "Then Dick Williams told me Sunday I was catching Monday night. This game was the biggest of my life."

He's playing because Howard is not hitting. No matter that Howard has had the kind of career that a Dick Williams could only dream of, or that he arrived in Boston with a résumé no one else on the club could match. Williams doesn't care about any of that. Howard can get in Williams' doghouse too.

The team leaves Detroit after the game and flies to Cleveland. They arrive at their hotel at 2:30 in the morning, play the next night. Only this time there's no large crowd, no festive atmosphere. Once the Indians were one of the American League's glamour franchises, back when the pitching staff had names like Feller, Lemon, Wynn, and Garcia, and the Indians were setting attendance records at Municipal Stadium. One day in 1954, the last year the Indians won the pennant, they put over 84,000 people in the stadium, the largest crowd in baseball history. But ever since general manager Frank Lane sent hero Rocky Colavito to the Tigers for Harvey Kuenn eight years ago, the Indians have suffered through hard times. Tonight, less than 7,000 people rattle around in the huge stadium. Yaz gets four hits, including a home run off Sam McDowell, the left-handed fastballer who is one of the most dominating pitchers in the league. The Sox again win it in the ninth inning.

The magic is back.

The only down note is that Lonborg doesn't have his good fastball, and appears tired. It's the third time he's failed to get his 21st victory. Already he's pitched 74 more innings than he did a year ago, and when he reached for the fastball it wasn't there. One of the big hits off him is by Tony Horton, who reports that though he's happy with the Indians, he's rooting for the Red Sox, has no resentment because they traded him.

The next afternoon Williams, Yastrzemski, and Lonborg go with broadcaster Ken Coleman to a meeting of the Wahoo Club, the Indians' booster club. Coleman, who used to broadcast the Indians' games, uses the opportunity to illustrate the difference between the fan interest in Cleveland and Boston, telling the story of the man who held up traffic on the busy Callahan Tunnel because he wanted to hear what Yastrzemski did before he went into the tunnel and lost radio reception. He also tells them of a South Boston man who tried to give the police the time of a nearby crime by using an incident in a Red Sox game as a benchmark.

Yastrzemski tells the group that the biggest difference in him is his ability to pull the ball, that he never felt he was strong enough to pull the outside pitch before, and that forced him to adopt two different hitting styles. In Fenway he would try to hit the ball to left field, in order to take advantage of the Wall. On the road he would try to pull. Now he tries to pull everything.

He also has a humorous interplay with Lonborg, the roots of which go back to Yaz's old habit of not turning around when a home run goes over his head in left field. Unlike other outfielders, who run back to the fence creating the feeling, at least for a few seconds, that the ball might be catchable, Yaz is infamous for never turning around. Many pitchers think this shows them up. "You could at least look like you could catch the ball," Lonborg says, a reference to a home run by Max Alvis.

"I might have if they moved the stadium back a 100 yards," Yastrzemski quips.

The Sox also come back to win the next night in a rain-delayed game that takes four hours to play. They then head off to Baltimore as a considerably looser team, some of the pressure off. Petrocelli was right. Getting out of Fenway and away from the large crowds has helped. He and Ryan sing in the back of the bus. There are Polish jokes aimed at Yaz and Popowski. Nothing makes a team happier than winning, and where just a few days ago the Red Sox had seemed to be as gone as last week's hit record, once again they've found another life.

While the Red Sox have been on the road in Detroit and Cleveland, in the middle of the baseball spotlight, there has been another drama taking place back in Fenway Park. It's the ongoing struggle of Tony Conigliaro to come back from his severe injury of the month before. Even though repeated trips to doctors and numerous tests have shown he still has a blind spot in his left eye, he clings to the faint hope he can return—ride out of the dugout on a white horse one day and win the pennant for the hometown team. On this morning he goes to Fenway, knowing the clubhouse boys will be there. Even if the team is on the road, they are there every day, doing chores, and sometimes working out with Yawkey.

One of the boys is Keith Rosenfeld. He's 18, a shade under five foot five, an owlish kid with horn-rimmed glasses who's been a Red Sox batboy since he was 15. He is from Quincy, and got the job because his father is a Quincy politician and knows someone in the Red Sox organization. To get the job Keith told the Red Sox he was 16, and he takes it very seriously. He loves to play pepper with Yawkey and considers him a Southern gentleman. It bothers him whenever someone denigrates Yawkey, or chastizes the Red Sox for being the last team in baseball to integrate, because "Mr. Yawkey doesn't have a prejudiced bone in his body and with a name like Rosenfeld you know something about prejudice."

He's old enough to realize that many of the players are

not very worldly, that they read the sports section of the newspapers and little else. He hardly ever sees anyone reading a book, with the exception of Lonborg, whom he spied one day reading a copy of *Bury My Heart at Wounded Knee*. He likes all the players, although he feels a little tension around Williams because he knows Williams would love to have his eleven-year-old son, Ricky, be a batboy, and that might one day affect his job. Williams already has brought Ricky along on some trips, and Rosenfeld can see the writing on the wall. But he is probably most friendly with Yastrzemski. He even drives Yaz's Thunderbird around when the Red Sox are on the road, the deal being that he gets the use of the car as long as he picks Yaz up at Logan when the Red Sox return home. And on the couple of trips he takes with the team every year Yaz always includes him in things, once even taking him to the beach with him in Los Angeles.

Since Keith does take his job seriously, he's eager to oblige Conigliaro when he asks him to throw some batting practice. The park is empty, just a few people at work cleaning the grandstand. Conigliaro is nervous, feeling the same anxiety he used to feel before a game. Rosenfeld throws some pitches. Conigliaro hits them weakly, and can't tell whether an outside pitch is a ball or a strike. He tries hitting with one eye closed. He tries concentrating on the ball until it hits his bat, overly concentrating. He tries everything he can think of. And still he can't hit the tosses of a 120-pound batboy with any real authority. In four major league seasons he has hit 104 home runs, and now he can't hit anything hard, even on a still morning in Fenway Park, surrounded by thousands of empty seats.

"Memorial Stadium?" blares a newspaper headline. "Will It Be a Burial Ground for the Red Sox?"

Before the first game of the series starts Oriole manager Hank Bauer is standing in Memorial Stadium, looking at the media crowd around Dick Williams. "That was what I was doing a year ago," he says somewhat wistfully. "We won and everyone wanted to talk to me. It's something I had to do. I didn't mind it much. I wish I was doing it now."

Williams is talking about the differences between managing in the majors and in the minors. He believes the majors is easier, and there are three reasons why: There are more players to maneuver with; you're able to use your relief pitchers earlier, because you have more of them, and they're better; and there are more coaches to help you.

The Sox are scheduled to play a doubleheader, and in the first they lose 10–0 in one of those inexplicable games that don't seem to make any sense. They come back to win in the nightcap, though, as Williams once again changes his lineup, this time emptying his doghouse and going back to Howard, Harrelson, and Foy. Santiago, who'd been the pitcher of record in the two Detroit victories, coming out of the bullpen both times, starts and pitches a complete game this time. It is a welcome tonic to a beleaguered pitching staff, and the well-liked Santiago is ecstatic.

"It's my first great big game," he says, "but I was in a pennant race before. In Puerto Rico, in 1960, we won the championship, then we went to Venezuela for the Caribbean World Series. Jerry Adair and Roberto Clemente were on that team with me."

Although he's Puerto Rican, Santiago speaks perfect English. Not that he considers such proficiency integral to being a major league pitcher. "It doesn't make any difference how you do in your speech if your fastball doesn't get them out."

He says he's the fourth most popular player in Puerto Rico, behind Roberto Clemente, Orlando Cepeda, and Juan Pizzaro, but "If I win a few more games like this I'll move up."

The other player who's had a big game is Foy, and maybe no one needs it more. He's in the lineup because Andrews has a sore elbow, and Adair has been moved to second to replace him. Foy has had three hits. "I was making errors in the field on easy plays," he says. "I'd lost my confidence and I was saying to myself, 'I hope they don't hit the ball to me.' But now I got my confidence back. I worked hard in practice with Bobby Doerr hitting at me, and now I'm ready to play again."

Foy admits he's spent much of the past few weeks brooding because he's been in and out of the lineup, mostly out. "I was lackadaisical and so many strange things happened. A couple of easy balls went under my glove, strange things. And I don't like to pinch-hit. I just don't have an idea when I'm a pinch hitter. I'm lost up there."

The Sox are back on the roller coaster the next afternoon, dropping a 7–5 game to the Birds. The only bright spot is Yaz's 42nd homer. The loss drops them into third place, a half game behind the Twins, and only a percentage point behind the Tigers. The White Sox are one half game behind them. What's so tough about baseball is the emotional strain it puts on everyone. The season is so long, there are so many games, so many highs and lows, that a team must be resilient, able to bounce back emotionally as well as physically.

Even now, in the middle of a pennant race in the dying days of the season, the Red Sox still seem as if they're doing it with mirrors. They have stretches when they don't hit. Conigliaro's absence has taken a large portion of their power out of the lineup, increasing the pressure on Yastrzemski. The pitching staff, suspect all year, is tired. Yet, every time they seem on the verge of collapsing, something happens. It's been that way the entire season, and it remains that way, symbolized by Yastrzemski's dramatic home run in Detroit.

Then there is Williams, who doesn't seem to be able to make a bad move. In Detroit he put Jones in the lineup and he hit a game-winning home run. He put Foy back into the lineup in Baltimore and he responded with three hits. He keeps juggling a pitching staff that's both thin and tired. He keeps falling out of trees and landing on his feet.

Harrelson remembers one unique moment. The Sox had lost a close game, one in which Harrelson had missed a cutoff man, an error that eventually allowed the runner to score. Afterward, he sat in front of his locker, tears in his eyes. Everyone else was in front of their lockers too, the room silent, funereal. Unlike years past when losing was discarded as easily as a uniform, now it seemed to stay in the clubhouse like some foul odor. Every game was so important each error seemed to stand out in bas relief, and now Harrelson was thinking he might have just lost the pennant. He sat there staring, alone in his grief, when he heard cleats on the floor, the only sound in the quiet of the room, and he knew it was Williams. The cleats seemed to be coming in his direction and he dreaded the sound. Dreaded the thought of Williams chastizing him in front of his teammates. He was feeling too fragile. He had arrived knowing he was supposed to fill Conigliaro's shoes, not only displaying his power at the plate, but also his star quality, and he was being paid big money to do it. But he'd been forced to play right field when it wasn't his natural position, and there were times when he felt scared. Not that he's alone in this. Sometimes he looked around the room at his teammates and knew many of them felt scared too. For so many of them this was the first time: the pressure of a pennant race, the pressure of each inning being important, complete with a manager who keeps pushing. And now those cleats were coming toward him, ominous sounds against the floor, getting closer.

Williams stopped near Harrelson, but instead of addressing him, he took a beer from a nearby cooler, opened it, took a long swallow, then said in a voice brimming with confidence, "Fuck it, it's just another game. We'll get them tomorrow."

"I think he won us over right there," says Harrelson. "It was a very significant victory he gained with us then."

Of course, the money involved adds to the pressure. The team that wins the pennant gets $10,000 a man, and that's more money than some of the marginal players make in a season. On the blackboard in the visitors' locker room in Baltimore is scribbled "$10,000." On this Sunday, the last Red Sox road game of this long season, Lonborg writes $10,000 on the pocket of his glove. He's still seeking his 21st victory, and the Sox stake him to a 7–0 lead as Jones, Adair, and Scott all come up with four hits. Lonborg throws six innings of shutout ball and Williams pulls him, so he can be rested for the final week of the season. The Sox have finished the road part of their schedule at 43-38, the first time they've been over .500 on the road in 11 years.

The trip that many thought would end the Red Sox season has been a success. The Sox won both games in Detroit, both games in Cleveland, and have earned a split of the four-game series here in Baltimore. They're now tied for first with Minnesota.

But it hasn't been easy. Nor has it relieved the pressure. Williams isn't happy with his bullpen. He's not very happy with Andrews, whom he didn't play today because of some defensive lapses the day before. Once again he has Foy on the bench in favor of Jones. He's decided to go with Lonborg, Bell, and Santiago as his starters for the remaining four games, Bell and Lonborg going against the Indians on Tuesday and Wednesday, and probably Santiago on Saturday against the Twins. That would leave him with Lonborg on Sunday. One writer asks him if he regretted his decision to take Lonborg out of the game after six innings with a 7–0 lead, especially since the Orioles then scored seven runs, before the Sox eventually won 11–7.

"I know I put myself on the hook when I did that," he says, "but, hell, I put myself on the hook when I took this job."

He's sitting in his office in the visitors' clubhouse, tongue now firmly in cheek. Around him are a group of New England writers who've been on the road trip since Detroit, the biggest press contingent to travel with the Red Sox in years.

"This has to be frustrating for you Boston writers," he says. "You've had to write too many nice things about the Red Sox and there have been too few opportunities to knock."

There is some mail in front of him. "You're a choker," one letter says. "Your pitching staff is gutless," says another. "Unless you get Adair in the lineup you won't win," says a third.

He picks up another one.

"Thank you for a wonderful year," it says. "God bless you."

"Who wrote that one?" he's asked.

Williams doesn't miss a beat.

"Why, my wife and kids, of course," he says.

The only bad news is that Bill Landis left today for a six-month army stint in Fort Polk, Louisiana. His season is over. His highlight has been the strikeout of Mathews, and it's not to be underestimated. In this year when everything counts, everything starts carrying the same weight, the daily greatness of Yaz, Tartabull's throw that cut down Berry in Chicago, Landis' striking out Mathews. All depend on the other; all feed off the other. The small moments as well as the big ones. Without all of them, the season already would be over.

Now there are only four games left: two with Cleveland, two with the Twins over the weekend—both series at home in Fenway Park, where this incredible Red Sox team, which began the season as a 100-to-one shot, returns for four games that will determine the pennant.

Boston	90-68	.570	—
Minnesota	90-68	.570	—
Chicago	89-68	.567	½
Detroit	88-69	.561	1½

It is Tuesday, September 26, a couple of hours before the Red Sox are to play the Cleveland Indians. The radio is on in the clubhouse. It's tuned to a rock station, and the song is a haunting ballad set in Mississippi about someone named Billy Joe McAlister who one day goes up to someplace called Choctaw Ridge and mysteriously jumps off the Tallahachee Bridge. It's sung by Bobbi Gentry. It's called "Ode to Billy Joe," and it's the number one song in the country. Some of the players are in Buddy LeRoux's training room. Harrelson is looking through his mail. He gets nearly 15 to 20 letters a week from soldiers in Vietnam, guys who are rooting for the Red Sox, and they always make him feel a little strange, not quite guilty, because that's the wrong word, but somehow more serious. Despite his swinging image, he really is a bit of a loner, possessing a reflective side that usually gets overwhelmed by the force of his personality.

Nearby is Scott. He's talking to a sportswriter. Lost in the hubbub of the pennant race is Scott's quietly garnering the fourth best batting average in the American League. He's now hitting .307.

"I'm satisfied with the season I've had so far and now we just have to win," says Scott, his gold teeth visible as he talks. "Last year they would pitch me under my chin, and then throw it outside on the corner. And when the ball was low I was going for it. Now, for the most part, I've learned to lay off those pitches. When I first broke in they fed me nothing but fastballs and I learned to handle them. That's why I had such a good first half last year. Then they started me on a diet of breaking balls, and it got me. I was swinging at too many bad balls. In the winter league I tried to learn my strike zone. Everyone tells me to let the pitch come to me and I'm trying to learn that. I know I'm a better hitter than the .245 I hit last year. Nobody can hit balls in the dirt. They were practically bouncing up at me and I was swinging at them. None of that now."

Scott has also survived a year with Dick Williams and that hasn't been easy either. Scott is a fragile personality, one who needs constant reassurance, and that isn't Williams' strength.

Williams isn't about to change, of course. It's doubtful the players would really want him to. After all, he has them in the thick of things in the last week of the season. People around the league are saying that if the Sox hadn't lost Conigliaro they would have won by four or five games. Williams believes this too, but he's also been around baseball long enough to know it's irrelevant. You play with what you're dealt. All year he's managed as if he's had a game plan written by the baseball gods, and now he's here in sight of the finish line, just needing one more push.

As do all of the three other teams still in contention. All have had their chances; all have squandered them. The Twins have played all year using a form of cruise control, as though they believe that all they have to do is step on the gas whenever they desire and win. They might be right. After their slow start, one that got Sam Mele fired, they've fought themselves back to the middle of the pennant race. A couple of weeks earlier reliever Al Worthington had said their World Series experience two years earlier would be the difference in the final days, that when the race got to the wire the intangibles would count. The Tigers have lost three games in the ninth inning within a week, each one like a body blow to manager Mayo Smith. They've also lost Denny McLain to the injured list—a toe dislocation supposedly caused by getting off the couch in his living room when his foot was asleep. It's been that kind of year for Detroit: Kaline out for a while when he broke his hand smashing a water cooler, now McLain getting hurt on a couch.

"Why did I get back into managing?" laments Smith, who'd managed the Phillies and Reds in the '50s and returned this year. "It's a disease, you know. Once you get hooked it's addictive, almost impossible to stop the craving. Maybe I should form Managers Anonymous."

Smith also tells this story about Stanky: "Let me tell you what happened when we scored seven runs in the ninth to beat his White Sox. I went upstairs in Comiskey Park to watch the finals of a golf match on TV and someone came in to tell me of one of the strangest sights he's ever seen. Seems the ballpark was empty when Stanky comes out of the runway in full uniform with a dog on a leash. He walked out to center field and he walked back. Why? How should I know? But anyone who knows Eddie pays no attention to him. He enjoys intimidating people. He's a great little agitator and a wonderful actor. If he were in Hollywood he'd get an Oscar every day."

Stanky also probably has the best chance of sneaking the pennant, with two games with Kansas City, three with Washington. Just like the Brat, the thinking goes, lucky enough to finish the season with five games against two bad teams that are impatient to go home.

The Red Sox–Indians is an afternoon game. Gary Bell against the Indians' Luis Tiant, he of the showmanship and the twisting, twirling motion. He inherited the showmanship from his father, one of the stars of the old Negro Leagues, one of the best and most popular pitchers in Cuba. The senior Tiant was a junkball pitcher with a strange, herky-jerky motion. His son picked up all his moves. Luis will eventually become one of the most popular players in the club's history, his omnipresent cigar one of the enduring symbols of the mid '70s. Now, in his fourth season in the majors, he possesses the same traits future Red Sox fans will find so endearing.

When the Indians score two runs off Bell in the second inning, Fenway Park suddenly becomes as quiet as inside the old North Church. By the seventh, with the Sox down 6–0, the suspense is gone. Bell is gone after four innings, outpitched by Tiant, who twists and turns and strikes out eight Red Sox, in command the entire afternoon. Strangely, there are only about 16,000 fans in the park, and right from the beginning it seems like bad karma. The final score is 6–3. The only bright spot is Yastrzemski's 43rd homer in the bottom of the seventh. It ties him with Ted Williams.

Afterward, Dick Williams sits in his office in his undershirt, alternately sipping a beer and smoking a cigarette. He's outwardly calm. The radio in the clubhouse is announcing that the Twins have won.

"We need help," he says. "We got a shot at Minnesota, but we have to get help from either Kansas City or Washington. It doesn't look good, but we've battled back before and we can battle back again."

Bell is getting ready to leave the clubhouse. He is wearing a burgundy turtleneck underneath a blue double-breasted sweater. He is carrying a box.

"I got a bomb in the box," he says. "I've got it timed for 16 seconds after I leave here and I'm going to blow off my head."

Yastrzemski is surrounded by writers, as he's been the past month. He is going to have a quiet celebration at home in honor of his 43rd home run. He'll play with his son, Michael, and his dog, Shag, for a while, then barbecue a couple of steaks and drink some wine. Beaujolais.

"It's expensive," he says. "I only use it for special occasions. It's a little celebration when it could have been a big celebration."

Seconds later the radio reports Killebrew has just hit his second home run of the game, his 43rd.

"That ends the celebration," says Yaz.

Somehow it seems fitting.

Making the day worse is that both the Twins and Tigers win, Minnesota over California 7–3, and Detroit edging New York 1–0.

Minnesota	91-68	.572	—
Chicago	89-68	.567	1
Boston	90-69	.566	1
Detroit	89-69	.563	1½

Lonborg is the Red Sox pitcher the next afternoon, and he has to win, even if he's only pitching on two days' rest. He must atone for the day before and a lousy Bell performance that got the Sox in a hole early. He must keep the Indian bats silent in hopes the Sox eventually can get to Cleveland starter Sonny Siebert. The Sox are running out of tomorrows. Conigliaro is on the bench for the first time, in uniform and wearing dark glasses. Everyone hopes it's a good luck charm. Conigliaro doesn't want to talk about his injury. There have been too many questions already. He parries them, changes the conversation away from his eye. He says he's taken up golf. "I can see the golf ball all right. It's smaller than a baseball, but it's sitting there."

But after a scoreless first, Lonborg gives up four runs in the second and the Sox are down early. They never recover. Eventually they squander some chances, and get beat 6–0.

Afterward, the clubhouse is doom-laden. Lonborg is in a rage. All season he has come through, been the stopper, and now, in the biggest game of the season, he's failed. He's mad at himself, mad at the world. Yastrzemski quickly leaves.

The season seems over. The Sox had come home for two games against the Indians and not only have they lost both, the two games weren't even close. Both Bell and Lonborg fell behind early. The bats were silent. They had their chance, and now it appears it's over, the Impossible Dream dying on a Wednesday afternoon in late September at the hands of the Cleveland Indians of all people. Wasn't this just like the Red Sox? Wasn't this just like '48 and '49 all over again, to be so close only to see it all go slip-sliding away at the end. On this afternoon, in the last week of the season, it all seems so.

The players certainly think so. Yastrzemski and Lonborg thank each other for a great season. Others do the same thing. Yastrzemski is already starting to think what the club has to do next year to be able to win the whole thing.

"We just played poorly," Williams says. "As poorly as we've played all season."

"Why?"

"That's all I can say."

Immediately after the game the writers hadn't been able to find him, because he's been hiding, having a sandwich. Now he's back in his office, a scene similar to the day before, trying to come up with answers when there really are none. All year he's whipped and cajoled, pleaded and pushed, and now it's the last week and there's nothing more to say, nothing more to do. It's all been said, and as he sits here in this small office it's as if he knows this, knows that in the end even someone who has prided himself all year on being in control now has very little. So he is not angry, not upset.

"They're probably pressing," he finally admits. "They've been so close all year and it's near the end."

"What did you think of the fans booing a team that was a 100-to-one shot?"

He shrugs.

"Well, we didn't play too well and I don't expect them to applaud, do you? I'd say this was as poorly as we've played all year."

Williams says he's not sure who will pitch the last two games, but that Lonborg will pitch one of them.

Over in the visiting clubhouse Indian manager Joe Adcock says the Red Sox's only problem is pressure. "When you've got a chance to win a pennant that's pressure. Once you've gone through it it's easier the next time. I'd be lying if I said I didn't see it. They're the same ballclub, but they're different."

* * *

And then, almost miraculously, the Red Sox have another life.

The Sox certainly are feeling the pressure of this long, grueling pennant race. So are the other contenders. The Twins lose to the Angels 5–1, as Dean Chance gets knocked out after trying to pitch on only two days' rest, just as Lonborg had done. The White Sox are scheduled to play a doubleheader against the A's in Kansas City. Peters and Horlen, their two aces, are scheduled to pitch.

Williams tries to get the game on the radio in his apartment in Peabody, but it's full of static. So he takes a six-pack of beer and goes and sits in his car in the parking lot. The reception is better, and he sits by himself in the car, listening to these faraway games coming through his dashboard shrouded in static, these distant games that now mean so much. The White Sox lose the first game, then they lose the second. All the while Williams sits in his darkened car, sipping his beer.

All year the White Sox's Achilles heel has been their lack of offense, a deficiency they've tried to mask with pitching, defense, speed, and Stanky's presence. Today, they couldn't mask it anymore, only getting seven hits in the two games. After the second loss Stanky stalks through the clubhouse for 10 minutes, unapproachable. Then he sits at the end of a table and starts eating potato chips. A group of sportswriters stand in front of him. Finally, one of them asks Stanky about his pitching rotation for the rest of the series.

"It's been posted for a week, where were you?" he asks. "How old are you? Twenty?"

A writer cautiously asks if his players might have tightened up a bit.

"How many games have you seen us play?" Stanky asks belligerently. "What did you say your name is? Where were you born?"

"Do you think you have a chance?" he's asked.

"Do I think we have a chance? How do I answer that one? I've been in baseball 30 years. I've seen seven runs in the last of the ninth. I've seen a winning streak of 10. I've seen us in first place, and I've seen us in sixth place. Why, I was drowning one time and a newspaperman threw me an anchor. Can you imagine that?''

He names John, Peters, and Horlen to face the Senators. They are his three aces. "All we can do is win three straight and pray," he says.

The next day, back in the clubhouse at Fenway, Yastrzemski proclaims the Red Sox the luckiest team in America. "I thought we were gone. Dead. Not only dead. Buried.''

He is part of an informal workout that includes only a few players. Most of the players stay away from the park. There has been too much baseball, too much drama, too much pressure, and the team welcomes the day's respite. Williams is huddled in his office with his coaches. It's Thursday, the 28th of September, and there are two off-days before the Twins come to town for the weekend. The standings now look like this:

Minnesota	91-69	.569	—
Detroit	89-69	.563	1
Boston	90-70	.563	1
Chicago	89-70	.561	1½

The next day, Friday, a full workout is scheduled, but it rains, and the players hang around the clubhouse killing time, waiting. The rain also causes the Tigers to get rained out in Detroit, a fact that will be important over the weekend. Williams announces his lineup for Saturday. It has Adair at third base instead of Foy, and Gibson as the catcher instead of Howard. Santiago will be the pitcher, Bell will be the first man out of the bullpen. Williams has selected Santiago for three reasons: He's pitched well the past couple of weeks, and he's well rested, and both Bell and Lonborg failed this past week against the Indians. It's a controversial decision, for what good is a rested Lonborg on Sunday if the Red Sox don't win Saturday?

But the big news is that the White Sox have lost 1–0 to the Washington Senators in Chicago, eliminating them from the pennant race. Once again the White Sox have not hit

This lack of offense had been their demise in Kansas City when they'd lost the doubleheader. Now it's eliminated them. Stanky is in tears in the clubhouse.

"I don't want any flowers when I go to the mortuary," he says. "I could chase all you newspaper guys out of here and be justified. We're out of it now, and Detroit and Minnesota and Boston feel relieved. The laughingstock of the American League is no longer a contender. It's true, but for 150 games these guys made a joke out of it and I enjoyed every minute of it. All year long the elephants feared the mice. Well they can have it all to themselves with a sigh of relief. We're out of it. And don't ask me who I want to win it now. I don't care. And when they play the World Series I guess I'm supposed to root for the American League team. I could care less who wins it. I'll be at the Instructional League.

"There's only one thing I wanted. I wanted to hang in until the final day. To make every one of them sweat until the final minute. I told the boys how proud I am of all of them. I told them they will go back to their hometowns proud, and with their heads high. We've had some tough losses the last two weeks. Most of you know I'm not a rah-rah manager. I'm not a Knute Rockne guy. But we've had a helluva run and I'm proud of that. It's just too bad my guys couldn't play in a World Series. I played in three of them and I would have traded all of them to see these guys play in one."

With that, he walks away, the tears streaming down his face.

The Brat's season is over.

It has all come down to these last two games, all the road trips, all the weekend series and night games, all the plane rides and living out of suitcases and other innumerable day-to-day things that come with being a major league ballplayer; all the tumult and shouting, and Yaz's great year and Williams' doghouse; all of it. It has all been reduced to these two baseball games to be played at Fenway Park in Boston, between the Boston Red Sox and the Minnesota Twins, on these Saturday and Sunday afternoons, September

30 and October 1. The Red Sox have to win the two games to have a chance for the pennant, and they need Detroit to lose two out of their four games with the California Angels.

Everyone concedes the Twins have the best talent in the league. They already have beaten the Red Sox 11 out of the 16 times they've played this year. They have two great pitchers in Jim Kaat and Dean Chance. They have the home run power of Killebrew and Bob Allison. Killebrew is the premier home run hitter in the game, the onetime bonus baby from Idaho who, at 31, already has 379 career home runs and is ahead of Babe Ruth's pace. Allison, the American League Rookie of the Year in 1959 when he hit 30 home runs, is a big, strong right-handed hitter.

They also have several Latins, are an organization that realized early that south of the border is a brave new frontier of talent. One is 27-year-old Tony Oliva, the Cuban who won the batting title his first two full years in the league, in '64 and '65. Another is rookie Carew, who, although he grew up in New York, was born in Panama. Soon he will be named the league's Rookie of the Year. There is Cesar Tovar, a five foot nine Venezuelan who has played both the outfield and three infield positions this year, and next year will play all nine positions in a game. Then there is shortstop Zoilo Versalles, the league's MVP two years ago. He is 26, and grew up dirt-poor in Havana, living in one room with his brother, mother, and stepfather. He quit school in the second grade because everyone else in the family was working and someone was needed to put the beans and rice on the stove. He learned to play baseball in his bare feet, because when you were poor and growing up in Havana you saved your shoes for church on Sunday. By the time he was 15 he was playing semipro in Cuba, in the same league with men. One day his mother took him to the Pan-American Building in Havana to see a scout for the Washington Senators named Joe Cambria, known as "Papa Joe," whose beat was Cuba. Versalles signed a contract, one which amounted to little more than a pittance.

"Bonus?" he laughs. "Sure we all get bonus. You know the bonus we get? Carfare, that's the bonus. Everybody knows us [Latins]. They know we have the poverty. We have the hunger. All we want is to play ball. So no bonus. Latin boys never get no bonus. I don't like this thing but I don't tell you for complaint. I tell you so that you will know the way it is.''

Three years later he was in the major leagues with the Senators. Two years later the team moved to Minnesota and became the Twins. Versalles had his problems early. He was showy, excitable, adrift in a strange culture. In 1961 he went AWOL for a while, hiding in his room, complaining of stomach trouble, unwilling to play. The bad rap increased, a perception growing that Versalles was trouble. Then two years ago, before the season, he had a talk with Twins coach Billy Martin, the former Yankee second baseman. Martin told Versalles he could be great, that he had the ability to be the league MVP. Versalles thought he was kidding. The seeds had been planted, though, and with Martin's constant urging, Versalles responded with the best year of his career. Afterward, when he was named the league's MVP, he was the first Latin player to be so honored.

Taking the mound September 30 for the Red Sox is José Santiago. He's nervous. Last night he'd taken two sleeping pills, but they hadn't done a lot of good. He's never pitched in a game of this magnitude. Yesterday he said pressure didn't bother him. That was yesterday. Those were just words. Now he has the ball in his hand and he is understandably nervous.

He quickly gets in trouble. Versalles opens the game with a single. After Tovar flies out, Santiago pitches too carefully to Killebrew and walks him. Oliva follows with a single to right that scores Versalles and the Sox are quickly down a run. Is this going to be a repeat of the two Cleveland games, the Sox getting behind early, climbing into a hole they spend the rest of the afternoon trying to get out of? Allison follows with another single, loading the bases. Still, Santiago is not worried. He's nervous, but knows he has good stuff today. He tries to calm himself down. He tells himself he has to get the ball lower. It works. He gets Carew on a soft liner. He doesn't know it, but Williams has already decided that if Santiago walks Uhlaender he's gone. Williams knows that if Santiago self-destructs he'll never be allowed to forget it, will be second-guessed forever for selecting Santiago to pitch. He then gets Ted Uhlaender after falling behind three and one.

Santiago's counterpart is the big, raw-boned left-hander Jim Kaat. Last year he won 25 games, was named the best pitcher in the American League by the *Sporting News*. Throughout this month he's been the Twins' hottest pitcher, and he starts the game the same way. In the third inning he's breezing along comfortably, pitching shutout ball, silencing the Fenway crowd, already having struck out four, when he hears something pop in his left elbow. He doesn't know what it is. Only that it's serious, and it scares him. He motions to the Minnesota dugout. Twins manager Cal Ermer comes out to the mound. He has no choice but to take Kaat out, and as Kaat walks dejectedly across the green infield grass toward the dugout, he's replaced by Jim Perry, older brother of Gaylord, who pitches for the San Francisco Giants. Perry is 31, and so far in his career has alternated between starting and the bullpen. Three years from now he will be the Cy Young winner in the American League, but now he's the Twins' Man Friday, called on to do a little bit of everything.

Perry breezes through the rest of the third and also the fourth. In the bottom of the fifth Reggie Smith leads off the Red Sox part of the inning with a double. Williams decides to pinch-hit Jones for the weak-hitting Russ Gibson. Jones hits a slow roller in the direction of Carew at second base. It appears to be an easy play even for a Little Leaguer, but at the last second the ball takes a weird bounce, comes up and hits Carew on the shoulder, allowing Jones to reach first. Runners on first and third, no outs. Fenway is in an uproar. But Perry comes back to fan both Santiago and Andrews, bringing Adair to the plate. As he's done so many times over this long season the gritty Adair comes through again. On the first pitch he bloops a single into shallow right.

Smith scores to tie the game at one run apiece and Yastrzemski comes to the plate. The crowd is delirious.

So many times this season he's been in this situation, so many times he's delivered. Anticipation runs through the park like some kind of electric current. Perry pitches him inside, and Yaz, attempting to pull, comes over the top of the ball and hits a ground ball toward first that goes off Killebrew's glove and bounces away. Carew picks it up, but Perry has not come over to cover first base and Carew can do nothing. The pitcher's obligation to cover first on any ball hit to the right side of the infield is basic baseball, one of the first things practiced in spring training, a drill that's worked on ad nauseum. Perry has not done so. Throughout the season the talented Twins had been plagued by mental errors, a malady that had largely contributed to the slow start that had gotten Sam Mele fired back in June. This is another one. It not only puts Yastrzemski on first and allows Jones to score, it seems to change the game's delicate momentum as the Sox now lead 2–1.

The Twins tie the game in the top of the sixth on two singles by Uhlaender and Rich Reese, but once again Santiago saves himself from further trouble with a big pitch. This time it's a sidearm curve to Versalles, who pops it up with the bases loaded. Santiago escapes. Then in the bottom of the inning Scott blasts one of his taters. This one goes into the bleachers in center field, and comes off Ron Kline, who's replaced Perry. It is Scott's most dramatic moment of the season and as he runs around the bases, Fenway is a cacophony, for it's becoming apparent there now will be a tomorrow that means something.

In the bottom of the seventh, with one out, Andrews hits a checked-swing roller to the left side of the mound that he beats out for a base hit. Adair then grounds the ball back to Kline, who quickly pivots and throws to Versalles, who's standing on second waiting to turn the double play. But Versalles drops the ball, and both runners are safe as Yastrzemski is due up at the plate. Ermer wants a left-hander to pitch to Yastrzemski and he goes with Jim Merritt, a starter whose record on the year is 13-7.

Yastrzemski and his wife, Carol, had stayed at the Colonial last night, the same hotel that he'd used for his workouts with Gene Berde last winter. There are too many relatives staying at his house. But he still hadn't slept very well. He'd spent the night tossing and turning, running everything through his mind, how his father had first taught him the game, how he'd spent winter nights in his cold garage hitting a baseball attached to a string, the long road that had brought him to this weekend. He'd gotten up early and had gone for a walk alone on the golf course at the Colonial, thinking all the time about the events in his life that had shaped him.

Now he waits for Merritt to come to the mound, as the roar of the large crowd washes over him like a warm wave. All afternoon the crowd has been deafening, thunderous, as if the volume had been turned up for this weekend. It's impossible to overestimate Yastrzemski's popularity, an affection that's come to even transcend baseball. He has become a certifiable hero, something to believe in. The new rallying cry in Boston is "Yaz sir, that's my baby." If nothing else in the country seems to make sense, Yaz at the plate does. Seeing him there in his familiar stance, tugging at his cap, adjusting his belt, digging in his back foot—all the mannerisms he goes through each time he comes to bat—becomes somehow reassuring. It makes people believe, and that's important. In these times when America's ability to do anything it sets its mind on is being increasingly questioned, along comes Yaz, an old-time hero, Frank Merriwell in cleats, someone who always seems to come through.

Now he is due up again in another big moment. Before the game Yaz and Santiago had made a pact. Santiago promised not to give up any gopher balls to Killebrew and Yaz promised to hit one out.

As Merritt warms up, Yastrzemski stands on the dugout steps and talks to Conigliaro, both of them trying to figure out what Merritt will throw, a habit they've had for years, even when there was a certain friction between them. Now the friction is over, and Conigliaro is a witness to Yastrzemski's amazing ability to deliver when he has to, whether it's the big hit, the big play in the field, whatever.

"He'll throw you a breaking ball," Conigliaro says.

"That's right," Yastrzemski says. "It will be a breaking ball all right, but it will be his slider."

Earlier in the season Merritt had shut out the Sox in Minneapolis, and had handcuffed Yastrzemski with sliders. So as Yastrzemski steps into the batter's box he's thinking about hitting a slider back up the middle. He has hit over .300 against lefties this year, the best in his career, but only has three home runs against them. Merritt misses on the first pitch, a slider, and Yastrzemski starts thinking fastball, feeling Merritt doesn't want to risk falling behind oh and two in the count. Again it's a slider. Again it misses. Yastrzemski feels even more strongly that now Merritt has to come in with a fastball, and probably is going to have to catch a good part of the plate with it. He is looking to attack it, to pull it, for he has come to learn that when you're going for a home run you're looking for a pitch you can pull sharply.

But Merritt again throws a slider, this time low for ball three. Yastrzemski looks down at Popowski in the third base coaching box, sees that he has the green light. Again he looks for a fastball. He knows Merritt doesn't want to load the bases with Scott up next, is essentially in the game to pitch to him, the left-handed pitcher against the left-handed hitter, by-the-book baseball. He gets the fastball this time, but it's not where he wants it, and he doesn't swing. It's a strike. He's guessing fastball again, gets it, and as soon as he hits it he knows it's gone. It goes into the visitors' bullpen in right-center, his 44th home run of the season, putting him one ahead of Killebrew in the home run race and also ahead of Ted Williams in the Red Sox record book. The Sox now have a 6–2 lead, and the Impossible Dream lives. At least for another day.

Williams lifts Santiago for Bell after Santiago opens up the eighth inning by walking Allison. It's been a gutsy performance by Santiago, who has made great pitches when he's had to. Bell's only mistake is giving up a home run to

Killebrew with two out in the ninth, a homer that ties him with Yastrzemski for the American League lead, and Williams blames himself for that.

"I was partly responsible for Killebrew's homer," says Williams. "Bell got behind in the count. When I went out there I said, 'Get it over. I want this man to swing.' So I called all three pitches, including the fastball that Killebrew hit out of the park. I told Gary we couldn't afford to walk him and if he hit it in the nets it was my responsibility. We had to take the chance. We couldn't let them get set for a big inning. I thought maybe Bell could throw a fastball by him and surprise him. I knew if he didn't surprise him then Killebrew likely would hit it out of the park and tie Yaz for the home run lead. But I wanted the game more than Yaz wanted the home run lead."

The clubhouse is raucous. The Sox have won 6–4. Santiago calls it the greatest day of his life. The Tigers have split a doubleheader, and now will have to win both games of another doubleheader tomorrow to tie the winner of the Sox-Twins game.

Only Lonborg is subdued. He has never beaten the Twins, has lost three times this year. "This is the biggest game of my life. I haven't seen a big game until tomorrow. Never."

He tries not to think about tomorrow. He wants to approach the game like he approaches every game, try to blot it out until he actually comes to the park. As he sits here in the clubhouse, amid the celebration of a win that saves the season, at least for another day, he doesn't want to feel anything now, roughly 21 hours before he's scheduled to pitch, because he knows emotion can't help him.

The next day is sunny, seasonably warm. Before the game the narrow little streets around the old ballpark are full of people. They pour out of the subway station in Kenmore Square, a mass of humanity spanning all ages—from kids in windbreakers and Red Sox caps to men and women in their Indian summer clothes. There is no generation gap here, no sign of the troubles that have tormented the summer.

There's a common purpose, a common energy, a sense of anticipation that is palpable, alive. The Red Sox have united New England as nothing else has done in years, brought people together all summer, made them aware, if only for a few months, that beneath the clothing styles and the hair lengths, maybe they aren't that different after all. The vendors on Jersey Street, which runs in front of the ball-park, are doing a big business, their cries of peanuts and ice cream piercing the air. There are policemen on mounted horses. It all seems like a carnival, summer's last stand. This is the game for the American League pennant, and there is a feeling among the throngs that course through the narrow streets that history will be made today, one way or the other.

Williams talks to the team in the clubhouse before they go out on the field. He'd started the day by going to an early Mass in Peabody. Usually, he goes to Mass at the Polish church where his kids also go to school, but the Polish church doesn't have an early Mass on this Sunday morning, so he'd gone to the other Roman Catholic church in Peabody. Also there was Petrocelli. After the service Petrocelli came over to him and asked, "Do we have a game today?" Williams considered it a good omen. Now he stands in front of the players in the silence of the clubhouse. He congratulates them, thanks them for a great season. Then he tells them he thinks they can win.

But no one thinks it will be easy.

Scheduled to pitch for the Twins is Dean Chance. He's 26, and one of the more colorful players in the league, a onetime bonus baby who came off an Ohio farm, made it to the bigs with the Angels, and never met a party he didn't like. He claims he throws a fastball, smokeball, snakeball, and something called a super-snakeball, and that he loves to play pool. He came to the Twins at the start of the season after leaving his Anaheim-Hollywood stomping grounds where he cavorted with the notorious Bo Belinsky, the swashbuckling pitcher who's become baseball's premier playboy. Three years ago Chance won the Cy Young Award as the best pitcher in baseball, but had slumped the last two years with the Angels, no doubt a victim of L.A.'s slow days and fast nights. But the trade to the Twins has rejuvenated him. He's 20-13.

The Twins score in the first inning. With one out, Lonborg walks Killebrew on four pitches. Oliva follows with a drive to left that goes over Yastrzemski's head, Yaz making a futile dive. Yastrzemski quickly retrieves the ball and throws to Scott, the cutoff man, as Killebrew is waved around third. Killebrew appears to have no chance to beat the throw, since he doesn't run well, but Scott tries to aim the ball, instead of throwing naturally, and his throw to Gibson is high and to the left of the plate; 1–0, Twins.

It's an unearned run, the kind that ages managers before their time, and in the third inning the Twins get another. This time Tovar walks with two out, and scores when Yastrzemski misplays Killebrew's single, charging in and letting the ball get by him. Now it's 2–0.

Fenway is quiet, the large crowd silenced. Its silence is a capsule version of what is occurring throughout the entire region. New England waits, and holds its collective breath. There have been so many near misses before, so many times the Red Sox just couldn't get it done . . . From small fishing towns along the Maine coast to tiny Vermont hamlets, from the White Mountains in New Hampshire to Cape Cod in Massachusetts, from cities to suburbs, New England waits. The people, old and young, sit in front of television sets and huddle by radios hoping that somehow today will *not* be like the past, that somehow today will be different. One is Bob McGarry, who lives in Providence. All summer he's followed the Red Sox with all the devotion a 12-year-old can give. All summer he's watched the games with his father, and at times when it seemed hopeless, when it seemed this dream was going to die, his father had told him to keep believing, that everything will be all right. So he's come to rely on his father's judgment, learned to wait for some encouraging word. But now as he watches on television, the Sox down 2–0, he turns to his father and his father just shrugs. He's so upset that he can't watch anymore. He takes his glove and a rubber ball and goes into the backyard and starts throwing the ball against the wall. But he has to stop after a few minutes because he can't see the ball through his tears.

No one can really know it now, but for the rest of their lives millions of New Englanders will remember where they were on this day. As so many other days blur together, this one will remain clear and in focus.

The Twins continue to lead 2–0 through five innings, Chance throwing a shutout, Lonborg victimized by those two runs.

Then comes the bottom of the sixth.

Lonborg is the scheduled hitter, and he stares at Williams in the dugout. It's a stare that says don't you dare take me out. Williams has no intention of doing that. He knows Lonborg is pitching his heart out, has only given up two hits and those two unearned runs.

"Come on," Williams says to no one in particular, "let's get something going here."

Lonborg hears this, feels relief. He knows he's still in the game. He steps in the batter's box and sees third baseman Tovar is a little back. He decides to bunt. He gets a fastball out over the plate and lays it down the third base line. He's decided to bunt on his own, going with his instincts. It catches the Twins' infield by surprise and he is on first with a single. Pitchers never like to see pitchers get on base, and Lonborg's move seems to upset Chance. Adair follows with another single, this time up the middle. There are runners on first and second, no outs. Dalton Jones at the plate.

The strategy calls for Jones to sacrifice the runners to second and third, but he fouls off two bunt attempts before Williams signals Popowski at third base to take off the bunt sign. Jones atones by singling into left field, but it's not deep enough in Fenway's short left field to enable Lonborg to score from second. Bases loaded. Yastrzemski up. As if Red Sox fans everywhere had written the script. Chance likes to throw him hard sliders low and away and Yastrzemski knows those are pitches virtually impossible to pull, but he so wants a home run now that he's momentarily frustrated. The error he's made weighs heavy on his mind and a home run will atone for that. Should he give it a big swing anyway, go for the home run, though the odds are squarely against it? Or should he just try to hit the ball solidly through the middle, go for the base hit? For a few moments he battles with himself, then decides to try to just hit the ball up the middle. He keeps telling himself *base hit* over and over, a personal mantra as he stares out at Chance.

On a one and oh count, he strokes a clean single to center and two runs score. Harrelson follows with a high chopper over second base. Versalles, the shortstop, has no play on Yaz at second since the count on Harrelson had been three and two and Yaz was running. So he elects to go to the plate in hopes of catching Jones. He throws wide.

Williams sends in Tartabull to run for Harrelson. Ermer counters by removing Chance in favor of his ace reliever, Al Worthington, one of the best in the league. Cat-and-mouse baseball, Williams and Ermer going back and forth, as the tension increases. Worthington is 38, has already been in the major leagues for 14 years. But his first pitch to Scott is in the dirt, wild, allowing Yaz to go to third and Tartabull to second. Three pitches later Worthington uncorks another wild pitch and Yastrzemski scores, with Tartabull advancing to third. Worthington fans Scott, but walks Petrocelli. This brings up Reggie Smith, as people dance in the Fenway aisles, knowing the momentum has changed. He hits a sharp ground ball to first. It's right at Killebrew, but he can't handle it, and Tartabull scores the fifth run of the inning. It is pandemonium in Fenway Park as the scoreboard reads 5–2.

As the Red Sox come out on the field in the top of the seventh, organist John Kiley—the answer to the longtime Boston trivia question, "Who is the only man to play for the Red Sox, Celtics, and Bruins?"—plays "The Night They Invented Champagne." The crowd is on its feet, bursting with wild and enthusiastic applause. Sitting in the dugout, George Thomas has never heard Fenway so loud. Lonborg responds with a strong inning. Then comes the eighth. With a runner on second Tovar grounds to Adair at second. He charges the ball, scoops it up, has the presence of mind to tag the runner, Rich Reese, and still get the ball over to Scott to get Tovar. It's another smart, heady play in a season of them for Adair, only this time he pays for it by getting spiked. He leaves the game to a thunderous standing ovation. Andrews runs out to replace him. The Red Sox are only four outs away.

But it's not over yet. Killebrew and Oliva both single, so Allison at the plate becomes the tying run. Allison hits a liner into the left-field corner. It looks like a sure double, but the ball is now in Yastrzemski's personal playpen, the part of Fenway he all but has a patent on. As Killebrew heads home to score and Oliva is nearing third base, Yaz, seeing that Allison is on his way to second, quickly decides to go there since he knows it's Allison who's the only potential run that counts. His throw to Andrews is a strike. Allison has no chance. He tries to hook-slide, but Andrews is there with the ball and the Red Sox are out of the inning. Killebrew has scored, but Yastrzemski has stopped the big rally. Once again he's made the big play, this time with his glove and the magic in his right arm. It's now 5–3, and the Red Sox are only three outs away from their place in baseball history.

The season has come down to these three outs. Lonborg is tired. Last night he'd slept in the Sheraton Boston, going to a hotel because he wanted to change his luck against the Twins. He figured that if he pretended this was a road game he'd be better off. He'd been nervous, but in a positive way. He'd gone over the Twins' lineup in his head, visualizing their hitters at the plate, watching himself get them out, batter by batter. It's a trick he'd learned from Sandy Koufax late in the season, something he calls "psycho-cybernetics," a device he uses to alleviate tension, so that when he actually gets to the mound it's as if he's already been there. Then he'd fallen asleep reading *The Fall of Japan* by William Craig, the same writer who'd profiled him earlier in the summer for the *Saturday Evening Post*. He woke up that morning feeling rested.

But he hasn't had his best stuff. The great fastball hasn't

been there, so he's relied more on his breaking ball. It's worked. The Twins are a fastball-hitting team and his breaking pitches have been effective. He's made up for Wednesday's game when he'd been shelled by the Indians. He stands on the mound, as the late-afternoon shadows fall across Fenway, only three outs away. The batter is Uhlaender, and he hits a routine ground ball to Petrocelli at shortstop. But at the last second it takes a bad hop, comes up and hits Petrocelli in the face. He falls down, in pain. He gets up, though, stays in the game. Carew is at the plate and he bounces one to Andrews. It's the same chance Adair had two innings earlier and Andrews replicates it. He tags Uhlaender as he runs by, still has time to get Carew at first. The Red Sox are one out away.

Ermer wants the right-handed Rich Rollins to bat for the left-handed Russ Nixon, going against the book. Rollins hits a pop-up toward Petrocelli. It seems to hang in the air forever as Rico waits for it. His mind is racing with myriad scattered thoughts as he waits for a routine pop-up, which now has become one of the most important pop-ups in Red Sox history. As he catches it, squeezing it extra hard because he knows this is it, Fenway explodes. It's as if there's been too much pent-up emotion, too much waiting, too many past failures, too much bad history. Lonborg sees Rico catch the ball and he leaps in the air, his arms over his head. Suddenly, Andrews and Scott reach him and start to lift him. The next moment it's as if all the Red Sox are there around him in joyous celebration. Then come the fans, and suddenly they too are everywhere, the infield a sea of people. The fans are coming from all over—from the right-field grandstand, through the bullpens in right-center, running across the outfield, wild with joy. Lonborg is riding on someone's shoulders, his hat off, laughing at the incredible sweetness of it all, a king among his subjects, when all of a sudden he senses it's getting out of hand. He's being carried out toward right field, a toy ship on a stormy sea, and now he's wondering if he's ever going to get out of here. People are tearing at his shirt, hugging him, clawing at him.

His cap is gone. His shoelaces are gone. He's getting scared.

Several policemen are trying to get at him, rescue him. Finally, they're able to run interference as he manages to get into the dugout and down the runway that leads back to the clubhouse. By this time he's angry. It's been too much, too out of control. He knows he came close to getting hurt. The crowd is still going berserk. They try to dismantle the scoreboard in left field. Some dig up the field, in search of some souvenir from this day that will live forever in Red Sox history. Some kids are climbing the screen behind home plate. The grounds crew eventually turns on the sprinklers to quiet the crowd, which spills out onto Jersey and Lansdowne streets, then Kenmore Square, the busy interchange a block away from the wall in left field. Thousands of people are in Kenmore Square now. People dance in the streets, hug strangers, yell and scream into the late-afternoon sky. The next day the celebration will be called the second biggest in the city's history, second only to the night seven years ago when John F. Kennedy was elected the president of the United States.

For this is more than just a baseball team winning a pennant. It is a region's redemption. Forgotten are those last-minute losses in '48 and '49, those times when the Red Sox were like some lover who promises to stay forever only to sneak out in the morning. Forgotten are the decades of frustration, all those years when a pennant race was always something that was taking place in some other city, and the Red Sox were known as a country club, full of spoiled, pampered players who usually were out of the pennant race before it was time to go to the beach. Forgotten are the hated Yankees, the franchise that's always been what the Red Sox wanted to be. The Red Sox have beaten the Twins in this storybook finish, this game that's come right out of some longtime Red Sox fantasy, and for now their past has been cleaned, the slate erased. This incredible team that began the season as a 100-to-one shot has defied the experts, the form charts, even baseball logic. They've proven that dreams do come true if only you wish hard enough, wait long enough.

The players are in the clubhouse and there is shaving cream and spilled beer everywhere. They are throwing each other in the showers, yelling and screaming. All season they've been like Sisyphus trying to push the large stone up the hill, only to have the stone keep rolling back, and now it's finally there at the top, and they are celebrating accordingly. The petty squabbles, the dislikes, the small tensions that affect every team over a long season have been forgotten.

"Lonnie really didn't have his great stuff," says Russ Gibson. "But he pitched with guts. He had a good breaking ball and we nursed it."

Yaz is beside himself with joy. He and Yawkey have embraced, the owner and his surrogate son, two men who've always been loyal to each other, through the good times and bad, two men who realize what this means to the other.

"I'm on a cloud, a trip, LSD, I don't know," Yastrzemski says excitedly. "I'm delirious."

Scott is yelling and spraying shaving cream on whoever comes near him. He's asked if he'd been nervous.

"Nervous? Sure I was nervous. I wouldn't have hit my mother that last time up. But this is a great team. I'm proud to be a part of it. Yaz is great. So is Conig."

Conigliaro is nearby, and he is the only sad moment, the hometown hero whose fate it is to have been reduced to little more than a spectator. He starts out whooping and screaming, a part of the celebration, when suddenly a feeling of depression sweeps over him. It's probably inevitable. For the past seven weeks he's been in the middle of an emotional maelstrom, his life turned upside down. This is supposed to be the greatest moment of his life, the culmination of every adolescent baseball fantasy, and yet nothing is what it should be. All around him his teammates are celebrating this incredible victory, catharsis after a long season, and he realizes he may never play baseball again. He feels alienated from everything swirling around him, as if in some inexplicable way the Red Sox season's become a parade that's passed him by. He sits in front of his locker and starts to cry. Mike Ryan sees him. He comes over and puts his arm around him.

"What's wrong, roomie?" he asks.

"Just what the hell did I do?" he asks. "What did I contribute?"

Yawkey also comes over to comfort Conigliaro, once more in the role of the kindly old uncle with the soothing voice, the one who always knows the right thing to say. "Tony, you helped," he says. "You were a part of it."

But he is uncomfortable, and he soon leaves. On this momentous day in Boston baseball history, Tony Conigliaro has become an asterisk.

The celebration goes on.

"This is the greatest moment of my life," Yawkey says, as he moves around the clubhouse, hugging players, thanking them.

"Better than '46."

"No comparison."

"How much has it cost you?"

"I don't think figures are important at a time like this. You can't figure the money. You can lose a million dollars a year with a baseball team. But how can you tell which dollar is the right one? Where would we be without people to find the players and develop them? People like Bots Nekola. Imagine if he didn't find some of the people he's found for us, like Yastrzemski."

This has been the season that's rekindled his lifelong passion with baseball. He sees Lonborg and gives him a big hug. Lonborg tries to tell Yawkey how much this moment means to him, choking on the words as he sees tears in Yawkey's eyes, but Yawkey quiets him. "You did your talking on the field today."

But all this celebrating comes with a catch. It's as though nothing can come easy for this Red Sox team; there always seems to be another hurdle they have to somehow get over. The Tigers have won the first game of their doubleheader against the Angels 6–4. If they win the second there'll be a playoff between the Red Sox and the Tigers. Williams already has said that if there's a playoff the pitcher will be Lee Stange. He's already told Stange not to do much celebrating, because he might have to pitch tomorrow. He's told *everyone* to be careful about how much they drink because of what tomorrow may bring. If the Tigers lose the second game, the Red Sox will win the pennant outright.

So the Red Sox wait. They sit in the clubhouse, amid the celebration, and listen to the Tiger game on the radio. The Tigers are ahead 3–1, but it's only the second inning, a long way to go. There's no place for the players to go anyway. It's still a madhouse outside, a never-ending party on the streets around Fenway that will last well into the night.

Yastrzemski is wearing a curious assemblage of sneakers, full-length hose, shorts, and warmup jacket. He sits near one of the radio speakers. He's had four straight hits today, has gone seven for eight in these last two games. He finishes the year at .326, with 44 home runs and 121 RBIs. He's won the batting title over Frank Robinson, won the RBI title with eight more than Killebrew, and he tied Killebrew in home runs. He's won the Triple Crown, only the 14th player in baseball history to do so. He's had one of the great seasons in baseball history. Ricky Williams, Dick's nine-year-old son, comes over and puts his hand on Yastrzemski's shoulder, listening to the radio. As his father has done so many times this season, Ricky leans on Yaz.

In the fourth inning, the Angels, who are now leading by one, push three more runs across. It's looking good for the Red Sox. Mayo Smith, the Tigers manager, will say later that he wasn't thinking of any possible playoff game with the Red Sox, that he only was managing to win the double-header and if there was a playoff game he'd have had to start "Joe Blow or somebody."

The crowd around the radio speaker grows. They sit on benches, on the floor, expectant. Others sit in the trainer's room where there's a radio. Still others are in Williams' office. They listen and wait. Players. Clubhouse kids. Red Sox officials. Sportswriters. They all sit and wait.

The Tigers' Bill Freehan opens the bottom of the ninth with a single. Everyone groans. Don Wert walks and there are more groans. Lenny Green is announced as a pinch hitter, and California manager Bill Rigney counters with left-hander George Brunet, a Michigan native who later said he felt sorry for the Tigers.

"If Brunet does it, what do you say we buy him a year's supply of beer," Yastrzemski says.

Brunet gets Green to fly out, and there are cheers and whistles. The Red Sox are only two outs away from the American League pennant, even if the game is being played in Detroit and all they can do is listen on the radio.

The Detroit batter is Dick McAuliffe, a good contact hitter, a tough out.

"A ground ball," says Ernie Harwell, the announcer, above the crowd noise.

Everyone in the room jumps up, tense.

"Over to second, one out," Harwell yells. *"To first."*

There is a pause.

"Come on," someone shouts.

"In time," Harwell says.

A war dance begins in the center of the room. A group of people come out of Williams' office. It is complete pandemonium. Williams is barefoot, wearing only long underwear and a T-shirt. He hugs Dalton Jones, and while they embrace Adair pours champagne on his head. Bell adds shaving cream. Then there is Williams kissing Santiago on both cheeks, both their faces covered with shaving cream.

Williams says that before the game Popowski had come into his office and told him he'd just come back from church where he'd lit two candles. Why two, Williams had asked. "Because some so-and-so might blow one of them out," Popowski said.

Williams continues to move around the room, hugging players, thanking them. Eventually, he comes over to embrace Yastrzemski.

"I've never seen a perfect player," he tells him, "but you were one for us. I never saw a player have a season like that." They embrace, two men who've both depended on each other, needed each other, and because of that have reached the pinnacle of their profession.

Williams will never again be viewed in the same way he was in the beginning of the season, the new guy with all the question marks hovering over him. He's won a pennant in his first time out of the box, doing it with a 100-to-one long shot no less. In this tough game when all managers are inevitably graded on whether they win or lose, he's won. It's now there on his résumé, and no one will ever be able to take it away from him, regardless of what happens in the future.

Yastrzemski is now seen as one of the elite players in all of baseball, right there with Clemente and Aaron and Frank Robinson. He'd gone into the season with the reputation that he wasn't a clutch player, having knocked in over 90 runs only once in his career, that he was someone who was bad on the base paths and sulked when things didn't go his way. Ironically, it was only a year ago he'd confessed to a sportswriter that there was too much pressure on him in Boston, that the burden of replacing Ted Williams as the next designated superstar was too oppressive. He'd said then that he never was going to be another Mantle or Frank Robinson, never going to be someone who hit a lot of home runs.

He stands on a table. Someone yells for him to give a speech. He looks around at his teammates. In a corner of the room is his father, the man whose own baseball dream had been handed down to his son, maybe the only family heirloom he had to give him. "Thanks for not quitting," Yastrzemski tells his teammates. "Thanks for giving me the thrill of my life."

It's also the biggest thrill of Williams' life. At one point, he was so overcome by emotion that he went into the trainer's room to lie down for a few seconds. He's had a year out of some storybook script, and now he's making the rounds, thanking his players. He feels especially close to kids like Smith and Andrews, Russ Gibson, the guys who'd been there in Toronto with him last year, back when all that's happened in the past year was a million-to-one shot.

As he stands amidst the jubilation, he's approached by Yawkey. Yawkey has tears in his eyes. He borrows a paper cup from a writer.

"I haven't had a drink in four years," Yawkey says, "but I'll have this one with you. Here's to you, Dick."

They had been the opponent the last time there'd
been a World Series in Boston, back 21 years ago
when the Red Sox names were Pesky, Doerr, York,
and another Williams, back when there'd been another
Red Sox team with the same dream and the St. Louis
Cardinals had been the dream crusher. Once again it's the
Cardinals who stand in the way of the Red Sox's first
World Series since '18. Once again they're expected to
crush a dream.

The Cardinals come to Boston for the start of the World
Series as overwhelming favorites. They rolled to the Na-
tional League title. The consensus seems to be that only
Yastrzemski and Petrocelli would start on the Cardinals; that
Orlando Cepeda would get the nod over Scott at first, Julian
Javier over the Andrews-Adair combo at second, Mike
Shannon over the Foy-Jones duo at third, Curt Flood over
Smith in center, Roger Maris over Harrelson in right field,
and Tim McCarver over the Howard-Gibson tandem.
Yastrzemski would get the edge over Lou Brock in left, and
Petrocelli over Dal Maxvill at shortstop. The Cards have a

better, deeper pitching staff that revolves around right-handed fireballing Bob Gibson, while baseball people still regard the Red Sox as a one-pitcher club.

The Cardinals believe they're the best team in baseball.

McCarver, only 25, is being called the best catcher in baseball, with the exception of Joe Torre. Midway through the season he was leading the league in hitting, and though he slumped afterward, he still finished with 14 home runs and a batting average just a few points away from .300.

It is still three years away from when Flood will file suit against major league baseball challenging the reserve clause that binds players to a team, claiming that being owned by a major league team is similar to "being a slave 100 years ago." He eventually lost the suit, which went all the way to the U.S. Supreme Court. But the suit helped to provide the climate that resulted in an arbitrator ruling that pitchers Andy Messersmith and Dave McNally were free agents, a ruling that brought on free agency and changed the game forever. He's rebounded from a bad year to hit .335, and combines with Brock to give the Cards excellent speed and one of the best defensive outfields in the game. Brock is also one of history's best base stealers. His mere presence on base upsets opposing pitchers, changes a game's rhythm.

Then there is Cepeda, "the Baby Bull," one of baseball's superstars. He's called Baby Bull because his father, often referred to as the Babe Ruth of Puerto Rico, was known as "Bull." Cepeda's also known as "Cha Cha" because of his exuberant personality. Ever since he was the Rookie of the Year in 1958 with the San Francisco Giants, Cepeda's been one of the game's great hitters, routinely combining power and average. Six years ago the numbers were 46 home runs and 142 RBI's, one of the truly great seasons, but he hurt his knee in '65, and it started to go sour. He was regarded as a malcontent, the principal reason for the Giants' supposed bad chemistry. He had trouble with managers Alvin Dark and Herman Franks, trouble with the front office over his salary, trouble with his knee.

Certainly, the fact he is Latin contributed to the controversy that seemed to swirl around him. The proliferation of

Latin players is still a relatively new phenomenon, the adjustment not always smooth. The players must deal with a different culture, a different language, problems that transcend baseball. Management, in turn, often views Latins differently, sees them as temperamental, excitable.

Cepeda was traded last year to the Cardinals for Ray Sadecki, and this year he's found his career again. He's hit .325, knocked in over 100 runs, and is seen as a positive force in the clubhouse, an outgoing, charming man who always seems to be listening to jazz and Latin music. He also has brought a Latin tinge to the Cardinals, who are now often called El Birdos in honor of Cepeda.

"I found love here," Cepeda said earlier in the season. "There are a great bunch of guys here and the manager showed me respect, that I'm a man. He said, 'Do your job, give 100 percent.' We don't talk much, but we are friends. That's what I was looking for. If I do something wrong he comes to me and tells me. He has respect for me. He helped me in many ways. He let me play. He appreciates what I do. In two years I never had a sour day on this ballclub. It's so easy to play here. When I came here I was looking for a new life. We Latins, we like people to appreciate what we do. We live on love. I found love here."

St. Louis has been installed as 3–1 favorites, and they arrive in Boston with a certain sense of style, a mixture of arrogance and confidence. They are only three years removed from being the world champions; they are good and they know it. They expect to make short work of the upstart Red Sox, and officially prove what they've felt all summer, namely that they are the best team in baseball. Gibson predicts the Cardinals in five games.

Yastrzemski, once again writing in the *Boston Globe*, picks the Sox in six games. It's already been decided he'll get $100,000 next year, a $50,000 jump from this year's salary. Not to be outdone by Yastrzemski's scribblings in the *Globe*, the *Herald-Traveler* grabs Lonborg for his thoughts. Both Williams and Conigliaro are doing columns for the *Record-American* and pick the Sox to win, Williams guessing in five games. The columns are all ghost-written, of course.

Clif Keane of the *Globe* has been rewriting Yastrzemski all along, usually transcribing the notes Yaz talks into a tape recorder. The *Herald-Traveler*'s Bill Liston is Lonborg's ghost, and Larry Claflin and Fred Ciampa do it for Williams and Conigliaro respectively. Boston is still regarded as a good newspaper town, with strong rivalries among the competing papers, and the various papers tout their guest columnists, promising their readers special insight into the Series.

They all joke about it.

"I never read those other guys," Yastrzemski says. "I don't even plan to read Lonborg."

"Now, considering this Series from the standpoint of American Literature, how would you rate the writers on your team?" Williams is asked.

"Well, I'm the best," he answers. "I don't read what the others are writing. In fact, I haven't even read my own."

Later, he'll amend that to say that the only reason he reads his column the next morning is to remember what he said the day before.

Virtually every pronouncement by one of the guest columnists is bannered in a headline, utterances which inevitably start to rankle the Cardinals.

But even before it starts, the World Series seems almost anticlimactic, as if nothing can match the drama of the weekend. Yastrzemski certainly feels it. The two games over the weekend had been the apex of his baseball life, a rising crest of emotion and frayed nerves and wonderful release. Afterward had come the inevitable letdown.

Wednesday, the 4th of October, is a bright, clear day in Boston, an Indian summer day that brings back memories of summer. Casualties in the Vietnam War continue. A federal judge calls for the easing of legal penalties concerning marijuana use, saying he believes the public greatly exaggerates its evil. Cass Elliot of the Mamas and Papas is arrested in London for allegedly stealing two hotel keys. You can buy a pair of Bond's "new breed" permanent press slacks for $8.95, and an upcoming concert by Donovan is already being advertised.

It's also the start of the World Series, the eyes of the baseball world focused on Fenway Park. All hotel rooms in the greater Boston area are full. Red-white-and-blue bunting hangs along the Fenway railings. Two dozen people sit on an Old Grand Dad billboard visible out past the Wall in left, across Lansdowne Street. It's been 21 years since there was a World Series game in Boston and the crowd is ready, if the team really isn't. Politicians, including the Kennedy brothers and father Joe, the patriarch of the most famous political family in the country, sit in box seats. So does baseball commissioner William D. Eckert. His special guest is a wounded Congressional Medal of Honor winner, a member of the army's special forces who's been flown in from Fort Bragg, North Carolina, for the game, a visible reminder that the war goes on. The nation's sportswriters are shoehorned into the press box that sits high above home plate.

Gibson gives ample testimony why he is one of the best pitchers in all of baseball. He's a great athlete, a former college basketball player at Creighton, with a rangy, sinewy body, and a fastball that seems to explode as it approaches hitters. He'd been the MVP of the '64 Series, and the only reason he's only 13-7 now is he broke his leg earlier in the summer when hit by a Roberto Clemente line drive, missing a little over seven weeks. The Red Sox hitters are overmatched, Gibson in complete control. Watching him, there's the feeling that as long as he's on top of his game the Red Sox never will be able to hit him. He strikes out 10.

Santiago pitches well, holding the Cardinals to only two runs in seven innings, but Gibson is too tough, and St. Louis wins 2–1. The only Sox run is a fluke, Santiago hitting a hanging curve for one of his rare home runs in the third inning. The other St. Louis star is Brock. He gets four hits, walks once, steals two bases, is a thorn in the Sox side all afternoon, speed personified. The Red Sox know they have to keep Brock off the base paths. They haven't. Both Cardinal runs are driven in by Maris, now 33, and already assured of baseball immortality by breaking Babe Ruth's record of 60 home runs in a single season. He'd signed back in 1953 after high school in Fargo, North Dakota, broke into the major leagues with the Cleveland Indians four years later. He went over to the Yankees in 1960, after an interim stint with Kansas City. At the time he was regarded as a fine outfielder with power. That was back in the era when the Yankees continued to pluck many of the best young players off the Athletics. Maris certainly fit the stereotype. His first year with the Yankees he hit 39 home runs and nipped teammate Mantle as the league MVP. It was the next year that he broke Ruth's record, teaming with Mantle to cut a wide swath through the ranks of American league pitchers. He and Mantle were neck and neck in pursuit of Ruth's ghost as the summer surrendered to September. Then Mantle got hurt and Maris became the biggest story in baseball in years, put under a media microscope he not only didn't want, but also wasn't very good at handling. Some of his hair fell out. Every at bat became news. Every home run seemed to split the baseball world even more, half of the fans rooting for him, the other half viewing Ruth's record as sacrosanct, a part of baseball lore that should remain pure forever, inviolate. When he finally did hit the 61st, off a young obscure Red Sox pitcher named Tracy Stallard, it came with an asterisk. Literally. Baseball commissioner Ford Frick ruled that an asterisk follow Maris' feat in the record book since Maris had played in 161 games in a 162-game season while Ruth had played in 151 of his team's 154 games.

He continued to be one of the most feared home run hitters in baseball until he hurt his hand in 1963 and injuries began taking the luster off his performance. By this time he'd grown unhappy in New York, wanted a change of scene. Last December he was traded to the Cardinals for a journeyman infielder, and the Cardinals moved Shannon to third base, installing Maris in right field. As a Cardinal Maris has been reborn. He's a veteran now, so different from when he'd come to the Yankees as the new kid. Now he's one of the stars of this first World Series game.

The Red Sox clubhouse is subdued, but not glum. It's only one game, nothing more, and to a team that spent the summer achieving the impossible what's being down one game?

"The Cardinals weren't a surprise, but they all swing the bat, that's for sure," Lonborg says. "That's good for me."

He'd spent the afternoon intently watching Santiago work the Cardinal hitters. He not only studied each of them, he tried to think of their counterpoint in the American League.

"How about Cepeda?"

"I'm not going to tell, but there are corollaries with several of them."

"You are perhaps the only pitcher in the game who can use 'corollary' and know how to spell it too," he's told.

He just smiles.

Shortly after the game ends Yastrzemski, Petrocelli, and Harrelson take extra batting practice. Foy pitches. Pitching extra batting practice is one of the things Foy does a lot of, one of the reasons his teammates like him, even if he's been in and out of Williams' doghouse all year. Yastrzemski, in particular, wants to do some hitting. He's not happy with his own performance, not happy with the fact that he'd arrived for the game emotionally spent.

"I wasn't sharp today," Yastrzemski says. "My hands were slow. Real slow. We went through a lot emotionally the last few days."

So as much of the nation's sporting press sits upstairs in the press box, still working on their stories, Yastrzemski and the others take batting practice. Yastrzemski stings several of Foy's gentle offerings on lines out toward right field, feels his good stroke coming back.

Over in the Cardinal clubhouse Gibson downplays Yastrzemski.

"You've been making too much of Yastrzemski," he tells the assemblage of writers. "He's a good batter, that's all."

In Boston, that's like blaspheming the Pope.

It is 10:30 in the morning, Thursday, October 5, the game still nearly three hours away. In the Pennant Grille adjoining Fenway Park baseball bats hang over the men's room door. Faded, yellowed pictures of Ted Williams and other Sox players from the past stare down from the walls. There are about 60 men already here, and the talk is of baseball and the upcoming game. It's overcast, with intermittent drizzle.

The crowd continues to swell for a couple of hours, the streets outside the stadium once again jammed with throngs of people. Everyone knows the Red Sox must win today, or in all probability they'll never return from St. Louis, site of the next three games.

The pitchers are Lonborg and Dick Hughes, the Cards' 29-year-old sensation, who spent nine years in the minors, but has gone 16-6. Throughout the summer he was the staff's stopper, helping to make up for the loss of Gibson.

In the bottom of the first Yastrzemski draws a walk, and stands on first base.

"Did you get your $100,000 contract for next year?" Cepeda asks.

"Yeah," Yaz says. "Did you get yours?"

"No," Cepeda says, turning his attention back to the game.

Lonborg has slept 90 minutes in the clubhouse before the game, blocking everything out, the pressure, the importance of the game, everything. Again, he'd spent the night at a hotel, for he is a man of ritual, especially when he's pitching well. He also had gone over the scouting report on the Cardinals with Dennis Bennett, the ex–Red Soxer who's familiar with many of the Cardinals from his stint in the National League. He keeps a little golden paper horseshoe that was given to him by Darrell Brandon.

As he toes the rubber for the first pitch he feels nervous, quickly gives himself a small pep talk, reminding himself that it's just another baseball game, no different from all the ones that have come before. His first pitch to leadoff hitter Lou Brock comes in at Brock in the general direction of his right ear, and sends him scurrying out of the way, a pitch that sets the tone for the rest of the Series. Brock had gotten four hits yesterday, a constant presence on the base paths. Now Lonborg sends him sprawling and the Cardinals rush to the dugout steps in outrage. "You bush . . ." someone yells at him. Lonborg just smiles back. He learned the hard way he can't give hitters home plate and he's certainly not going to change now. He's just sent them a message, the same message he's given the hitters in the American League all summer. Don't dig in on Gentleman Jim. From his vantage point in center field Reggie Smith sees the pitch zoom in toward Brock and thinks that Lonborg has just taken control of the game.

Lonborg has his great stuff to go along with pinpoint control and the Cardinals can't do anything against it. Like Gibson the day before, Lonborg is a textbook example that good pitching beats good hitting. He sails through seven innings without giving up a hit, the only Cardinal to reach first being Curt Flood on a walk in the seventh, and in the press box there are references to the perfect game the Yankees' Don Larsen pitched against the Dodgers in the '56 Series. Which is not without its own irony. Elston Howard, who is catching Lonborg, also caught Larsen that day, and Larsen's opponent that day was Sal Maglie, now Lonborg's pitching coach.

But with two outs in the eighth Lonborg throws a high slider to second baseman Julian Javier. As soon as he throws the ball he wishes he had it back. He actually covers his face as if looking at a bad automobile accident. Javier doubles to left, a ball Yastrzemski has no chance on. The chance for the no-hitter is over, and the Fenway crowd erupts in a loud ovation for Lonborg, this young pitcher who's once again put his imprint all over the game.

Still, the Red Sox win 5–0, evening the Series. Lonborg at first says it was agony when Javier ruined his no-hit bid, but quickly recovers. He tells the cluster of sportswriters around him that he never gave a thought to Larsen's perfect game. "To me, it was the victory," he says. "Get guys out any way we can, one at a time. Listen, when I'm out there pitching, I don't worry about perfect games or no-hitters. I think about winning. I think about keeping the guy from getting a hit. I make pitches that are going to win for me no matter where I go."

Lonborg is pressed against the side of Yastrzemski's locker in the corner of the room as the reporters keep coming after him in wave after wave, different faces with the same questions. He wishes he had a sign that says

"Javier hit a high slider." Yaz is in front of his locker, standing on a stool, speaking loudly and clearly, in what has become his customary pose. He has hit two home runs, and knocked in four of the five runs, and admits he'd been swinging for the fences all day, referred to in the Boston papers as "going for the Downs," a local colloquialism for trying to hit a ball in the direction of Suffolk Downs, the racetrack in East Boston. In the first game he'd been just trying to meet the ball because he didn't feel quite right, and he knows that when he's not sharp it's better that he cut down on his swing. The Cardinals' book on Yastrzemski is to pitch him high and inside, but both home runs have come on high inside pitches, one off Hughes and one off reliever Joe Hoerner.

It's an incredibly busy time for Yaz. His parents are staying with him, as are his wife's parents. He's spent $1,500 on tickets. After Wednesday's game he took 24 people out to dinner at Stella's, a tab that cost him nearly $200. He's still staying at the Colonial because there are too many people at his house. He also let his kids take off from school today to watch the game because "you never know what's going to happen in baseball" and they might never get a chance to watch their father play in another one. He already is scheduled to be on the Ed Sullivan show, Merv Griffin, and *The Match Game* when the season ends. Celebrity has found him.

"The two days off before the opener hurt me," he says. "I didn't feel good. That extra batting practice helped me."

He felt so good when he came to the park that he elected not to take batting practice, opting for a nap instead.

Once again, as it has been over the weekend, the Red Sox clubhouse is a happy place. Petrocelli is particularly pleased. He hadn't played well yesterday, and Williams had taken him out because he thought he looked helpless against Gibson at the plate, striking out three times. He's come back today to make a great play in the field against Cepeda and knock in the insurance run. It's significant that Rico didn't get down on himself, a key difference from past years when being pulled for some failure would have shaken his fragile confidence and put him into a tailspin.

Williams is asked if he feels pressure.

"Pressure? You should have been here last weekend. That was pressure. This is fun."

Both teams fly to St. Louis that night.

It's the first time Yawkey has traveled with the team in 17 years. He has invited the players' wives along, some of the office help, and Yastrzemski's parents, and he and his wife, Jean, spend much of the flight going through the aisle thanking everyone. Lonborg sits by himself in the back of the plane, looking spent. He's one of the few single players on the team, a fact his teammates often kid him about. This time he answers that maybe he'll think about getting married when he pitches a no-hitter.

In a sense it's a homecoming for Dick Williams, who spent the first 13 years of his life on St. Louis' north side.

"Do you think the St. Louis fans will give you a standing ovation?"

"I don't think so," he says, smiling. "I think they'll boo me more than anything else. But you know, as a youngster I liked the Browns a little better than the Cards because the Browns would let the knothole kids in on Sundays. The Cards wouldn't because they got big Sunday crowds. But my favorite player was a Cardinal, Ducky Medwick. He was my boyhood hero. And I was at the first game Stan Musial ever played. Even when we were in school in the spring and fall I'd still get to the games. School wouldn't get let out until 3:15 and the games started at 3. Our school was about a mile from the park so as soon as we got out the door I took off for Sportsman's Park. I usually got there about the second or third inning."

Williams has never been to Busch Stadium, though.

"I know the section of the city where it is, but I've never seen it except on television. It will be interesting because when I think of baseball in St. Louis I think of Sportsman's Park."

The Red Sox arrive in St. Louis about 8:30, are met by a

handful of people who cheer when the players walk down the steps. The team is staying at the Sheraton-Jefferson. The players' wives also are there, and the coffee shop in the hotel lobby is full by midmorning. Shortly after 11:30 a bus arrives to take the players to Busch Memorial Stadium for a workout.

The stadium opened a year ago, a ballpark of the future, a circular multipurpose facility with symmetrical outfield fences. It's near the arch and is named for the brewery family that bought the Cardinals 14 years ago, a move that was the brainchild of August Busch, grandson of the founder of the Anheuser-Busch brewery.

It's so different from Fenway Park, with wide expanses of pink and red seats that are far away from the playing field. The only problem is the field itself. It's chewed up, ragged, particularly the infield—the aftermath of games contested by the football version of the St. Louis Cardinals.

The two starting pitchers for game three are Bell and Nelson Briles, the veteran and the Young Turk. The knock on Bell always has been that he doesn't take baseball seriously enough, that he's constantly living up to his image of "Ding Dong," and Bell uses this time to defend himself.

"It's only newspapermen who say I might be a better pitcher if I was more serious," he says. "I've never had a manager or the guys I play with say that. They know I'm always trying. But it's not my style to worry. Tonight, I'll go out to dinner, relax, have some fun. About the time I walk out to warm up, that's when I'll turn myself on."

Briles is a former theater major at Santa Clara where he once performed in Shakespeare's *Twelfth Night,* a handsome twenty-four-year-old with dreams of one day being an actor. He'd begun the year as a reliever but Gibson's injury had made him a starter, and he's been one ever since. He wastes no time causing some controversy in the third game, hitting Yaz in the lower back in the first inning. Yastrzemski falls to the ground, holding his left calf, as Williams runs toward plate umpire Frank Umont.

"What's going on?" shouts Williams. "Is this the way it's going to be?"

Umont motions for Schoendienst to come out of the Cardinal dugout. Red Schoendienst is 44, the former second baseman for the Cardinals and Giants among others, now in his third season as the St. Louis manager. The "Old Redhead," in his second year in the Cardinals' starting lineup in 1946, had played the Red Sox in the World Series. He later became the roommate of legendary Stan Musial, now the Cards' general manager. Schoendienst always had been a good, steady ballplayer, but nine years ago his plight became a national story, when he battled tuberculosis, missing most of the '59 season. As soon as he arrives at the plate, Schoendienst starts talking about how he'd read in the Boston papers that Red Sox pitchers had thrown at Brock. Umont calms them both down. The game resumes.

The Series has changed, probably changed the minute Lonborg's opening pitch headed in Brock's direction to start the second game. Afterward, Flood had said publicly he didn't like Lonborg's throwing at both Brock and Dal Maxvill, and warned that the Cards could play that kind of baseball too. "And we're not going to get Petrocelli, we're going to get Yastrzemski," he said. So it wasn't surprising that many of the Cardinals tried to downplay Lonborg's performance, saying they thought Juan Marichal of the Giants was a better pitcher; that Lonborg is good, but not exceptional.

Bell has his good fastball, but his breaking stuff is shaky. He's also having trouble getting the ball down. Brock, quickly becoming the Red Sox's nemesis, leads off the game with a triple, then quickly scores on Flood's single. The Sox go deeper into the hole in the next inning when Shannon, one of the top RBI men for the Cardinals, hits a high breaking ball out of the park. Ironically, the book on Shannon is he's a fastball hitter.

Brock comes back to haunt the Sox again in the sixth. It's a typical Brock sequence, a tribute to just how important speed can be in manufacturing runs. He beats out a bunt. His very presence on base seems to rattle Lee Stange, the third Sox pitcher, who eventually throws wild to first in hopes of keeping him close. That allows Brock to get to third where he soon scores, giving St. Louis a 4–1 lead, a large enough cushion. They eventually win 5–2, once again leading in the Series.

"I wasn't trying to hit Yaz," Briles says afterward, trying to defuse the growing enmity between the two teams. "I was so nervous I was gripping the ball too tightly and having some difficulty releasing it. Having watched their batters in two games I had a better idea about pitching to them. In the late innings I was throwing easily and good. I was real nervous in the beginning, but I guess anyone would be. You have to fight yourself sometimes. You get so keyed up for a game like this, and you can't slow yourself down. I could feel the adrenaline pumping, but I couldn't do anything about it."

Nonsense, says Williams.

"There's a lot of difference between a brushback pitch and a knockdown," he snorts, "and I've seen enough of each to know the difference."

The only encouraging sign for the Sox is that pitcher Gary Waslewski pitches three great innings in relief. His performance so impresses Williams that Williams tells reporters Waslewski might even get a start later in the Series.

"We're down 2–1," Williams says. "That doesn't mean the world's coming to an end. Now instead of winning it in five like I said, we'll win it in six like Yaz said."

The next day is Sunday. It is cold, raw, 55 degrees. Dark clouds hover over the park, low, threatening. Santiago starts, but he's in instant trouble, giving up six hits and four runs in the first inning. The onslaught starts when Brock beats out an infield hit, once again using his speed to advantage. Santiago is chased before he can retire anyone in the first, and with Gibson pitching, the Red Sox might as well wave a white flag.

The final score is 6–0, Gibson not allowing a Red Sox runner to advance as far as second base until the ninth inning. The only encouraging aspect of the Red Sox's performance is that Dave Morehead and Ken Brett combined for a one-hitter over the last four innings. Only 19, Brett had pitched just two innings in the big leagues before today.

Now the Sox are down 3–1 in the Series, and can't escape the hard, cold fact that only two teams in baseball history have come back to win the Series after trailing 3–1, the '25 Pirates and the '58 Yankees.

"We've been coming back all year," Williams says. "No reason why we can't do it again."

No one seems so sure.

Williams is planning to go with Harrelson in right, Andrews at second, and either Foy or Adair at third, wanting to get as many right-handed hitters in the lineup against Steve Carlton, the young Cardinal lefty who's been anointed the best young left-handed pitching prospect since Sandy Koufax. Carlton has been erratic, but already he's shown he can be a big winner in the big leagues.

There's some question as to just how many times Lonborg can be called on to save the Red Sox. Already, the strain is showing on him. On the flight from Boston to St. Louis he'd seemed drawn, tired. Now he sits in the clubhouse, once again knowing that it's all up to him tomorrow, and already he is dreaming of losing himself on some Caribbean island where nobody knows him. These past two weeks have been a little too hectic. During most of the season he'd pitch, take a shower, and go home. Now there are always writers, photographers, television cameras, attention. It has worn him down, and there is a part of him that wishes it were over.

"When this is over I'm going to go to some islands—the Bahamas, maybe Jamaica—where they don't care about baseball there and no one will know who I am. Jim who? I'll just plain do nothing."

The Red Sox season already seems over.

Certainly there has been too much Gibson. There's also been too much Brock, the 28-year-old who had been signed out of Southern University in Louisiana for a $30,000 bonus in 1961, and was in the majors full-time a year later with the Cubs, one of the quick, young black players who were turning the National League into a speed league. In 1965 he came over to the Cardinals in a trade that included pitcher Ernie Broglio going to Chicago, and quickly became one of the stars of the Cardinals' '64 World Series champions. Last year he stole more bases than anyone in the National League with 74. This year he led the league again with 52 and also led in runs scored with 113.

"I was a pitcher in high school," says Brock, "not too bad either. In college I went out to pitch, threw some, and the coach said why don't I try first base. After a couple of ground balls went through me, he said, 'Lou, why don't you try the outfield?' "

Lonborg does it again in the fifth game. This time it's a three-hitter. He likes Busch Stadium, especially its wide, spacious outfield where there is ample room to run down fly balls, and considers it fun to pitch in a place where he doesn't always have to look over his shoulder and see the Green Monster beckoning seductively to hitters like some baseball version of Bali Hai. In his pocket is his lucky horseshoe, one he thought he'd lost until Darrell Brandon found it and gave it back to him right before the game.

But Carlton is just as tough on the Red Sox. After eight the Sox only lead 1–0, Foy scoring in the third when he parlayed a single, an error, and a Harrelson hit. It's a redemptive moment for Foy, who's seen his playing time decrease dramatically in the last weeks of the season as Williams has gone more and more with either Jones' hot bat or Adair's experience. Even when the pennant was won he felt he'd been an insignificant part of it. Later he'll say that no one can know what it feels like to have been a regular player only to see it all change, complete with long moments on the bench wondering if you'll ever be a regular again.

In the ninth inning, with Ron Willis now pitching for the Cards, Scott walks. With everyone expecting bunt, Smith doubles down the left-field foul line. Petrocelli is walked intentionally. The batter is Howard. He's struggled at the plate ever since coming to the Sox, clearly at the end of his great career, no longer able to catch up to the good fastball. But Williams decides to let him hit. He tells him to choke up on the bat and just try to slap the ball. Willis throws a low pitch to Howard, and Schoendienst replaces Willis with Jack Lamabe, who'd once pitched for the Red Sox, back a few years ago in the country club days. Lamabe delivers his pitch and Howard bloops it through the drawn-in infield into shallow right field. Maris fields the ball, but his throw to the plate is wild. Two runs score. The Sox eventually win 3–1 after Maris homers in the bottom of the ninth, ending Lonborg's string of 17 scoreless innings.

"It was a real blast," Howard says of his hit after the game. "Really, it was a dying quail, but I'll take it."

"Did you think Williams was going to pinch-hit for you?"

Howard looks at the questioner.

"Look, he's the boss, and the way I've been hitting I wouldn't have blamed him. He's got a guy sitting on the bench in Dalton Jones who's been hitting real good in the Series. I wouldn't have argued about it. Besides, he's the boss. What he says, I do."

Once again, Williams is surrounded by the press. "Why does it keep happening?" the reporters ask, referring to his amazing ability to keep taking players off the bench and see them come through.

"They're hungry," he says. "That's why it keeps happening."

He takes a long sip of Budweiser, leans back in his chair, a contented look on his face. "How does it happen Augie makes the beer so flat one day, and so good the next?"

The Red Sox are met by fifteen hundred people when they disembark at Logan Airport.

"Go get 'em, Dick," a woman yells at Williams.

"We'll get em, lady," he answers back. "We'll get 'em."

Yastrzemski, wearing sunglasses, tells the crowd the Sox aren't out of it yet. Outside the terminal, most of the traveling party is getting on a bus that's to take them back to Fenway Park. Lonborg walks unnoticed by the crowd, gets on the team bus.

"That's Lonnie," a teenager screams.

Lonborg, seeing the crowd start to rush for him, looks like a frightened deer. He leaps on the bus and finds a seat. People bang on the windows by his seat. Police blow whistles, and a siren wails, but no one seems to pay any attention as the bus moves slowly through the hordes of people.

Williams has tapped Waslewski as the next day's starter. He tells the inquiring press he has every faith in Waslewski because he pitches like Lonborg. This is Williams at his best, fearless, innovative, not afraid of being second-guessed if it doesn't work out. He says he'll have everyone but Lonborg in the bullpen.

Waslewski is 26. He grew up the son of a tool and die maker in Connecticut where he was a baseball and basketball star at Berlin High School. The Pirates tried to sign him when he graduated from high school, but he chose instead to go to the University of Connecticut. A year later he changed his mind and called the Pirates back. So began an odyssey through such minor league ports-of-call as Kingsport, Hobbs, Kingston, Reno, Asheville, Pittsfield, Toronto. Along the way he was lost in the draft to the Red Sox, and this March, after winning 18 games last year in Toronto, he was brought to spring training with the Red Sox. He quickly developed a sore arm, and when the Sox came north to start the season in Boston he went further north to Toronto. He'd been recalled in June, won a couple, lost a couple. His arm started hurting again, and soon he was back in Toronto, back on the pendulum. Now he finds himself in the middle of the media spotlight.

"When Waslewski was with me in Toronto last year I told him to stop trying to be Thomas Edison," says Williams. "Stop experimenting. Finally, he got rid of his slow curve and stuck to his fastball."

"Did you have to do a lot of talking?"

"I had to insult the devil out of him."

"He was on me all the time," Waslewski says, "and far as I'm concerned it didn't do a bit of good."

"It got you to the major leagues, didn't it?"

"In a way, yes, but I think I would have gotten there

266 • Bill Reynolds

anyway. They were using all kinds of psychology on me, hollering and yelling all the time. All they're going to get from that is a sore throat.''

Waslewski pauses.

"Still, I think he's a darn good manager."

He has sat and watched Lonborg beat the Cardinals, and he knows there's only one way he can beat them. It's nothing very complicated. He has to keep the ball down, throw strikes, and not walk anyone. He also is going to throw what Howard tells him to.

Not that the nation's sporting press expects him to win.

After commenting that Waslewski's great-grandmother was a full-blooded Cherokee, columnist Red Smith writes, "as any adult who watches television knows, the Indians never win."

The next day is an off-day, both teams back at Fenway Park for more workouts, more interviews. Yastrzemski takes batting practice, works on hitting the outside pitch to left field. The Cardinals have changed their book on him, now virtually throwing exclusively on the outside part of the plate, and he wants to be ready. He knows that it's usually futile to try to pull outside pitches, especially ones down and away.

Williams is telling a group of writers that one of his main functions on the Brooklyn Dodgers was to serve as manager Charlie Dressen's "yeller."

"During a game Dressen would call me over from my seat on the bench and say to me, 'Williams, call Westrum, or this one, or some other guy, a jerk. So I'd go to the top of the dugout and yell, 'Westrum, you're a jerk.' "

The conversation starts to meander, eventually focuses on the time Ted Williams came back from an injury to play a doubleheader, going three for three in the first game and four for five in the second.

"Do you remember what you did when you came back from your injury?" Dick Williams is asked.

"Easy," he says. "I went to the top of the dugout and yelled, 'Westrum, you're a jerk.' "

* * *

"It's pure fantasy, of course, to dream up a team called the Boston Red Sox," writes Red Smith, "whose capacity for futility is exceeded only by the Mets one year, then have them win the pennant in the dizziest race the American League ever knew."

Wednesday, October 11. The pitchers are Waslewski and Dick Hughes, and as fate would have it they've pitched against each other a few times before, in Triple A, when Waslewski was pitching for Toronto and Hughes for Toledo. Waslewski's last start has been September 3 against Syracuse, but he gives the Sox five strong innings, before Williams takes him out in the sixth. The Sox have a 4–2 lead at the time, thanks to four home runs: one by Petrocelli in the second and one each by Petrocelli, Yastrzemski, and Reggie Smith in the fourth.

Waslewski doesn't object to coming out. He has not pitched much for an entire month and he is tired. His legs are weak. His arm is weary. Howard knows Waslewski is tiring because his ball is starting to drift on him, a sure sign to Howard that his pitcher is losing it. But Waslewski has given Williams what he was looking for. He is replaced by John Wyatt.

The Cards tie the game in the seventh when Brock hits a two-run homer off Wyatt. The Sox, though, come back with four more in the seventh, the two key hits being a single by Jones and Foy's double, as people dance in the Fenway aisles. The Sox get a scare in the eighth when Bell, now in for the ineffective Wyatt, loads the bases, but Yastrzemski makes a sweet running catch of a McCarver fly, eliminating the threat. They get another scare in the ninth when Brock hits a long drive that appears headed for the Sox bullpen in right-center, but little-used George Thomas, in right field for defensive reasons, snares it out of the bullpen and the Sox win 8–4.

Petrocelli has hit two home runs, making a Conigliaro prediction come true. Tony C. had written in the *Record-American* that Petrocelli "is due to bomb one into the nets." He becomes only the 16th player to hit two homers in a World Series game, and it couldn't have come at a better time for him. He's not been happy with his hitting lately, feels he's been striking out too much, and has been another Red Sox player who's gone to Bobby Doerr for advice. Doerr thinks he's been uppercutting the ball too much, tells him to try to get on top of the ball a little more, just to try to hit the ball hard up the middle. Today it's worked. Both home runs have come on fastballs.

The only negative on this greatest of days for Petrocelli is that his wife couldn't be at the game, due to problems getting a babysitter for their two infant twins and their 20-month-old. Life's realities. Even in the middle of the World Series.

The Series is now tied at three games apiece. Tomorrow the Red Sox play the Cardinals for the world championship. One game at Fenway Park. Lonborg will pitch. It all seems longer than just 11 days ago when it was the Red Sox and the Twins for the American League pennant. They beat the Twins on the last two days of the season in Fenway to win the pennant. Now they only have to beat the Cardinals in Fenway in the last two games of the World Series, and they've already won one of them. Certainly everyone in Boston believes. John Gillooly of the *Record-American* writes Williams "could pull rabbits out of a skullcap" and who's to argue?

For there is a new variation on an old Boston song:

> *Here's to the Red Sox of Boston,*
> *Home of the bean and the cod,*
> *Where Cabots now cheer Yastrzemski,*
> *And Old Beantown is suddenly Mod.*

"LONBORG AND CHAMPAGNE" is the big, bold headline in red on the front page of the *Record-American*. Underneath is a large picture of Petrocelli, Yastrzemski, and Smith, all laughing. Petrocelli is barechested, the other two still have their uniforms on.

"My pitching rotation for the final game is Lonborg and champagne," writes Dick Williams. "I'm going to listen to those corks pop."

In the same paper Conigliaro writes, "Cream also rises to the top."

Outside Fenway Park there are even a few hippies. They are here with their long, stringy hair and colorful clothes, a postcard of Haight-Ashbury suddenly come to life on Jersey Street. One carries a sign that says, "The Red Sox Are Incredibly Beautiful People." The counterculture has come to Fenway Park.

The stage is set. Gibson against Lonborg, the dream matchup, the one the country has been waiting for. The only catch is that Lonborg has had just two days' rest. The last time he'd tried to get by on that, in the last week of the season against the Indians, he'd been shelled in the second inning. Williams doesn't expect Lonborg to go nine innings. Like he has so many times before, he tells Lonborg to go as hard as he can for as long as he can, nothing more. He'll have the entire staff in the bullpen, with Santiago tapped as Lonborg's replacement.

At 12:40 Lonborg, who's been warming up in the bullpen in right-center, starts the long walk in from the bullpen. He walks through applause every step of the way. Before the game both teams are introduced. Conigliaro gets a prolonged and thunderous ovation, his biggest ever in Fenway Park.

But by the third inning Lonborg is laboring. The light-hitting Dal Maxvill, whom Lonborg has thrown the ball by in his previous two games, leads off the inning with a triple off the center-field fence. Lonborg gets the next two batters before Flood singles to center, scoring Maxvill. Maris then singles past Scott, sending Flood to third, where he soon scores on a wild pitch. The Sox are down 2–0 and it's apparent Lonborg's not sharp, that he's paying a price for trying to pitch on only two days' rest. Around the fourth inning he knows he doesn't have it. Warming up in the bullpen before the game he thought he was going to be all right, but now he tries to snap off a good breaking ball and nothing happens.

Gibson, on the other hand, is brilliant again. He walks Foy to begin the game, then retires 13 in a row until Scott triples in the fifth.

The Cardinals get two more runs in the fifth. Gibson helps his own cause with a long homer into the center-field bleachers near the flag pole. It's now 3–0. Brock, the Sox nemesis throughout the series, singles to left, steals both second and third, and scores the Cards' fourth run on Maris' sacrifice fly to right. In the sixth inning it's obvious Lonborg is finished. The Cardinals have two men on, Javier up. Williams comes out to the mound to lift him. He'd said before the game that he wouldn't let Lonborg take a beating, but Lonborg wants to stay in. He tells Williams he thinks Javier is at the plate to bunt and that he can get him out. Howard agrees. He too realizes Lonborg doesn't have it today, but in all his years of catching great pitchers he's never seen anyone want it more. Williams finally agrees.

It's a mistake.

Lonborg hangs a pitch and Javier hits a three-run homer into the screen.

At the end of the inning Lonborg comes out to a thunderous ovation. As he walks across the infield, heading for the dugout, his shoulders seem to sag from utter weariness. Tears stream down his face. He is devastated. He hears the cheers and he doesn't know how to respond. He comes down the steps of the dugout and starts to walk up the ramp toward the clubhouse. Williams yells some words of encouragement, but he doesn't hear them. Maglie tries to console him on the walk up the ramp, telling him that he gave everything he had, and that's all anyone could have hoped for. Maglie tells him to keep his head up, but he can't. He walks into the clubhouse and sits down in front of his locker. He starts to take off his uniform, still in tears. The game is on the television at the other end of the clubhouse, but he doesn't look at it. He knows it's finished.

Fenway is quiet. The dream is over and everyone knows it. In the top of the ninth, Bob Gibson comes to the plate—Bob Gibson, who is in the process of winning his third Series game, the one man most responsible for the fact the Red Sox are going to lose this Series. He's given a rousing ovation. When Brock comes up he gets the same treatment.

Then, as the Sox come in from the field for their last time

at bat, the capacity crowd begins a long and deafening ovation, cheering as if the Red Sox are conquering heroes, a thank-you for the summer no one will ever forget.

Yastrzemski leads off in the bottom of the ninth, his last appearance of the season, and is given a standing ovation, the applause washing over him, one last goodbye. He singles hard to right field as the applause continues, but Harrelson quickly hits into a double play. At 3:25 in the afternoon Gibson strikes out Scott to end both the game and the season. Gibson has pitched a three-hitter. The final score is 7–2.

As the game ends the Cardinals mob Gibson. A few mounted police come out on the field, but there is no real use for them. A fan jumps over the railing and breaks toward first base, where he steals Cepeda's hat, but it's all pretty much subdued. The Red Sox disappear down the tunnel that takes them to their clubhouse. Thousands of fans remain in their seats, staring out at the field, this field that has provided so many unbelievable moments in an unbelievable summer. One of them is Yastrzemski's six-year-old son, Michael, dressed in a blue Red Sox jacket. A half hour after the game he is still sitting in the family's box seat behind first base. He continues to sit there until his mother, Carol, and his grandparents lead him away. Slowly, almost reluctantly, the crowd starts to file out of Fenway for the last time. Outside, the streets around the park are jammed.

"The glass slipper that everyone thought belonged to Cinderella wound up on her stepsister's foot," Clif Keane of the *Globe* will write the next day.

The celebration planned for the Red Sox clubhouse is taking place in the visitors' clubhouse under the grandstand behind third base. Yawkey comes into the room to congratulate the Cardinals. Gussie Busch, the St. Louis owner, goes around the room shaking hands with his players.

"We're drinking Lonborg and champagne," chant several Cardinals in their locker room. "We're drinking Lonborg and champagne."

There is no mistaking the sarcasm in their voice. It's been a nasty series, full of brushback pitches and bench-jockeying.

The Cardinal players haven't liked the pronouncements by the various "columnists" on the Red Sox. They believe the Red Sox have disparaged them, and this is their moment of retaliation. So they go around the room chanting "Lonborg and champagne" as they celebrate their second world title in four years.

"It's Gibson's champagne," shrieks McCarver.

To McCarver, this World Series is so much better than the one three years earlier against the Yankees because of the lack of respect tendered by the Red Sox.

"This team belittled us in the papers."

He starts ticking off the imaginary headlines:

" 'Yastrzemski Says Sox Will Win in Six.'

" 'Scott Says We'll Kayo Gibson in Five.'

" 'Williams Says Cards Pitching Staff Is Gibson and Five Other Guys.'

" 'Lonborg and Champagne.'

"You want more?" he asks. "I can read them back to you. They never should have done that. Now it's our turn to belittle them."

Brock is asked what the turning point of the game was.

He thinks for a second. "Gibson," he says.

Flood peels off his uniform, a bottle of champagne in his hand.

"There was a lot of jazz in the newspapers," he says. "I've never seen anything like it in my whole life. Everybody had something to pop off about. They could have finished fourth on the last day of the season. They forgot about that."

Throughout the room is the chant of *"Lonborg and champagne, hey; Lonborg and champagne, hey."*

In the middle of the Red Sox clubhouse is a large platform, set up earlier for the TV cameras and interviews in case the Red Sox won. No one uses it. The players seem to avoid it as though it's been condemned. There are victory cakes on a table, but no one touches them. The champagne is nowhere in sight. Harrelson weeps openly. Yawkey, O'Connell, and Haywood Sullivan go throughout the room, thanking players. Yawkey is wearing a tan windbreaker, still could pass for one of the clubhouse men. He'd been crushed when he lost in '46. He isn't now. This summer, this culmination of an Impossible Dream, has been his greatest thrill in baseball. He's come to love this team, love its heart, the fact it blossomed out of the ruins of seasons past.

The mood is solemn, but there's no real grief. The Red Sox have acquitted themselves well. There's no way anyone can know that a season like this will never come again. They're a team whose core is young, and as they sit here in this clubhouse on this last day of the season, they no doubt think they'll be here again sometime soon. It's still too soon for them to realize what all teams realize on the last day of any season, namely, that they'll never be together in quite the same way again. That next year will bring new faces, change.

Yastrzemski stays in the trainer's room for roughly 20 minutes. Eventually, he comes out and starts going around the room thanking his teammates. Then he talks to the writers:

"It's not the ending I'd like to have, but great ballplayers like Al Kaline have never played in a World Series. If we could have stayed close to Gibson it might have made a difference in the final innings. In a way it's a great disappointment, but in a way it gives us something to look forward to next season."

Once again, as he's done so many times over the course of this long season, he credits Williams for making them a winning ballclub. "He never can be second-guessed for anything he's done this season."

There are a bunch of people outside the clubhouse. They pound on the door and chant. "We want Carl ... we want Carl." Over and over they chant, almost like a mantra.

Yastrzemski glances over at Lonborg.

"You can't always put heart in your arm," he says.

Lonborg is soaking his arm in a bucket of ice water. Reporters surround him. One of the questions is whether having to pitch with only two days' rest is more physical or mental?

"It has to be physical," he says. "That's why I'm

soaking my arm. If it was mental I'd be soaking my head."

He's had time to compose himself.

"Dick was thinking of taking me out in the sixth but I wanted to pitch," he says. "That's the funny thing about this job, you always think you can go on. I suppose it's a little like a politician who keeps running for office time after time even though he keeps getting beat. He does it because he feels eventually he will be successful. That's the way I was out there today. I felt that I could get these batters out. I knew I wasn't right, but you don't have to be right sometimes to get hitters out."

Lonborg is understandably down, but already he has this long and incredible season in perspective.

"It will take some time to forget this," he says finally, "but I will. To me, this is all part of life. I've learned a lot this year. Now I'm going to put what I've learned together and try to use it to make me a better pitcher next year. Now I just have to take a deep breath, and start all over again. It would have been great to win it for all those wonderful people, but this is not the end of the world. There will be good times for me. There will be happiness."

Williams is asked if he made a mistake in pitching Lonborg.

"There is not a thing I've done this season I would have done differently," he says. "Lonborg is our best and we had to have our best today. Probably he didn't have his stuff today, but he's still our best."

A reporter sticks a microphone in Williams' face and says, "Some people would say you stayed too long with him."

"Some people," says Williams icily, biting off the words, "would say that."

But he quickly calms down. The one thing he regrets is leaving Lonborg in to get rocked, because he knows Lonborg didn't deserve that. But he also knows that today's game doesn't detract from what he's done all year.

"Well, the season is over now. We played every game we possibly could, but we lost the last one. I was wrong. I said it would be a rotation of Lonborg and champagne. It wasn't.

It was Lonborg and beer. But I can speak for every player on the team when I say that we wish we could have won the last one for Mr. Yawkey. And we wish we could have won it for those wonderful fans in Boston. There never has been a year like this one for me, and I guess for any other guy on the team. I hope the people in Boston are as proud of those players as I am. Somehow I think they are.''

Outside, it's already getting cold. The sky is starting to darken. There are still many writers up in the press box overlooking the field. The field itself is empty, a silent cathedral, just a few workmen already starting to move through the bleachers cleaning up. The fans have left, the fans who began giving their hearts to this team in midsummer and got rewarded with a season that will live forever in Boston baseball history. Already they're undoubtedly thinking of next season and all the future seasons this young Red Sox team figures to own. Yastrzemski has said this team should be good for the next eight to 10 years, and if Yaz said it, then it must be true, right?

The corner of Jersey and Van Ness streets, where the entrance to the players' parking lot is located, is still jammed, complete with mounted police and security guards. There are adults and teenagers and kids. They are swaying back and forth, singing, ''Red Sox, we love you.'' They raise homemade signs, including two that had been put together late in the game. They say, ''Thank You for an Unbelievable Year'' and ''Number One—No Matter What.'' The signs were made by Beth Braveman of nearby Newbury Street, who'd been watching the game on television in her apartment with some friends. When it became apparent the Sox were going to lose, she and her friends decided someone had to show the Red Sox that people still loved them. So they quickly made the signs, and rushed down to Fenway only to find thousands of others who had the same idea.

The people huddle there, waiting for one last look at the players, one last chance to cheer. About two hours after the game Yastrzemski and Carol come out into the small parking lot, visible to some of the crowd gathered around the entrance. Carol has tears in her eyes, but the fans start cheering enthusiastically.

"You'll get 'em next year, Yaz," they shout. "You'll get 'em next year."

Nearby, old wrappers and debris lie in the gutters like confetti after some long-gone parade.

EPILOGUE

The Tet Offensive, the attack on Saigon by the North Vietnamese, began in January 1968. It was the turning point in the war, ending Lyndon Johnson's hope that it would soon end, and dramatically increasing opposition to a conflict that was beginning to seem more and more unwinnable. Three months later Johnson went on national television, looking somber and old, and announced he would not be seeking reelection. The Vietnam War would continue for seven more years.

Less than a week later, on April 4, Martin Luther King was assassinated in Memphis, shot by James Earl Ray as he stood on a motel balcony. Following King's death there were uprisings in virtually every black ghetto in the country. In June, on the night he'd won the California primary, Robert Kennedy was shot by Sirhan Sirhan moments after finishing his victory speech at the Ambassador Hotel in Los Angeles. With the void left by Kennedy's death, Hubert Humphrey beat out Eugene McCarthy, the so-called peace candidate, for the Democratic nomination at the Democratic National Convention in Chicago. His selection was over-shadowed by the ugly spectacle of antiwar protesters and clashes with police, massive disturbances that television brought into the nation's living rooms. The protesters chanted "The whole world is watching" as the Chicago police, with their mace and dogs and riot control gear, fought with thousands of America's children. This was not some inner-city clash, some ghetto riot. These were white America's sons and daughters. It was the war coming home, with all its far-reaching implications.

By the following fall the country seemed polarized: young versus old; long hair versus short; marijuana versus alcohol; black versus white. Within two years the effects of the new culture would be wide, influencing everything from fashion to values. Throughout the '70s the counterculture would be incorporated into the larger culture; to the point that rock music, once seen as rebellious and symbolic of social change, would be used by Madison Avenue to sell products to mainstream America. The aftershocks of the '60s reverberate to this day.

Baseball changed too of course. Expansion and thus divisional play came into being in 1969, taking some of the luster off the pennant races. In 1973 the American League adopted the designated hitter rule, a fundamental change in how the game had always been played. Free agency came two years later, and that too would change the game forever. It basically allowed players to be able to sell their services to the highest bidder when their contract was up, thus creating the climate that eventually led to huge money for superstars, and the escalation of salaries for everyone. The rise of the Players Association also changed the way opposing players related to one another. They were all brothers in the same union now and Yastrzemski later said it lessened the frequency of brushback pitches.

The Red Sox began spring training in '68 full of the optimism of the year before, convinced they could somehow keep the lightning in the bottle, but already things were different. Conigliaro still had his vision problems, would miss the entire season. Lonborg, who'd fallen and hurt his knee while skiing near Lake Tahoe over the winter, was not the same pitcher, finishing 6-10. Adair and Wyatt, two players who'd overachieved the year before, had bad years. Santiago tore a muscle in his pitching arm, then had it surgically attached. When it ripped loose again his career was over. Never again would Williams be able to have the same impact on the Red Sox, the same dramatic effect. He'd taken a spoiled, pampered team that had no clue how to be successful and he'd taught them how to win. He'd taught them to be tough and resourceful and never back down, taught them to believe in all those clichés that were taped to the locker room walls of their youth. He too couldn't replicate that again. Perhaps it was inevitable. There was a sense among the players that though Williams had spurred them on the year before, they didn't need him now. It was as if Williams' caustic, sarcastic approach had a short half life, could best work with a team that hadn't experienced success.

Shortly after the World Series ended, Williams was given a new three-year contract by Yawkey, the first real security he'd ever had in his baseball life. He was so happy that day that he was halfway home before he remembered he'd left his son, Ricky, back in the clubhouse. He talked about managing the Red Sox for years.

But the Sox finished the '68 season 17 games back of the pennant-winning Detroit Tigers, and the alliance between Williams and Yastrzemski, so key to the success of '67, began showing strain. In August of '69 Williams benched Yastrzemski after a game in Oakland and fined him $500 for not hustling. On September 23, 1969, Williams was fired, just two years after the Impossible Dream. He eventually was replaced by Eddie Kasko. The team that seemed poised to begin a dynasty just two years before had become a mere shadow of its former self.

Within five years many of the '67 Red Sox already were no longer playing baseball: Howard, Fischer, Santiago, Bell, Morehead, Stephenson, Adair, Russ Gibson, Rohr, Tartabull, Horton, Thomas, Osinski, Siebern, Stange, Waslewski, Landis, Wyatt.

Howard returned to the Yankees as a coach in 1969, remained there for 11 years. Bell was drafted by the expansion Seattle Pilots in '69. Adair went to play in Japan in '71, then returned and eventually coached for both the A's and the Angels. Russ Gibson finished his career with the Giants in '72. Waslewski was traded to the Cardinals after the '68 season for infielder Dick Schofield and went on to also pitch for the Expos, Yankees, and A's, through '72. Lee Stange went back to the bullpen in '68 where he led the staff with 12 saves, before finishing his career with the White Sox in '70.

In October of '68 the Red Sox lost Foy to the expansion draft, but not before he called Williams "a two-faced sneak who tried to start trouble to make the players play better." Williams was unperturbed. "It's not the first time I was called that," he said. Foy was later traded to the Mets in 1970, but was no longer playing two years later after a year with the Senators.

Tony Horton, who'd been traded to Cleveland midway through the '67 season, hit 27 homers in 1969 for the Indians and seemed on the way to actualizing his great potential. But he went into a slump the next year, and the subsequent booing contributed to a nervous breakdown and the end of his career.

Andrews stopped playing after the '73 season, as did Darrell Brandon. Andrews, who'd been traded to the White Sox in December of 1970, had landed with the A's, having been picked up by Dick Williams, their manager at the time, to bolster their infield. Brandon, bothered by arm woes, had been sent back to the minors before he surfaced in the early '70s as a reliever for the Phillies. Mike Ryan, who went over to the Phillies after the '67 season, was not playing after the '74 season. Dalton Jones was traded to the Tigers following the '69 season, where he remained a utility player through 1972, then finished that year with the Texas Rangers— the first year of that team.

None of them ever duplicated the summer of '67.

In 1968 Harrelson hit 35 home runs and led the American League in RBI's, becoming the darling of Fenway fans. By this time he'd established himself as one of the game's first "flower children," one of the prime examples of "counter-culture meets baseball." He was traded the next year to

Cleveland, a controversial move that resulted in many fans picketing Fenway. He broke his leg the next year, and in 1971 he quit baseball in a futile quest to land on the PGA tour as a professional golfer. In the mid '70s he returned to Boston as a broadcaster where he quickly recaptured his old popularity. He later became the general manager of the White Sox.

Sparky Lyle, a bit player in '67, emerged as the ace of the Sox bullpen in '68, one of the few bright spots in a dreary season. The next couple of years he established himself as one of the best young relievers in the American League, but was traded to the Yankees for Danny Cater before the '72 season in one of the worst trades in Red Sox history. Lyle immediately led the league in saves, and went on to become the league's Cy Young Award winner in 1977.

Ken Brett, just 19 when he became the youngest player ever to pitch in a World Series game, went on to pitch for 10 major league teams. He pitched in the 1974 All-Star game and lasted in the big leagues until 1981. It was his fate, however, to be overshadowed by his younger brother George, one of the best hitters in baseball for the past 15 years.

Rico Petrocelli used the '67 season as a springboard to a solid career. He was moved to third base in 1971 after the Sox acquired veteran shortstop Luis Aparicio. He played in the '75 World Series, before an inner-ear problem ended his career in 1977. He then became a Red Sox broadcaster for a while, and later a minor league instructor in the White Sox organization.

George Scott had a horrible year in 1968, hitting just .171. He was traded to Milwaukee after the 1971 season in a 10-player deal. Four years later he tied Reggie Jackson for the American League home run lead with 36, and led the league in RBI's with 109. Before the '77 season he was traded for Cecil Cooper and came back to Boston. He hit 33 home runs, and again was a fan favorite in Fenway. The Boomer was back—back with his gold chains and his taters.

But when it ended for him, it ended badly. By 1979, overweight, and no longer able to get around on the fastball, he'd become a sad parody of himself as a player. He came to the plate, waving his big black bat, just like in the old days, but he no longer seemed able to hit the ball to the left side of the field. Maybe that was the final irony. George Scott, who'd always tried to pull everything, much to the consternation of many of his managers, no longer could. He was booed and ridiculed in Fenway Park, the place that had once given him his best moments. He was traded to the Royals and then finished his career playing 16 games for the Yankees.

Reggie Smith went on to realize much of his awesome potential, but by the early '70s he was routinely booed in Fenway and took to wearing a batting helmet in center field to protect himself from fans throwing things at him. He battled publicly with Carlton Fisk, the Sox's young catcher whom the fans loved. Fisk called Smith one of the major causes of friction on the club. The fans perceived Smith to be lazy, seemed to blame him for not having become a superstar. Smith, in turn, called Boston a racist city, and the Red Sox an organization that failed to promote black players.

"The fans react to that," he said. "I've been here eight years and had to fight to get on TV and get the kinds of endorsements that players like Yaz, Carlton Fisk, and even Billy Conigliaro get. I'll bet Fisk got more money in endorsements in two years than I got in eight."

He was traded to the Cardinals in October of 1973 for Rick Wise and Bernie Carbo and soon had two All-Star seasons for the Cardinals. He then was traded to the Dodgers where he hit 32 homers in the Dodgers' pennant-winning season, then came back and hit 29 more the next year. He lasted in the major leagues until 1982 when he went to play in Japan.

Tony Conigliaro missed all of '68 with his vision problems, but returned the next season to win Comeback Player of the Year honors. He wrote a book called *Seeing It Through*. In 1970 he hit 36 home runs, but was traded that October along with pitcher Ray Jarvis and catcher Gerry Moses to the California Angels for Ken Tatum, Jarvis Tatum, and Doug Griffin. Midway through the following year, the vision in his left eye disintegrated again, and he quit baseball. He tried a comeback in 1975, but it failed and he began a career as a television sportscaster. He worked a while for a television station in Providence, where he also owned a bar called Tony C.'s, then for a TV station in San Francisco. In the early '80s, while home in Boston auditioning for the job as color man on Red Sox broadcasts, he suffered a near-fatal heart attack while being driven to Logan Airport by his brother Billy. The heart attack left him in a wheelchair, seriously debilitated.

Dick Williams went on to manage the Oakland A's in 1971, leading them to the divisional title. The next year he took them to the world championship. He won the World Series again the following year, but got into a dispute with owner Charlie Finley over Finley's decision to put Mike Andrews on the disabled list. He quit at the end of the year. In 1974 he became manager of the Angels in the middle of the season, later became the manager of the Expos, and then the Padres in 1982. Two years later he won the pennant. He finally retired early in the 1988 season after three years as manager of the Seattle Mariners.

It was a heady time for Lonborg following the '67 World Series. He went on a Caribbean vacation. He appeared on *The Dating Game*. After he hurt his knee skiing, he never seemed to be the same pitcher. In the next four years he'd win just 27 games for the Red Sox, before being traded to Milwaukee in October of '71 in the 10-player Scott deal, with Brett, Billy Conigliaro, and two others, for Marty Pattin, Tommy Harper, Lew Krausse, Pat Skrable, and a minor leaguer. He ended up with the Phillies where he won 18 games in '76 before retiring in '79.

By the spring of '68 Yastrzemski was almost as big a hero as Batman and James Bond. He'd done the Johnny Carson and Merv Griffin shows, as well as *The Match Game*. He had his $100,000 contract, an autobiography called *Yaz* in the bookstores, and enough endorsements to supply him with more money than he was getting to play baseball— everything from T-shirts to ice cream to Yaz Bread. He benefited, of course, from being a white superstar at a time when blacks had started to dominate the game. In a time when racial tensions were high, it's not surprising that advertisers reacted positively to white stars. Frank Robinson had won the Triple Crown in 1966 and received no endorsements. Yastrzemski was quickly plugged into the American Fame Machine.

He won the batting title again in '68, hitting .301 in what was called the "year of the pitcher." But never again in his long career did he match his accomplishments of 1967. He hit 40 home runs in both '69 and '70, but began to hear boos the next year when he hit .254. He continued to play 12 more years, hitting over .300 only once, .301 in 1974. He went on to become an extremely solid player, but never a superstar. But when he retired in 1983 he'd become one of the game's all-time greats, largely because he'd played for over 20 years. He'd won three batting titles and played in 18 All-Star games. He ranked first in career games with 3,308, and was the only American League player to have both 3,000 hits and 400 home runs. He'd won seven Gold Gloves. On his last day in baseball, he trotted around Fenway Park in a ceremonial farewell, the cheers following him every step of the way. He was inducted into the Hall of Fame in 1989. In August of that summer his number was officially retired in Fenway Park, joining those of Doerr, Joe Cronin, and Ted Williams.

It would be eight years before the Red Sox returned to the World Series, and when they did the only two players left from the '67 team were Yastrzemski and Petrocelli. This was the year Conigliaro had started one last comeback attempt—one last effort to discover what had been lost that August night in '67. But he was beaten out of the designated hitter spot by Jim Rice, in his first full year, and soon retired for good. The marquee names became Rice and fellow rookie Freddie Lynn, and Carlton Fisk and Rick Burleson. The ace of the pitching staff was Luis Tiant, the same Luis Tiant who'd beaten the Sox in the last week of the '67 season.

This time the Cincinnati Reds were the opponents. Again, the Red Sox would lose in seven games. In July of the next year, 1976, Yawkey died. He'd been battling leukemia, a fight he'd kept secret. He'd owned the Red Sox for 44 years, the longest any major league team had been owned by one individual. Four years later he was inducted into the Hall of Fame.

For about a year after his death the future of the team's ownership was unclear, as several syndicates bid for the team. Originally, Jean Yawkey had intended to sell the team to a group of investors headed by Haywood Sullivan, a Red Sox vice-president in charge of player personnel, and Edward "Buddy" LeRoux, the trainer of the '67 team who'd become a millionaire largely as the result of establishing a physical rehabilitation center in the Boston area. They were going to buy the team from the Yawkey estate for $15 million. Then she changed her mind and decided to be a limited partner. But the American League, which had to approve the team sale, turned the proposal down, feeling the price was too low. The group's next proposal was for $20.5 million, and included Jean Yawkey as a general partner along with Sullivan and LeRoux.

Right from the beginning the arrangement didn't work: Jean Yawkey and Sullivan on one side, LeRoux on the other. In June of 1983, a night when Conigliaro was being honored in Fenway Park, LeRoux came into the press room before the game and proclaimed that the limited partners had given him sole power. His plan was to bring O'Connell back as general manager. Jean Yawkey and Sullivan took LeRoux to court, eventually went to trial, and the litigation resulted in LeRoux being bought out four years later.

Baseball in Boston was never the same after 1967. The Red Sox became a phenomenon in New England, so that now they routinely draw over two million fans to Fenway Park every year.

It's now nearly a quarter of a century later, and the players who were young in that summer of '67 are no longer so. Some are no longer alive. Howard. Adair. Foy. McMahon. Conigliaro died in February of 1990, having never fully recovered from his heart attack.

The rest are all yesterday's news now, and most have gone back to the relative anonymity from which they came, back to the small towns and the mainstream jobs they probably would have ended up in if there never had been any baseball.

Mike Ryan is a coach for the Philadelphia Phillies. Russ Gibson works for the Massachusetts state lottery. George Thomas, who spent 10 years as the baseball coach at the University of Minnesota, now works in sales for an audiovisual company in the Minneapolis area. Reggie Smith is a minor league instructor in the Dodgers' organization. José Santiago broadcasts baseball games in Puerto Rico. Lee Stange is a pitching coach for the Red Sox. Ken Harrelson is a member of the White Sox's broadcast team. Dalton Jones lives in Plymouth, Massachusetts, where he works in financial services and also is associated with former Red Sox player Denny Doyle's baseball schools. Tony Horton is the president of a bank in Santa Monica, California. Gary Bell owns a sporting goods store in San Antonio, and has appeared for several years in Florida at the Red Sox Fantasy Camp. Darrell Brandon sells retirement insurance in the Boston area, and also runs a pitching school for kids. His pitching school is something he started back in the mid '70s in the Philadelphia area where one of his first pupils was a kid named Orel Hershiser, then the fifth starter on his Cherry Hill (New Jersey) East High School team. José Tartabull spent some time working for a minor league club in Florida; his son Danny plays for the Kansas City Royals. Billy Rohr is a lawyer in Newport Beach, California. Every year in the middle of April he gets phone calls from sportswriters wanting to ask about that game in Yankee Stadium. Every year on April 14 his name appears in newspapers under such headlines as "What Happened on This Date in Baseball History."

"I just hope that no one ever does anything important on April 14," he says with a laugh.

Petrocelli and Andrews now work for the Jimmy Fund in Boston, the official Red Sox charity for children with cancer whose main benefactor had been Yawkey. Petrocelli also runs a batting school in the Boston area. Andrews runs a baseball camp.

Jim Lonborg is a dentist in Hanover, Massachusetts, and

lives in nearby Scituate. Ironically, Rosemary Feeney, the woman he married, had visited Boston for the first time the last weekend of the '67 season. She was a high school student in New Jersey at the time, in Boston with her mother to look at colleges. She wasn't a baseball fan. She and her mother stayed in a hotel and were kept awake most of the night by drunken, celebrating fans, to the point that her mother almost didn't let her come to school in Boston because it was too rowdy. She met Lonborg, quite by accident, a couple of years later, had no idea who he was.

Williams is now living in Las Vegas. He's a part-time scout for the Padres and wrote his autobiography in 1990. It's called *No More Mr. Nice Guy*. His son, Rick, who so often had seemed the Red Sox's unofficial mascot in 1967, played his college baseball for Eddie Stanky at South Alabama, in a strange twist of irony. He's now the minor league pitching instructor for the Montreal Expos. Popowski still scouts for the Red Sox and works spring training for them.

Yastrzemski does promotional work for Kahn's meats, and is a part-time hitting instructor with the Red Sox in spring training. His son, Mike, spent some time in the White Sox organization.

They're all linked together by that long-ago summer. Like men who've been to war together, they're bonded in ways most of us will never be. All have come to realize that what they did has endured; that, in many ways, they've achieved a measure of immortality by virtue of that one baseball summer so many years ago.

"I am a part of something that meant so much to so many people and that's a great feeling," Rohr says. "If I was going to be famous for a few minutes I'm glad I picked the right day and the right year."

"It's like having a child, or getting married," says George Thomas. "It's a part of your life. A golden moment that never can be duplicated. It just never will. People say they know how you feel. But they don't. They can't."

"Everywhere I go people still bring up that summer, that team. It's unbelievable. It seems like we're playing today," says Russ Gibson. Looking back, that season was a dream come true for Gibson, who'd grown up in nearby Fall River, and had spent 10 years in the minor leagues before that summer. "I can't tell you how many times people look at my ring, and when they find out I played for the '67 Red Sox they can name all the players. They even remember specific games, things I don't even remember. People always are asking me if Williams was that tough, or about Scotty being overweight. It's like people inherited you, and you became part of their household."

Petrocelli thinks back often to that summer. He too lives in the Boston area, is still an intergal part of the extended Red Sox family, appearing at many charity events around New England in his job for the Jimmy Fund.

"It was like that one year you dream about," he says wistfully. "And we were all so young."

One of the reasons Lonborg decided to live in Massachusetts was the effect of that summer, the sense he'd been a part of something that has come to be embedded in the area's history. On a beautiful May morning in 1991 he was in the Red Sox clubhouse for an old-timers' day. He was putting on the white uniform, and if you looked real quick it could have been 1967. His hair is gray now, but he is still lean and in shape, still looks like he could go a few innings. Two of his young sons were with him, John and Jordan, and he said that one of the satisfying aspects of coming back to the ballpark for this old-timers' day was that his sons could walk on the field, sit in the bullpen, stand at the foot of the Green Monster, walk in their father's shoes, if only for a few minutes. His baseball now has been reduced to playing catch with his sons in the yard, watching them play Little League.

"Even when I come to some games I rarely come down to the clubhouse," he said, looking around. "It's all so different now, and when I come in here I feel like a bit of an intruder."

"When you do come in here, is it like jumping into your past?" he was asked.

Lonborg smiled, spoke softly, still Gentleman Jim after all those years.

"You remember," he said. "How can you not? There are so many memories here."

Also in the clubhouse, getting ready for old-timers' day, were Gary Bell and Dalton Jones. They, too, said that long-ago summer has a hold on them.

"How many people ever do anything that makes so many people happy?" asked Gary Bell. "There are only certain teams that capture everyone's imagination and we were one. And the older you get the more it means. I mean, how many times in your life are you really important? How many times in your life do you get the chance to pitch in the World Series?"

Dalton Jones still wears his World Series ring most every day. It serves as a reminder.

"It's nice to look at, especially when you're a little down," he said. "You think of that year and you realize that that's just life, it goes in cycles. We had been so down before that, and then we won. So it's good to think back to that season. Because it makes you remember that you were a winner, and that you played with winners."

Also in the clubhouse that morning was Yastrzemski. He was a little heavier, his face a little fleshier, starting to gray around the temples, but he didn't look all that different from when he retired. He never appears very comfortable at these events, and this day was no exception. He said how '67 was the high point of his career, that it was always good to see some of his old teammates, and that he owed so much of his success to Mr. Yawkey. While the other old-timers seemed to relish being in the spotlight again, it was obvious Yastrzemski didn't. Then again, Yaz never wanted to be a star, just a ballplayer.

About an hour later, when he was introduced at the start of the old-timers' exhibition, there in his white uniform with the familiar number eight on the back, he got a massive ovation as he trotted out to the first baseline. He waved to the crowd, finally appeared at ease, as if at last he'd found a place where he felt comfortable.

Old-timers' days aside, several players from that '67 team still get together frequently, especially those who live in greater Boston.

"Being on that team is an important part of your life that people have never forgotten, a wonderful memory that never can be taken away, the greatest year in Boston baseball history," says Mike Andrews. "It's helped me in my professional life, and it's amazing how many people today remember that I was the second baseman for the '67 Red Sox. I played for a world championship team with the A's in 1973, but the '67 season was clearly the most cherished moment of my baseball career. It's just too bad that it happened my rookie year. I didn't know it then, but it was like 'where do you go from here?' "

Through the years there've been several get-togethers of teammates, some official, some unofficial. He understands, as the others have, that they're all part of something that has transcended themselves.

"When you share something like that, you're bonded," he says. "You're together forever."

One day in the summer of 1990 George Scott was walking past Fenway Park, past the red-brick walls and the gates on what used to be Jersey Street. It was a bright summer day, and since the Red Sox were out of town there was little traffic on the narrow streets around the park. The neighborhood is essentially the same as it was in '67, a mixture of warehouses, a large souvenir store, and a few bars catering to the baseball crowd. Behind the Green Monster in left, no more than a short fly ball away, is Kenmore Square, an area that's still dominated by Boston University. Jersey Street, the small, narrow thoroughfare that runs along the front of Fenway Park linking Boylston Street with Brookline Avenue, is now named Yawkey Way. A small plaque honoring Yawkey and donated by his employees is on a brick wall in front of the building. High above it, on the top of the building in red letters against a tan-brick background, it says "Fenway Park," there since 1912.

The park itself is virtually the same. There's a giant electronic scoreboard that sits on top of the center-field bleachers, complete with all the accoutrements of the '90s.

The scoreboard obscures the "Buck Printing" sign, which was once a Fenway landmark, off in the distance, out past the bleachers. There is advertising on the electronic scoreboard, just as there are a few large billboard ads on what used to be the pristine dark green walls of the center-field bleachers. Two years ago a new and expanded press box was built high in back of the screen behind home plate, an addition that raised the height of the building and led to the theory that the wind currents have been altered. But everything else looks the same. The Green Monster is still there in left, so close you can almost reach out and touch it from third base, a sweet temptation to all those right-handed sluggers. The grandstands are still close to the field, only a few feet separating the fans from both the left-field and right-field foul lines. Fenway is still timeless.

On this warm afternoon, as Scott trudged along the sidewalk, the old ballyard was empty. If you closed your eyes you could almost hear the echoes of yesterday's cheers, back when Scott was the Boomer and Tony C. was in right field and Lonborg was on the mound. Back when Yaz patrolled left field as skillfully as some Old West sheriff, and Dick Williams stood in one corner of the dugout, squinty-eyed, trying to make his team play better than they had any right to play. Back in that long-ago summer that resurrected baseball in Boston, and made the Red Sox a passion again.

On this day Scott happened to be in the neighborhood, the Red Sox were in the middle of a pennant race, just as they had been 23 years ago, but now the names were Clemens and Boggs, Greenwell and Burks. Scott was just someone who sometimes hung around the ballpark, hoping the Red Sox would give him a job. He's heavy now, walks like an old man, the grace that once made him the best-fielding first baseman in the game just a memory.

"We saved baseball in this town," he said, "but none of us have any jobs with the Red Sox."

He shook his head sadly, regret in his high-pitched voice—a voice that always seemed incongruous coming from such a big body. Scott does some baseball card shows, appears every winter at the Red Sox Fantasy Camp in Winter Haven, where men pay money to play in the sunshine with the old Red Sox, pretend it's 20 years ago, when dreams still have a chance to come true.

A few minutes earlier he'd said how he loved all his teammates, how it had been a surprisingly close team. In most ways it *had* been, men brought together by their youth, and the magic of that summer, which now seems bathed in some soft orange light. On this warm afternoon, so many years later, Scott was effusive in his praise of Williams, as if to let bygones be bygones. He called him the best manager he ever played for, said he always knew Williams' prodding and pushing was to make him a better player, that it was nothing personal. He talked about his old teammates with obvious affection, as if he were an old man at the end of his life remembering old lovers.

"Baseball is huge around here now," he said, looking around. "But without us it wouldn't be the same."

Amen, Boomer.

Amen.

FINAL STATS

BATTING	AB	R	H	HR	RBI	AVG.
Osinski	9	3			1	.333
Yastrzemski	579	112	189	44	121	.326
Scott	565	74	171	19	82	.303
Conigliaro	349	59	101	20	67	.289
Jones	159	17	46	3	25	.289
Adair	415	47	111	3	35	.267
Andrews	494	79	131	3	35	.265
Petrocelli	491	53	127	17	66	.259
Harrelson	332	42	85	12	54	.256
Lyle	8		2			.250
Foy	427	64	106	17	48	.248
Smith	536	73	131	14	56	.244

BATTING	AB	R	H	HR	RBI	AVG.
Tartabull	246	35	58		10	.236
Thomas	88	9	18	1	6	.205
Gibson	138	6	28	1	14	.203
Ryan	224	21	45	2	26	.201
Santiago	42	5	8	1	4	.190
Brandon	44	3	8		1	.182
Howard	315	22	56	4	26	.178
Seibern	102	10	18		11	.176
Bell	74	7	12		2	.162
Lonborg	97	7	14		8	.144
Wyatt	11		1			.083
Morehead	12	1	1			.083
Stange	48	2	3		1	.063
Landis	2	1				.000

PITCHING	IP	H	BB	SO	W	L	ERA
Lyle	43	33	14	42	1	2	2.30
Osinski	64	61	14	38	3	1	2.53
Wyatt	93	71	39	68	10	7	2.67
Stange	182	171	32	101	8	10	2.77
Lonborg	273	228	83	246	22	9	3.16
Bell	226	193	71	154	13	13	3.31
Santiago	145	138	46	109	12	4	3.60
Stephenson	40	32	16	24	3	1	3.83
Brandon	158	147	59	95	5	11	4.16
Morehead	48	48	22	40	5	4	4.31
Landis	26	24	11	23	1	0	5.19

AMERICAN LEAGUE SEASON STATS:

BATTING	G	AB	R	H	AVG.
Yastrzemski, Boston	161	579	112	189	.326
F. Robinson, Baltimore	129	479	83	149	.311
Kaline, Detroit	130	453	93	140	.309
Scott, Boston	159	565	74	171	.303
Blair, Baltimore	151	552	72	162	.293
Carew, Minnesota	136	514	66	150	.292
Oliva, Minnesota	146	557	66	168	.289
Fregosi, California	150	585	63	168	.287
Freehan, Detroit	154	515	66	146	.283
Clarke, New York	143	533	74	160	.282

HOME RUNS

Yastrzemski, Boston	44
Killebrew, Minnesota	44
F. Howard, Washington	36
F. Robinson, Baltimore	30
Mincher, California	25
Kaline, Detroit	25

RBI's

Yastrzemski, Boston	121
Killebrew, Minnesota	113
F. Robinson, Baltimore	94
F. Howard, Washington	89
Oliva, Minnesota	83

BIBLIOGRAPHY

Angell, Roger. *The Summer Game*. New York: Popular Library, 1972.

Anson, Robert Sam. *Gone Crazy: The Rise and Fall of the Rolling Stone Generation*. New York: Doubleday, 1981.

Boston Globe. Newspaper stories, April–October, 1967.

Boston Evening Globe. Newspaper stories, summer 1967.

Boston Record-American. Newspaper stories, April–October, 1967.

Cole, Milton. *Baseball's Great Dynasties, the Red Sox*. New York: Gallery Books, 1990.

Coleman, Ken, and Dan Valenti. *The Impossible Dream Remembered*. Lexington, Mass: Stephen Greene Press, 1987.

Conigliaro, Tony, and Jack Langer. *Seeing It Through*. New York: Macmillan, 1970.

Fornatale, Pete. *The Story of Rock 'n' Roll*. New York: William Morrow, 1987.

Goldstein, Richard. *Reporting the Counterculture*. Boston: Unwin Hyman, 1989.

Halberstam, David. *The Summer of '49*. New York: William Morrow, 1989.

Hayden, Tom. *Reunion*. New York: Macmillan, 1988.

Hendler, Herb. *Year by Year in the Rock Era*. New York: Preager, 1983.

Hirshberg, Al. *What's the Matter with the Red Sox?* New York: Dodd, Mead and Company, 1973.

Lautier, Jack. *Fenway Voices*. Camden, Maine: Yankee Books, 1990.

Lee, Martin A., and Bruce Shalin. *Acid Dreams: The CIA, LSD, and the Sixties Rebellion*. New York: Grove Weidenfeld, 1985.

Lukas, J. Anthony. *Common Ground*. New York: Knopf, 1985.

McSweeney, Bill. *The Impossible Dream*. New York: Coward-McCann, 1968.

Pro Sports magazine. September 1969.

Providence Journal. Newspaper stories, March–October, 1967.

Providence Journal-Bulletin. Newspaper stories, March–October. 1967.

Riley, Dan., ed. *The Red Sox Reader*. Boston: Houghton-Mifflin, 1991.

Riley, Tim. *Tell Me Why*. New York: First Vintage Books Edition, 1989.

Shatzkin, Mike, ed. *The Ballplayers*. New York: Arbor House, 1990.

Shaughnessy, Dan. *Curse of the Bambino*. New York: Dutton, 1990.

Sports Illustrated. Vol. 32, No. 25, June 22, 1970.

Street and Smith's Baseball Yearbook. 1967.

Sport magazine. March 1966, August 1967, June 1968.

Super Sports magazine. June 1971.

This Fabulous Century. New York: Time-Life Books, 1988.

Walton, Ed. *This Date in Boston Red Sox History*. New York: Stein and Day, 1978.

Williams, Dick, and Bill Plaschke. *No More Mr. Nice Guy*. New York: Harcourt Brace Jovanovich, 1990.

Yastrzemski, Carl, and Al Hirshberg. *Yaz*. New York: Viking Press, 1968.

——— and Gerald Eskenazi. *Yaz, Baseball, the Wall, and Me*. New York: Doubleday, 1990.

INDEX

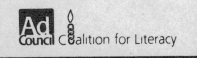